Contents

COLLECTED WORKS OF

BERNARD LONERGAN

VOLUME 6

PHILOSOPHICAL AND

THEOLOGICAL PAPERS

1958–1964

COLLECTED WORKS
OF BERNARD

LONERGAN

PHILOSOPHICAL AND THEOLOGICAL PAPERS 1958–1964

edited by
Robert C. Croken,
Frederick E. Crowe, and
Robert M. Doran

Published for Lonergan Research Institute
of Regis College, Toronto
by University of Toronto Press
Toronto Buffalo London

ISBN 0-8020-3473-X
ISBN 0-8020-3474-8

Reprinted 2005, 2012, 2013

Printed on acid-free paper

Canadian Cataloguing in Publication Data

Lonergan, Bernard J.F. (Bernard Joseph Francis), 1904–1984
Collected works of Bernard Lonergan

Partial contents: v. 6. Philosophical and theological papers 1958–1964 / edited by Robert C. Croken, Frederick E. Crowe, and Robert M. Doran.
ISBN 0-8020-3473-X (v. 6 : bound)
ISBN 0-8020-3474-8 (v. 6 : pbk.)

1. Theology – 20th century. 2. Catholic Church. I. Crowe, Frederick E. II. Doran, Robert M., 1939– . III. Lonergan Research Institute. IV. Title.
BX891.L595 1988 230 C88-093328-3

The Lonergan Research Institute gratefully acknowledges the generous contribution of THE MALLINER CHARITABLE FOUNDATION, which has made possible the production of this entire series.

The Lonergan Research Institute gratefully acknowledges the contribution toward publication of this volume of DOROTHY and DONALD NEWTON, given in memory of their parents, KATHERINE and THOMAS MONETTE, and ANNIE and WILLIAM NEWTON.

University of Toronto Press acknowledges the financial support for its publishing activities of the Government of Canada through the Book Publishing Industry Development Program (BPIDP).

Editors' Preface

Our preface will be limited to two points: a general comment on the lectures that are transcribed and edited in this volume, and a statement of the editorial policies that we have followed. Specific details regarding the record we are working from and the earlier work that has been done in transcribing and editing the material will differ for different lectures; this information will be presented in the first footnote of each lecture.

General comment. This volume, number six in the Collected Works of Bernard Lonergan, parallels so closely in outward form the three volumes published as *Collection* (CWL 4), *A Second Collection,* and *A Third Collection* (the latter two also to appear in the Collected Works, as volumes 11 and 13) that it might have been called 'A Fourth Collection.' There are differences, however, that suggest a distinctive title. For one thing the earlier volumes span Lonergan's writing career in successive periods (1943–65, 1966–74, 1974–82) and provide material for a preliminary overview of his life's work, while the present volume focuses on a few critical years at the end of the first period. More important, the *Collection* series benefited from Lonergan's own input as to titles, contents, and editing – nearly all the papers included had, in fact, been published in his lifetime – whereas the lectures in the present volume, with some exceptions, were delivered to a familiar audience in a free-wheeling way and were left on tape recordings without thought of subsequent publication. It fell to the present editors to put them into readable form.

The circumstances of delivery account, of course, for differences in style, which remain even after a good deal of editing; but it may also be a factor in the content itself of the lectures. For the period they cover was a time of important transitions for Lonergan: he was moving rapidly toward a new conception of theology and its method; his mind was churning out a steady stream of new ideas; new avenues for exploration were opening up for him; he was on the verge of what is now recognized as a major breakthrough in his thought on method, the idea that came to him in February 1965 of the eight functional specialties. What is more natural, therefore, than that in these lectures, nearly all of which were delivered to circles of close friends, almost *en famille*, he should try out his ideas with less concern for censors looking over his shoulder and so with correspondingly greater freedom?

In any case, while the lectures maintain a continuity with previous work, they also reveal new and significant ideas coming to birth or receiving new and creative application: philosophy of history, human historicity, the natural and the human sciences, the move from substance to subject, the notion of presence and the notion of mediation, a new analysis of meaning, of stages of meaning, and especially of meaning as constitutive of the human, the three fundamental human communities, intersubjectivity, differentiations of consciousness and the resulting worlds of the human subject, and always the drive toward a new conception of theology as a whole and of its method, with a particular concern for the relevance of theology to the spiritual life – these were some of the topics he was pondering in these six crucial years.

It should be noted, however, that the lectures are only selected spin-offs from the more integral thinking found in Lonergan's university courses and summer institutes at the time. The primary arena for his struggle with these new ideas was the set of graduate courses he gave at the Gregorian University in Rome between 1958 and 1964. Then this work was mediated to Canada and the United States primarily by the three great institutes at Regis College, Toronto, in 1962, at Gonzaga University, Spokane, in 1963, and at Georgetown University, Washington, in 1964. We have in those courses and institutes a gold mine of ideas still to be tapped, but while we await the publication of volumes 19 and 20 of the Collected Works, which will include some of this material, the lectures of the present volume provide a set of windows into the interior of a mind at work, and a kind of publisher's preview of what those courses and institutes hold in store for students of Lonergan.

For readers who would like to situate this volume in the total scheme of the Collected Works, we may say that a further volume of Philosophical and Theological Papers is planned (volume 14 in the series); this would cover the remaining years of Lonergan's life and would include any papers similar to those of the present volume that were not included in the three volumes of the *Collection* series. Further, we plan in volume 17 of the Collected Works to publish a large number of shorter papers and reviews spanning the whole of Lonergan's lifetime writings from 1928 on. In this way we hope to make available in these six volumes (the three Collections and the three volumes of Papers) all the dispersed items in Lonergan's writings and lectures; there will, of course, be special volumes (18 and, as already indicated, 19 and 20) for the integral lecture series of his university courses and his summer institutes.

We have to resist here temptations of the kind to which editors are subject: in our case to look backward and uncover the influences at work in the years from 1958 to 1964, to look forward and trace the assimilation and adaptation of the new ideas in the post–1965 work, and to undertake an analysis of what was going forward on the broad front of Lonergan's development at the time of these lectures. The study of such questions in detail and in overview we leave as a challenge to others. It is a study his ideas not only deserve but require, for we are still far from that combination of overview and competence in detail that is needed for a mastery of Lonergan's thought.

Editorial policies. The present volume follows the general policies of the Collected Works, where these are relevant, and adopts some particular decisions specific to our purpose here.

Lonergan lectured without thought of publication. Years later, when the question of publication arose, his wish regarding transcriptions of his lectures was that they not be verbatim (see the editors' preface to CWL 10, p. xvi). We have respected that wish in the present volume as we did in *Understanding and Being* and in *Topics in Education*. We have also added titles and subtitles to what seemed logical divisions and subdivisions of the material. Often Lonergan's own summary of his lecture or, when available, his separate outline notes for the lecture suggested the wording of these titles and subtitles.

Since in these lectures Lonergan frequently cited references from memory and did not have them quite right, we have made any corrections required in the text regarding the titles, dates of publication, and so on, of works referred to. Full bibliographical information is supplied in the footnotes. None of the lectures published here contained any footnotes written by Lonergan, and so the material in the footnotes is entirely our work; and it includes what otherwise would have been editorial notes.

Lonergan also cites scripture from memory. Unless we have indicated otherwise, we have retained his wording in the text and supplied the translation of the New Revised Standard Version (NRSV) in a footnote.

As in previously published volumes in the Collected Works series, we have used the *Oxford American Dictionary* and the *Chicago Manual of Style* as guides to many of the minutiae of editing. And once again we have added a lexicon of Latin and Greek phrases; these phrases are far fewer in the present volume – almost all occur in chapter 6 – but we judged that an English translation should nonetheless be provided.

We have also maintained our policy of providing a list of the works of Lonergan referred to in our notes. Again, too, *PL* is our abbreviation for reference to J.-P. Migne, *Patrologiae cursus completus ... Series Prima*, and *DB* or *DS*, depending on the context, for reference to H. Denzinger, *Enchiridion symbolorum* ... In keeping with another earlier editorial decision, we have not changed Lonergan's use of exclusive language to inclusive language.

Page references to *Collection* (CWL 4), *Understanding and Being* (CWL 5), *Insight* (CWL 3), and *Topics in Education* (CWL 10) are to the Collected Works editions. Volume numbers of these already published works as well as anticipated numbers of volumes yet to be published in the series are given in the list of Lonergan's works referred to.

It is time now to record our thanks, and our first word of acknowledgment goes to the Thomas More Institute in Montreal. The majority of the lectures in this volume were originally given at the Institute. Lonergan had a warm and close relationship with the Institute, and during his Roman years, on return summer visits to North America, he would gladly oblige his colleague and friend, the late Fr R. Eric O'Connor, and the Institute staff in giving a lecture to introduce a course. The staff of the Thomas More Institute has been extremely generous over the years in supplying us with copies of the tape recordings of these lectures and of interviews and discussions. More specifically for the editing of this volume, we are grateful to Charlotte Tansey, President and Director of Studies, and to Heather Stephens for responding to our questions (often requiring considerable detective work) regarding the context of a particular lecture in a course or series given at Thomas More.

Our further thanks, whether for initial transcriptions of tape recordings or for valuable editorial assistance, go to Ivo Coelho, Nicholas Graham, Joseph Komonchak, Jean-Marc Laporte, Richard Liddy, Howard Logan, Philip McShane, Mark D. Morelli, the late Michael O'Callaghan, Pierre Robert, Jacqueline Sheehy, Michael Shields, Bernard Tyrrell, and Sister Rose Wilker; and special thanks to Marcela Dayao, who typed the transcriptions on computer.

THE EDITORS

PHILOSOPHICAL AND THEOLOGICAL PAPERS 1958–1964

1

The Redemption[1]

1 Bibliography

It is impossible to cover adequately such a topic as the redemption in a single lecture, and I do not know just how far I will be able to take the subject in the time at my disposal. To indicate very summarily its magnitude, I would like to give a few bibliographical indications.

1 A lecture given 25 September 1958 at the Thomas More Institute, Montreal, in the course 'The God of Christian Teaching.' A transcription of the tape recording was made available at once by mimeograph (14 pp., $8\frac{1}{2} \times 11$), and was published seventeen years later as the first chapter (pp. 1–28) in the booklet *Bernard Lonergan: 3 Lectures*, ed. with intro. by R. Eric O'Connor (Montreal: Thomas More Institute, 1975).

At the time of the lecture Lonergan had just finished teaching the theology of the redemption for the third time at the Gregorian University in Rome (as part of his course 'De Verbo incarnato,' taught 1953–54, 1955–56, 1957–58). Furthermore, letters (to F. Crowe) show he had been planning a book on the redemption since 1956 (letter of 12 June 1956), had started actual work on it during the academic year of 1957–58 (17 November 1957), and by the spring had completed six chapters (25 May 1958). He may have brought this work with him to Halifax, where he spent the summer that year, but there is no evidence that he did so. If then he gave the Montreal lecture without reference material, it was an extraordinary *tour de force*, even though he was full of his subject from the work of the previous year. Two years later his first manual *De Verbo incarnato* was published (Gregorian University Press, 1960; 2nd ed., 1961; 3rd ed., 1964), with theses 15 to 17 devoted to the theology of the redemption; this work will be of use to us in locating references he made in this 1958 lecture.

Jean Rivière devoted his life to the question of the redemption. He published his doctoral thesis about 1905,[2] and he kept writing on the question until about 1949 when he died. He wrote the article on the redemption in volume 13 of the *Dictionnaire de théologie catholique*,[3] and at its end in fine print you will find several pages of bibliography up to 1937. Rivière's *Le Dogme de la rédemption dans la théologie contemporaine*,[4] published at Albi in 1948, adds further bibliography for the next ten years.

Anglican theologians particularly, and in general non-Catholic theologians in England, have written extensively on the redemption. A book of this decade by T.H. Hughes (a non-Catholic), *The Redemption in Recent Theology*,[5] gives at the end about sixty titles of books on the redemption written by non-Catholic authors in England. (English-speaking Catholics have a very low production in the field of theology, nothing to compare with France and Germany.)

In recent thinking on the redemption, an outstanding figure is Stanislaus Lyonnet, who, for the past fifteen years at least, has been professor at the Biblical Institute in Rome, publishing in the periodical *Verbum Domini*.[6] The articles are mainly in Latin, articles written by himself and by his doctoral students – for example, Fr David Stanley's study on Romans 4.25[7] was done under Fr Lyonnet. They give the exegesis, the study of the main scriptural texts relevant to the redemption, and the history of the exegesis of those texts, that is, the history of what has been said by the Fathers and the theologians and the exegetes during the whole history of the church.

2 Jean Rivière, *Le Dogme de la rédemption: Essai d'étude historique* (Paris: Librairie Victor Lecoffre, 1905); in English, *The Doctrine of the Atonement: A Historical Essay*, 2 vols., trans. Luigi Cappadelta (London: Kegan Paul, Trench, Trübner & Co., and St Louis: B. Herder, 1909).

3 *Dictionnaire de théologie catholique*, vol. 13/2 (Paris: Librairie Letouzey et Ané, 1937) cols. 1912–2004. Lonergan added: 'This is a fundamental work in all Catholic theology, composed mainly by professors in the five Instituts Catholiques in France: Paris, Lyons, Lille, Toulouse, Angers. Rivière taught at Strasburg, where the German system of Catholic university faculties holds.'

4 Jean Rivière, *Le Dogme de la rédemption dans la théologie contemporaine* (Albi: Lombard, 1948).

5 The reference is possibly to Thomas Hywel Hughes, *The Atonement: Modern Theories of the Doctrine* (London: George Allen & Unwin, 1949), which provides a bibliography of books on the atonement, pp. 325–26.

6 *Verbum Domini* (Roma: Pontificio Istituto Biblico, 1921–69), vols. 1-47.

7 David M. Stanley, 'Ad historiam exegeseos Rom 4, 25,' *Verbum Domini* 29 (1951) 257–74. (Fr Stanley was well known as a lecturer at the Institute.)

For books after 1947, there is a Spaniard by the name of Xiberta, who published in 1957 a two-volume *De Verbo incarnato,*[8] and he has about ten pages of bibliography of the last decade. There is also a book in Italian by Moraldi,[9] mainly a discussion in Italian of Hebrew words and customs. His thesis is that the notion of expiatory substitution does not occur in the Book of Leviticus. Charles Novel has written a doctoral thesis, published in 1954 – it is simply mimeographed – on the development of the notion of redemption in the Old Testament. It is in French, a doctoral thesis at the Catholic Institute of Lyons.[10] I would also like to mention Pirot-Clamer; you have probably heard of their work in any biblical courses you have had.[11] It is an edition of the Bible, Vulgate Latin and French translation about two lines per page; the rest is footnotes, and you have first-class exegesis all the way through. The best results of scriptural studies are pretty well there, though not the very latest. On the Epistle to the Hebrews, as a whole aspect of the redemption, there is the first-class commentary by Spicq in two volumes,[12] one as an introductory volume and the other as exegesis of the Epistle.

2 Redemption as Communication

The redemption is the outstanding expression of God to man. 'The Word was made flesh' was the incarnation. The words of St John refer primarily to the incarnation, to the fact that one person is both God and man. But it was not simply the fact of the second person of the Blessed Trinity assuming human nature; it was an act of communication. We express ourselves, we communicate, through the flesh, through words and gestures, the unnoticed movements of the countenance, pauses, all the manners in which, as Newman says, 'cor ad cor loquitur,' the heart

8 Bartolomaeus M. Xiberta. The reference is most likely to his two-volume *Tractatus de Verbo incarnato* (Madrid: Consejo Superior de Investigaciónes Científicas) of 1954 rather than to his *Enchiridion de Verbo incarnato* (Madrid: Consejo Superior de Investigaciónes Científicas) of 1957.

9 Luigi Moraldi, *Espiazione sacrificale e riti espiatori* (Rome: Pontifical Biblical Institute, 1956).

10 Charles Novel, 'Essai sur le développement de l'idée biblique de rédemption.' Thèse de doctorat présentée à la Faculté de théologie de Lyon, 1954.

11 Louis Pirot et Albert Clamer, *La Sainte Bible,* 2 vols. (Paris: Letouzey et Ané, 1946–64).

12 Ceslaus Spicq, *L'Épître aux Hébreux,* 2 vols. (Paris: Librairie Lecoffre, 1952, 1953).

speaks unto the heart.[13] And the incarnation and the redemption are the supreme instance of God communicating to us in this life. In heaven we shall know as we are known, but now our chief means of knowing God is through the fact of the incarnation and the act of the redemption. And it is not only God communicating with us, it is God giving himself to us. The Gospels repeatedly affirm that the motive of Christ's coming was love.

In Monsignor Knox's translation,[14] the First Epistle of St John, chapter 4, verse 9 and following, reads: 'What has revealed the love of God, where we are concerned, is that he has sent his only-begotten Son into the world, so that we might have life through him.' The sending of the Son is the revelation of the love of God. 'That love resides, not in our shewing any love for God, but in his shewing love for us first, when he sent out his Son to be an atonement for our sins.' And St John immediately goes on to the practical application: 'Beloved, if God has shewn such love to us, we too must love one another.' In 2 Corinthians, chapter 5, verses 18 and 19, we read: 'Everything has become new ... This, as always, is God's doing; it is he who, through Christ, has reconciled us to himself, and allowed us to minister this reconciliation of his to others. Yes, God was in Christ, reconciling the world to himself, establishing in our hearts his message of reconciliation, instead of holding men to account for their sins.' The sending of the Son is God's act in which he reconciles the world to him, reconciles us to him. Several similar emphases upon the love of God you will find in such notable texts as Romans 5.6–10 and Ephesians 2.4. St Augustine remarks in his *De Trinitate*, 'even when we were God's enemies, even when we were sinners, God loved us.'[15] It is not a matter of Christ earning God's love for us; God's love for us was the prime cause and mover of the redemption.

13 The motto Newman chose on being made a cardinal. See Wilfrid Ward, *The Life of John Henry Cardinal Newman* (London: Longmans, Green, and Co., 1913), vol. 2, p. 457.

14 *The New Testament of Our Lord and Saviour Jesus Christ: A New Translation* (New York: Sheed & Ward, 1945). R. Eric O'Connor (above n. 1) observes, p. 9: 'The only translation at hand in the lecture room.' Lonergan does not consistently follow this translation in subsequent scriptural references. Where he does follow it, we will simply leave his quotation without comment, but where he seems to be quoting from memory, we will give the quotation in the text as he stated it, but in the footnote will give the translation of the New Revised Standard Version (NRSV), as is our policy in the Collected Works.

15 We have not found this remark in Augustine's *De Trinitate*. Three times at least in that work Augustine refers to Romans 5.8, 'But God proves his love

Now that act that is found in the incarnation and in the death and resurrection of Christ is, above all, a personal communication. It is something directed to each individual soul. It is an object of his meditation, his contemplation; and each one must take from it his own fruit. As St Ignatius in the *Spiritual Exercises* urges, the retreatant in contemplating the mysteries of the life of our Lord is to do his own thinking on each mystery and to take from the mystery the fruit that suits him, the thoughts that come to him, the affections aroused in his heart, the acts of will that arise, that are presented as possibilities to his freedom.[16] The redemption is above all something that is accessible to everyone, no matter what his natural talents or opportunities, his cultural, intellectual, or spiritual development. It is an act of human communication performed by a divine person. It is a fundamental mistake to think of some theory, some analysis, some study of the redemption, as mediating between Christ's act and the individual soul. Moreover, that act of Christ's was above all a deed, something that can be seen, imagined, recalled, thought upon. It is not any abstract proposition but a deed accomplished for each of us. St Paul remarks incidentally, talking of scandal, 'Would you scandalize your brother for whom Christ died?' (1 Corinthians 8.11).[17] St Paul insists – he does so several times – on the relevance of the redemption to each individual.

It remains that the individual apprehension and appreciation of the word of Christ is apt to be an incomplete view. It is not wrong, mistaken, because it is incomplete. It becomes mistaken or wrong only insofar as it tends to be exclusive, as it tends to narrow down and to become fixed and static instead of growing and developing and becoming complete. And the utility of theology or of theological consideration, particularly in such a topic as this, is that it attempts to offer something of a total view, not for the purpose of replacing what one has already but for the purpose of indicating further possibilities.

---

for us in that while we still were sinners Christ died for us,' and adds his comments, but not in the words Lonergan uses. The puzzle is why Lonergan would refer to Augustine when the point was already explicit in Romans – was he perhaps thinking of one thing and, as happens, saying another?

16 Ignatius of Loyola, *The Spiritual Exercises of Saint Ignatius*, trans. George E. Ganss, SJ (St Louis: The Institute of Jesuit Sources, 1992) § 2, pp. 21–22.

17 NRSV: 'So by your knowledge those weak believers for whom Christ died are destroyed.'

3 Intelligibility of the Redemption

A view of the redemption is some act of mind, some act of understanding, and technically what is grasped when one understands is named an intelligibility. I wish to indicate first of all certain general aspects of the intelligibility of the redemption, because it is a mystery, and a mystery that is particularly complex. It involves things that profoundly trouble the mind of man: suffering and death and sin, forgiveness and law, and so on.

3.1 Not a Necessity

The first point to be noted is that, while the redemption is an intelligibility, it is not to be thought of as a necessity.

The early Protestants, the orthodox Lutherans and the orthodox Calvinists, mainly the thinkers who succeeded the first Reformers, flatly affirmed that God in his justice could not possibly forgive the sins of mankind, unless Christ became man and suffered and died. Calvin had even gone further. He was not content with the sufferings that Christ endured at the hands of the soldiers and of Pilate, but also required that the phrase in the creed 'He descended into hell' be taken to mean that Christ also suffered the punishment of the damned.

The doctrine – not Calvin's, but the doctrine – that suffering is a necessary condition limiting God's goodness can in some way be attributed to St Anselm. He frequently seems to be offering a theory that would explain why Christ's suffering and death were necessary. On the other hand, he also qualifies what he means by necessary. And it requires very nuanced interpretive efforts to determine what precisely St Anselm thought. As a matter of fact, his thinking, at the end of the eleventh century, was prior to any developed systematic distinction between philosophy and theology or any systematic attempt at determining the precise nature of theological thinking and the intelligibility that theology can grasp.

The Catholic tradition on the necessity of redemption by Christ is clear and uniform. St Augustine flatly stated that there were many other ways in which God could redeem man apart from the suffering and death of Christ. The same view was repeated by Peter Lombard, whose *Sentences* were the basic text in theology for about three or four centuries. It was repeated by St Thomas and Scotus and subsequently by all theologians.[18] And so, while there is something to be understood in connection with the redemption, this understanding is not grasping a necessity. It is not like understanding that 2 and 2 must be 4. It is like understanding the law of gravitation, which is a constant acceleration but might without any contradiction be some other mathematical formula. Intelligibility, then, is not the same as necessity.

3.2 A Dynamic Intelligibility

In the second place, that intelligibility is not static but dynamic, not a matter of deductive but rather of dialectical thought. Its fundamental element is a reversal of roles. In the book of Genesis, we read that God said to Adam when forbidding him to eat of the fruit of the tree, 'On whatever day thou eatest thereof, thou shalt die' (2.17).[19] Death is presented in the book of Genesis, and in the book of Wisdom, as the penalty for sin. The same doctrine is repeated by St Paul in Romans 5.12: 'By one man sin entered into the world, and by sin death.'[20] And again in chapter 6, verse 23, 'The wages of sin are death.'[21] Yet death is not simply and solely the wages of sin. It is by the death of Christ that we are saved. And our salvation through the death of Christ is reaffirmed continuously throughout the New Testament. As St Paul says in 1 Corinthians 15.21, 'A man has brought us death, and a man should bring us resurrection from the dead; just as all have died with Adam, so with Christ all will be brought to life.' The theme of death and resurrection takes many forms and is constantly returning in St Paul. And the meaning of that recurrence is that death is swallowed up in victory (the words in 1 Corinthians 15.54), that what was the consequence of sin became the means of salvation. That transformation of a penalty into a means of salvation is to be understood, I think, as the antithesis of the

18 It seems likely that Lonergan relied on Rivière for these historical statements denying the necessity of the redemption. At any rate, Rivière's *Le Dogme ... Essai* deals with Augustine on this question, p. 248 (*Doctrine of the Atonement* 1: 288–89), discusses Peter Lombard, pp. 81, 84 (ibid. 2: 80–81), Aquinas, pp. 364–66 (ibid. 2: 100), Scotus, pp. 368–69 (ibid. 2: 105); Rivière studies the ambiguous doctrine of Anselm in chapter 18 – see esp. pp. 314–16 (ibid. 2: 42–45).

19 NRSV: '... in the day that you eat of it you shall die.'

20 NRSV: '... just as sin came into the world through one man, and death came through sin ...'

21 NRSV: '... the wages of sin is death ...'

apocalyptic, eschatological, messianic expectations that were current in Judaism at the time of Christ. They were awaiting a Messiah that would transform, in the twinkling of an eye, the whole human situation. The wicked would be punished, and the just would triumph, in this world. But the Messiah that came did nothing startling to transform the world. He himself submitted to the evils of this world, to the injustice of the leaders of the Jewish religion, and to the injustice of the Roman procurator in Jerusalem. And as you no doubt have heard, 'sanguis martyrum, semen ecclesiae,' the blood of martyrs is the seed of the church.[22] There is in the death and resurrection of Christ a fundamental intelligibility that is not something like a deductive process but rather like a dialectical process: that sin leads to death, and death, through Christ, becomes the means of salvation. That means that conditions in this world continue despite the advent of the Messiah, but their very continuance becomes the means by which we proceed to eternal life.

3.3 An Incarnate Intelligibility

Again, the intelligibility to be reached in considering the redemption is not an abstract but an incarnate intelligibility. It exploits all the subtle relations that hold between body and mind, between flesh and spirit. Christ crucified is a symbol of endless meaning, and it is not merely a symbol but also a real death. It is again in the concrete, in the flesh of Christ, in his blood, and in his death that punishment is transfigured into satisfaction. And as you no doubt are aware, the notion of punishment is an extremely difficult notion to philosophize upon. The notion of the satisfaction of Christ contains all those difficulties and the transformation of them. I would like, in connection with that notion of satisfaction, to indicate a passage in St Thomas, in the *Summa contra Gentiles*, book 3, chapter 158. It occurs in the context of his treatment of grace, of the necessity of grace for liberation from sin. St Thomas asks how man is freed from sin. After pointing out that punishment follows upon sin by its nature, he goes on to say, in the last two paragraphs of that chapter:

22 Tertullian, *Apologeticus* 50 (*PL*, vol. 1, col. 535 in 1844 ed., col. 603 in 1879 ed.): 'Plures efficimur, quoties metimur a vobis; semen est sanguis Christianorum' ('We become more numerous every time we are hewn down by you; the blood of Christians is seed.') Tertullian, *Apology*, chapter 50, § 13, in *Fathers of the Church*, vol. 1, trans. Sister Emily Joseph Daly (New York: Fathers of the Church, Inc., 1950) 125.

> One must consider that when the mind, the soul, has turned away from sin, its displeasure in sin may be so vehement and the mind's clinging to God so firm, that there may remain no obligation to any penalty. For, as may be gathered from what has already been said about penalties, a penalty, suffered after the forgiveness of sin, is needed that the mind cling more firmly to the good and also that the order of justice be maintained. But the love of God suffices to fix firmly a man's mind in good, particularly when that love is vehement. And one's displeasure in one's own past sins can cause the greatest sorrow. Consequently through the vehemence of one's love of God and of one's hatred of one's past sins, there can be excluded the necessity of any satisfying or purgating penalty. And even if the love of God and the displeasure of sin does not attain that vehemence, at least it reduces the penalty required.

And he goes on:

> Further, since what we can do through our friends we somehow can do ourselves because friendship makes two people one in affection and particularly when the affection is charity, therefore, just as one can satisfy for one's own sins, so can one satisfy to God for another's. For the pain which a friend endures for another is taken, considered, by the other as though he himself were suffering. For your friend to suffer is for you to suffer. So, for a friend, a friend's sufferings are his own. And consequently the sufferings of Christ, contemplated by the sinner who is moved by charity, are at once an incentive to his love of God and the cause of the greatest sorrow for his own sins.[23]

I think one finds in that passage of St Thomas clues that solve not a few of the many difficulties that can be raised in connection with the notion of satisfaction. And it illustrates what I meant when I said that the intelligibility of the redemption is not an abstract but an incarnate intelligibility. One's suffering because of the sufferings of one's own friend is something that is intelligible, and yet it is something that can be seen by us to occur only when flesh and spirit are united in a single being.

23 Thomas Aquinas, *Summa contra Gentiles,* 3, c. 158. Lonergan's translation here is very free, at times a paraphrase, with several omissions.

3.4 A Complex Intelligibility

Again, the redemption is not a simple but a complex intelligibility; and I use the word 'complex' in the sense that the mathematician speaks of 'complex numbers.' The mathematician uses not only rational but also irrational numbers, not only real numbers but also imaginary numbers. And everything goes well, provided he does not mix them up, provided he does not consider that they are all numbers in exactly the same sense and manner. Similarly with regard to the redemption, we must not think of it as something that will fall into a single intelligible pattern. There is in this world the unintelligibility of sin. Sin is not something that is understood. It is not something for which you can give a reason. Why did the angels sin? Why did our first parents sin? Strictly, if there were a reason why, not simply a pretense or an excuse, it would not have been a sin. Sin represents a surd. It is the irrationality of a rational creature. It is not something that arises because God wants it to arise. To think of it that way is to think of it as though it were something intelligible, something that admitted an explanation. Everything that is, everything that is intelligible, has an explanation. But sin is not something that is; it is a failure. It is not something that is intelligible; it is an irrational. And so St Thomas can say that God in no manner whatever wills the evil of guilt, that is, the pure element that is simply sin and nothing more.[24] God in no manner whatever wills sin, and only indirectly does God will the evil of natural defects or of penalties, punishments. The divine will regards the good. The divine will permits sin. The divine will, as a consequence of willing an orderly universe, indirectly wills the accidents of natural defect and the natural consequences of sin. Consequently, in thinking about the redemption one must make an effort – and it requires an effort – to avoid the tendency to think that an explanation casts everything one can think of into a single intelligible pattern. It does that insofar as what one is considering is intelligible, has a reason. But the redemption regards sin, it presupposes sin, and it is the transformation of the situation created by sin. Consequently, in a consideration of the redemption one has to have in mind the existence not of a simple intelligibility but of the transcendent intelligibility of God meeting the unintelligibility of sin.

24 See Thomas Aquinas, *Summa theologiae*, 1, q. 19, a. 9, ad 3m.

3.5 *A Multiple Intelligibility*

Finally, the intelligibility to be reached in the consideration of the redemption is not a single but a multiple intelligibility. It is not something that is going to be fitted into some single formula, some neat reason. St Anselm's *Cur Deus homo?* does illustrate the tendency to try to reduce everything to a single formula. But it was followed by a much less celebrated work about a century and a half later, about the beginning of the first quarter of the thirteenth century, by William of Auvergne, Bishop of Paris, the title of which was not *Cur Deus homo?* why a God-man? but *De causis cur Deus homo,*[25] on the causes or the reasons why God was made man. What William wanted to put forward was that the redemption is not a matter of some single reason but of many reasons. And William represents one of the first notable attempts to introduce Anselmian thought into the theological tradition. Peter Lombard, writing about 1150, most probably knew about St Anselm's *Cur Deus homo?* but he wrote on the redemption without any mention of it or of the theories it contains. William of Auvergne belongs to the period when Anselm's work was beginning to influence the theological schools. St Thomas, in the third part of the *Summa theologiae,* question 1, article 2, after enumerating reasons for the incarnation – about five or six from three or four different points of view – ends off the main body of the article by saying that 'there are many other reasons also which transcend human comprehension.' When he treats of the nature of the redemption in the same third part, question 48, articles 1 to 5, he does not try to express the intelligibility of the redemption in a single formula, but he selects five different aspects. He asks whether Christ saved us by way of merit, whether he saved us by way of satisfaction, whether he saved us by way of redemption, whether he saved us by way of sacrifice, and whether he saved us by way of efficiency, efficient causality.

Such, then, are the general characteristics, the precautions that one must take, I think, in seeking a total view of the redemption. There is an intelligibility to be grasped, but that intelligibility is not a necessity. It is an expression of what God thought wise, what God thought good, and that is intelligible, but it is not an expression of what simply had to be. It is like an

25 *Les Oeuvres de Guillaume d'Auvergne,* tome 1 (Orléans et Paris, 1674) 555–70. William of Auvergne is not found in Rivière's *Le Dogme ... Essai,* nor in *Le Dogme de la rédemption au début du moyen âge.* We cannot determine whether Lonergan relied on some other secondary author or went directly to the source.

empirical law, not like a mathematical theory. In the second place, it is not a static but a dynamic intelligibility. It has to do with the reversal of roles: the death that is the consequence of sin becomes the means of salvation. In the third place, it is not an abstract but an incarnate intelligibility. It resides in the love Christ manifested to us and the effects of that love on us. In the fourth place, it is not a simple but a complex intelligibility; it includes the surd. There are elements to it, namely sin, that are simply nonintelligible, and there are consequences to sin that have, as it were, a devaluated intelligibility. And finally, it is not an intelligibility that can be put in a single formula but one that exhibits many aspects.

4 Aspects of the Redemption

Now I shall have something to say on the traditional five aspects enumerated by St Thomas. Obviously I cannot handle them completely. Each one could occupy several lectures. And I shall treat them more rapidly for a further reason, namely, that I wish to ask the question of how the many aspects can be brought into a single view.[26]

26 There is an apparent conflict between this 'single view' and the statement above that we are not dealing with 'an intelligibility that can be put in a single formula.' But it is more a conflict between aspects of thought growing toward unity than between two positions already taken and fixed for life. Three factors are involved here: the understanding of the redemption Lonergan inherited, his own habitual orientation toward a unified understanding, and the unity he was able to achieve by further thought.

What he inherited was the scriptural doctrine of the mystery hidden from all ages (Romans 16.25–26) and of the incredibly complex wisdom of God (Ephesians 3.10), to which was added the somewhat misguided effort of Anselm to see it all in unity, but under the heading of necessity, and the more cautious doctrine of Thomas who was content to leave his understanding spread over five aspects. Lonergan did not, then, inherit a unified understanding, but here the second factor comes into play: his own strong orientation, eloquently supported by Vatican I on the understanding of mysteries possible to us (*DB* 1796, *DS* 3016), toward a unified view, however imperfect, of what God is doing in redeeming us; there results a sense of the many-faceted reality of redemption, but also a striving toward the 'total view' that is as yet more a hope than an achievement. The third factor follows: the unity Lonergan actually achieved in his understanding of the redemption through the law of the cross; see his *De Verbo incarnato* (Rome: Gregorian University Press, 1964 – the same doctrine is found in the first edition of 1960) 574–79; brief references in English can be found in *A Second Collection*, ed. William F.J. Ryan and Bernard J. Tyrrell (London: Darton, Longman & Todd, and Philadelphia: Westminster, 1974) 7–9, 113.

4.1 *Sacrifice*

First of all, the death of Christ is conceived as a sacrifice. That conception is recurrent in St Paul. 'Christ our Pasch has been sacrificed' (1 Corinthians 5.7).[27] Again, 'Christ offered himself up as a sacrifice of sweet odor' (Ephesians 5.2).[28] It occurs, implicitly at least, in the statements in the synoptic Gospels and in 1 Corinthians, chapter 11, on the institution of the Eucharist: 'This is my body which is given for you; this is my blood which is to be shed for you for the remission of sin.'[29] But above all it is in the Epistle to the Hebrews that the death of Christ is presented as a sacrifice. Chapters 1 to 3 are devoted to presenting the new mediator between God and man. And a contrast is set up with Moses, who gave the old law. Chapters 5 and 7 are concerned with the new priesthood, chapter 8 with the new covenant, the new testament, chapters 9 and 10 with the sacrifice of the new law, which is the sacrifice of the death of Christ and the perpetual intercession of Christ for us before God. To go into details of the conception of the death of Christ as a sacrifice would be an enormous task. I could not even begin to enumerate the texts of the scripture relevant to it. But it is a conception of which no doubt whatever can be entertained by a Catholic.

However, the precise sense in which there is a sacrifice raises a question that has to do with the meaning of the Greek word *hilaskesthai.* On the meaning of that word, C.H. Dodd, a professor at Cambridge University, in *The Journal of Theological Studies,* about 1931,[30] drew attention to the fact that the usage of the word in classical Greek was quite different from that in the Greek translation of the Old Testament, the Septuagint. The root of the word permitted two different meanings. One meaning was used uniformly in the Septuagint, and the other in classical Greek. In classical Greek the word *hilaskesthai* means to placate the gods, to avert their anger or vengeance. In the Septuagint, *hilaskesthai* conveys the meaning of something that removes sin, that puts aside a barrier that prevents man's access to God. As you can see, the nuance in the different meanings of *hilaskesthai*

27 NRSV: '... our paschal lamb, Christ, has been sacrificed.'

28 NRSV: '... Christ loved us and gave himself up for us, a fragrant offering and sacrifice to God.'

29 1 Corinthians 11. 24–25. NRSV: 'This is my body that is for you ... This cup is the new covenant in my blood.'

30 C.H. Dodd, '*Hilaskesthai,* its Cognates, Derivatives, and Synonyms, in the Septuagint,' *The Journal of Theological Studies* 30 (1930–31) 352–60.

has considerable difference of implications for religious thought and religious feeling. The implications for the interpretation of the New Testament in some aspects are quite certain, in others less so. A clear example of *hilaskesthai* used in the sense of the removal of sins occurs in Hebrews 2.17, where it is stated that Christ became priest in order to *hilaskesthai* the sins of the people – in the Vulgate *propitiaret delicta populi. Hilaskesthai* is an action exercised upon sin, and that is the Septuagint meaning of the word. It is not an action exercised upon the feelings of a god, as in the rites of pagan Greece.

Another point to be noted about the interpretation or understanding of the redemption, the death and resurrection of Christ, in terms of sacrifice is that, on the one hand, the connection of sacrifice with liturgy, with prayer, with the piety of the people of God makes it an extremely helpful mode of thought, an aspect of the intelligibility of the death and resurrection of Christ, while on the other hand, because sacrifice is not traditionally, not in any but the most barbarous religions, human sacrifice – but the sacrifice of Christ is in his own blood – clearly the notion of sacrifice is not an intelligibility that exhausts the meaning of the redemption. A ritual meaning such as is connoted, a liturgical meaning such as is suggested, by the name 'sacrifice,' while it conveys enormously the aspect of personal relations between the sinner and God, still does not exhaust the meaning of the reality, insofar as Christ's sacrifice was not simply a ritual act, but his own suffering and death and glorious resurrection.[31]

4.2 Redemption

A second aspect of the redemption is connected with the word 'redemption' itself. In the New Testament, there are a variety of words employed to state that meaning. In Mark 10.45 and Matthew 20.28, Christ speaks of the Son of Man coming not to be ministered unto but to minister and to give himself in redemption for many. And the word *lytron* is employed; it denotes a ransom, a means of ransom. Again, in 1 Timothy 2.6, the word *antilytron*, a ransom in exchange, is used of the death of Christ. The verb

31 The two main points in this somewhat obscure passage are clear enough: the connection of sacrifice with liturgy helps us understand the redemption, but it does not exhaust the meaning of the reality. The reason for the second point seems to be this: the sacrifice of Christ goes beyond the usual liturgical sacrifice because it is in his own blood, and that is not the case in traditional sacrifice.

lytrousthai and the nouns *lytrôsis* and *apolytrôsis* occur repeatedly in the New Testament. *Apolytrôsis* is employed in a twofold sense, first of all of an immediate effect of the remission of sin, but also of a final effect. St Paul, in Romans 8.23, says we look forward to the redemption of our bodies. He means the resurrection of the body. The complete redemption is eschatological. It occurs not in this world but in the world to come. Besides, apart from *lytron, lytrôsis, lytrousthai,* there occur in the New Testament other words from the marketplace: 'You are bought with a price,' 'pretio redempti estis' (1 Corinthians 6.20),[32] *agorazesthai,* bought in the marketplace, and *exagorazesthai.* The word 'price' occurs, *timê.*

In connection with those frequent modes of expression and the meaning of the death of Christ in terms of the redemption, it has been noted that there are two possibilities of interpretation. The first is derived from Old Testament usage and the usage of Septuagint Greek. There are three Hebrew words mainly connected with the redemption. The first, *pâdâh,* occurs frequently in the text of the liberation of the people of Israel from Egypt. The second, *gâ'al,* is used predominantly in connection with their liberation from Babylon. And the third, *kipper,* is employed principally in connection with liberation from sin.[33] Hebrew tradition on the meaning of the word 'redemption' is primarily one of liberation, deliverance. It is not primarily a meaning in terms of a financial transaction. This meaning of redemption from the Hebrew viewpoint you will find expressed in the canticle of Zachary (Luke 1.68–79). Zachary, when he recovers his speech, sets forth the anticipation of deliverance, and employs in that context the word 'redemption.' And it is a fundamental mode of interpretation of what the word 'redemption' means.

> Blessed be the Lord, the God of Israel; he has visited his people, and wrought their redemption. He has raised up a sceptre of salvation for us among the posterity of his servant David, according to the promise which he made by the lips of holy men that have been his prophets from the beginning; salvation from our enemies, and from the hand of all those who hate us. So he would carry out his merciful design

32 NRSV: 'You were bought with a price.'

33 We follow the transliteration of the Hebrew that Lonergan used in his *De Verbo incarnato* two years later (p. 537), namely, *pâdâh, gâ'al,* and *kipper,* which is that of Stanislaus Lyonnet, *De vocabulario redemptionis* (Rome: Pontifical Biblical Institute, 1960) 142.

> towards our fathers, by remembering his holy covenant. He had sworn an oath to our father Abraham, that he would enable us to live without fear in his service, delivered from the hand of our enemies, passing all our days in holiness, and approved in his sight.

The expectation of pious Jews for a redemption included the very practical matter of being liberated from the hands of their enemies. But the purpose of that liberation was tranquility, so that they could pass 'all our days in holiness, and approved in his sight.'

> And thou, my child, wilt be known for a prophet of the most High, going before the Lord, to clear his way for him; thou wilt make known to his people the salvation that is to release them from their sins. Such is the merciful kindness of our God, which has bidden him come to us, like a dawning from on high, to give light to those who live in darkness, in the shadow of death, and to guide our feet into the way of peace.

Besides the Hebrew tradition on the meaning of the word 'redemption,' which is in terms of deliverance – deliverance for the sake of holiness – there is also a context, an interpretation, that, according to Fr Lyonnet,[34] is taken from the pagan marketplace and the ancient practice of buying and selling slaves and captives. In the Christian tradition, that has taken two forms. There is the form it took beginning with Origen, who conceived the death of Christ as liberating man from the devil. That view has been attacked as highly mythical, and perhaps not all the manners in which it was expressed among the Fathers are defensible. But at least that view has this quality, that it attributes to the devil his role; that it does not make it God the Father demanding the sufferings and death of Christ, but the devil. In that respect it is true to the fundamental picture presented in the New Testament: that it was the chief priests and Pharisees, that it was Judas and Pilate and Herod, that in the presentation of John it was the evildoer's hatred of the light, that led to the death of Christ; and what caused the resurrection was the Father. Insofar as the

34 Stanislaus Lyonnet, 'De notione emptionis seu acquisitionis,' *Verbum Domini* 36 (1958) 257–69; and later, *De peccato et redemptione*, vol. 2, *De vocabulario redemptionis* (Rome: Pontifical Biblical Institute, 1960) 49–66.

Origenist interpretation or theory of the redemption in terms of the second context, namely, that of buying and selling, is involved, at least it has this merit that the sufferings and death of Christ are thought of primarily as the work of the devil. That is also the New Testament view, and it squares with, it expresses as it were in terms of images and persons, the fundamental truth that redemption is concerned with sin, and sin is not intelligible.

The medieval reaction against the Origenist view was begun by Abelard in France and Anselm of Canterbury. Of course, discussions that concern Anselm involve volumes, and Anselm is not guilty of all the crimes attributed to him. But by the fact that he is presenting his view as just a single strand – in other words, he does not present his view as one element among many, although he does not deny it – there is perhaps a weakness in his presentation: that it contains a suggestion that God wants suffering and death as a means of forgiveness of sin, when in fact, in the redemption, God is making issue with wickedness and transforming sin and its effect into the forgiveness of sin and recovery.

We have considered two of the five aspects of the redemption that St Thomas singles out in the *Summa theologiae*, third part, question 48, namely, sacrifice and redemption. There remain three, on which I would like to make a few remarks.

4.3 Vicarious Satisfaction

The third of the five is the notion of vicarious satisfaction. I think it is well to divide it into two steps: first, the vicarious suffering, and second, the vicarious satisfaction.

The notion of vicarious suffering is very clear in the New Testament. Christ not only acted on our behalf, but he also suffered on our behalf. 'He suffered and died for us' is the type of expression (especially 'died for us') that occurs repeatedly. A person is a vicar, an agent, an attorney, when he acts for another. But Christ not only acts for another, he also suffers and dies for others. In this connection the fundamental text occurs in the Old Testament, in Isaiah, chapter 53. There is a sequence of passages, beginning in chapter 42, that are known as the songs of the servant, the 'Ebed Yahweh, but it is particularly in chapter 53 and also the last four verses of chapter 52 that there is set forth the vision of the suffering servant that in Christian tradition has been applied to Christ. I might mention that a translation in French, based upon an intensive study of the text, was recently published by Fr Cazelles in *Recherches de science religieuse* in 1955.[35] The exegesis of the passage is a matter on which volumes have been written; in addition, within this decade a bibliographical volume has been written on the works that have studied this text and have been published in the last century and a half.[36] The idea, then, may be taken most briefly by turning to the First Epistle of St Peter 2.20–25:

> If you do wrong and are punished for it, your patience is nothing to boast of; it is the patience of the innocent sufferer that wins credit in God's sight. Indeed, you are engaged to this by the call of Christ; he suffered for our sakes, and left you his own example; you were to follow in his footsteps. He did no wrong, no treachery was found on his lips; he was ill spoken of, and spoke no evil in return, suffered, and did not threaten vengeance, gave himself up into the hands of injustice. So, on the cross, his own body took the weight of our sins; we were to become dead to our sins, and live for holiness; it was his wounds that healed you. Till then, you had been like sheep going astray; now, you have been brought back to him, your shepherd, who keeps watch over your souls.

In that passage of St Peter, there recur (with minor, verbal differences) expressions from Isaiah 53: 'He did no wrong, no treachery was found on his lips,' and 'His own body took the weight of our sins,' and 'It was his wounds that healed you.' A similar notion is also found very briefly at the end of the fourth chapter of Romans: 'He died for our iniquities and rose again for our justification' (v. 25).[37]

The vicarious suffering of Christ is interpreted in the church, particularly through the influence of St Anselm, as the vicarious satisfaction of Christ. The word 'satisfaction' was employed in the church from about the third century in regard to the personal sins and the penance of the sinner after absolution. But with the possible exception of certain Spanish liturgi-

35 Henri Cazelles, 'Les Poèmes du Serviteur: Leur place, leur structure, leur théologie,' *Recherches de science religieuse* 43 (1955) 5–55.

36 Lonergan is probably referring to C.R. North, *The Servant Songs in Deutero-Isaiah* (Lund: Gleerup, 1951). This book is mentioned together with Cazelles's article in *De Verbo incarnato* (1960: 556; 1964: 470), where attention is called to its bibliography.

37 NRSV: '... who was handed over to death for our trespasses and was raised for our justification.'

cal works, it was not applied to the sufferings of Christ until St Anselm wrote his *Cur Deus homo?* at the end of the eleventh century. And the word 'vicarious' was first applied to the satisfaction of Christ during the nineteenth century. So the expression 'vicarious satisfaction' is not coeval with the life of the church itself.

The word 'satisfaction' in Latin has a variety of meanings, and there is a dictionary article of about twenty pages devoted to the matter, by Fr Deneffe, in the *Zeitschrift für katholische Theologie* of 1919.[38] Perhaps an influence that would prevent the word 'satisfaction' from being applied to a Christian interpretation of the death of Christ may be found in St Mark's Gospel, chapter 15, verse 15, in which it is said that Pilate, wishing to satisfy the people, liberated Barabbas and had Jesus scourged and condemned to death. The idea of satisfying the people is satisfaction in an evil sense, and to turn its meaning over to apply it to the suffering of Christ before God on our behalf required time.

The doctrine is implicitly Catholic doctrine. It occurs in the Council of Trent, in the sixth session on justification. In Denzinger it is stated: 'Christ by his most holy passion merited our salvation and satisfied for our sins.'[39] And further on, in the fourteenth session of the Council, on the sacrament of penance, we are given a clue to the meaning of satisfaction in the minds of the Fathers of Trent, when the Council states, 'When in satisfying we suffer for our sins, we are made similar to, we are conformed to, Jesus Christ, who satisfied for our sins.'[40] The Council is thinking of the satisfaction of the sinner whose sins have been absolved and forgiven, and who nonetheless must do penance. The Lutherans particularly, in their denial of good works, deny satisfaction for sin after the remission of sin. And the Council, reaffirming the doctrine of satisfaction, suggests that there is a similarity between the satisfaction of Christ for our sins and our own satisfaction for

38 We believe Lonergan is referring here to August Deneffe, 'Das Wort *satisfactio*,' *Zeitschrift für katholische Theologie* 43 (1919) 158–75.

39 'Iesus Christus ... sua sanctissima passione in ligno crucis nobis iustificationem meruit, et pro nobis Deo Patri satisfecit.' Henricus Denzinger, *Enchiridion symbolorum definitionum et declarationum de rebus fidei et morum*, 28th ed. (Freiburg im Breisgau: Herder, 1952; henceforth *DB*, with paragraph number) § 799. Lonergan added, 'Denzinger-Bannwart is a handbook that contains all the symbols and pronouncements of the councils and Roman pontiffs.' In the revised edition by Adolfus Schönmetzer (Freiburg im Breisgau: Herder, 1963; henceforth *DS*) the passage here referred to is found in § 1529.

40 '... dum satisfaciendo patimur pro peccatis, Christo Iesu, qui pro peccatis nostris satisfecit ... conformes efficimur.' *DB* 904 (*DS* 1690).

our sins. It puts the word 'satisfaction' in the context of contrition and confession; in other words, the three acts of the penitent in the sacrament of penance are contrition, confession, and satisfaction. And the occurrence of the word 'satisfaction,' the use by the Council of Trent of the analogy of the satisfaction of Christ, provides a solid basis for an interpretation of what the Catholic doctrine on satisfaction is.

Romans 8.3 reads:

> There was something the law could not do, because flesh and blood could not lend it the power; and this God has done, by sending us his own Son, in the fashion of our guilty nature, to make amends for our guilt. He has signed the death-warrant of sin in our nature, so that we should be fully quit of the law's claim, we, who follow the ways of the spirit, not the ways of flesh and blood.

In the Vulgate and the Greek, the passage that Monsignor Knox translates as 'he has signed the death-warrant of sin in our nature' reads literally that God has condemned sin in the flesh of Christ. The sufferings of Christ, then, are the expression of God's detestation of sin. They are also the expression of Christ's own detestation of sin. Contrition is, as you know, a matter of the detestation of sin, sorrow for sin, and purpose of amendment. And the Word was made flesh. As he loved his Father above all things according to the precept, 'Thou shalt love the Lord thy God with thy whole heart and thy whole soul and all thy mind and all thy strength,'[41] so also he loved us to whom he came. And that placed him in a divided position. We had offended God. We were turned away from God. We were not friends but enemies of God, and Christ loved both his Father and his Father's enemies. His love of us did not in the least, and could not, lessen his detestation of sin. On the contrary, his detestation of sin, combined with his love of us, caused in him the greatest sorrow that we had sinned. He was sorry for our sins because of his love for us in a manner that we can hardly be sorry, because we do not possess his knowledge of God and his love of God. Christ, the Son of God, because of his perfect knowledge and love of his Father, could detest sin as sin is to be detested, and because of his love of us could feel a sorrow such as no sorrow can equal. It is the combination of love and

41 Mark 12. 30. NRSV: '... you shall love the Lord your God with all your heart, and with all your soul, and with all your mind, and with all your strength.'

deepest regret involved in a single situation and about the same persons. That detestation of our sins and sorrow for them were acts that occur not only in the mind of Christ. Man not only thinks and wills, he also feels and acts. Christ accepted his sufferings and death. He did not ask his Father for twelve legions of angels to protect him from Caiaphas and Pilate and Herod, but accepted his sufferings because they provided an opportunity for him to communicate to us at once his love of us and his detestation of sin and his sorrow for our sins. That interpretation of what is meant by the satisfaction of Christ is just one aspect of the matter, but I mention it particularly because it fits in so well with the passage I have already quoted to you from St Thomas, in which he says that the sufferings of our friend can cause in us a sorrow greater, perhaps, than any other suffering we could have.

Now what I am saying so briefly on satisfaction is the sort of thing that is batted around for weeks in theological classes and not ended off as quickly as that. I am just giving you a few leading ideas on the subject.

4.4 *Merit*

A fourth aspect is the merit of Christ. The merit of Christ is affirmed in the documents of the church, the pronouncements of the councils. More emphatically perhaps than any other, the Council of Trent, in the section on original sin, states that 'against original sin, there is no remedy save the merit of Jesus Christ.'[42] And it reaffirms the merit of Christ again in the treatise on justification (in Denzinger, §§792 and 799).[43] St Paul, in the fifth chapter of Romans, verse 19, writes, 'As by the disobedience of one man all died, so by the obedience of one man all are saved.'[44] Christ's obedience is also Christ's merit. A merit is a good act worthy of a recompense. And when St Paul says that by Christ's obedience we are saved, by a very close implication one can conclude that there is an element of merit in the relationship of Christ's free act and our salvation. The freedom of Christ in dying is affirmed emphatically in St John 10.18. And the merit of Christ, not for us but for himself, appears in Philippians 2.7, in Hebrews 5.8, and also in Hebrews 2.9.

42 'Si quis hoc Adae peccatum ... per aliud remedium asserit tolli, quam per meritum unius mediatoris Domini nostri Iesu Christi ... [anathema sit].' *DB* 790 (*DS* 1513).

43 *DS* 1515 and 1529.

44 NRSV: 'For just as by the one man's disobedience the many were made sinners, so by the one man's obedience the many will be made righteous.'

4.5 *Efficiency*

Finally, there is the efficiency of the death and resurrection of Christ. Efficiency means something more than intercession. Intercession suggests what the man Jesus asks God to do for us. Efficiency is what he himself does. There are two aspects to it: what he does reigning in heaven, and what he has done as a historical person who founded a church and down the ages has exerted an influence upon the lives of countless millions, more intimate and more profound than any other historical figure.

5 Redemption as Mystery

Now I have been speaking of redemption in terms of particular aspects: merit and efficiency, redemption and sacrifice, and vicarious satisfaction. I would like briefly to suggest how one moves towards a total view. I think that the fundamental category is the word *mystery*, not in the theologian's sense of a truth that we cannot adequately understand in this life, nor in the sense of Christian piety that speaks of the mysteries of the life of Christ and meditates upon the mysteries of the rosary, but in the sense of the New Testament, where it refers to the secret counsel of God, the plan of God. In St Mark 4.11–12, it is stated that the apostles had been given the mystery of the kingdom of God. In Romans, at the end of chapter 16, St Paul speaks of 'a gospel which reveals the mystery, hidden from us through countless ages, but now made plain, through what the prophets have written, and published, at the eternal God's command, to all the nations, so as to win the homage of their faith' (Romans 16.25–26). The mystery hidden through all the ages and now made plain is mystery in the sense of 'secret counsel.' A Greek word has been used to translate a Hebrew conception of Persian origin, as is clear from the Old Testament and from the recent findings at Qumran. There are articles on this by Vogt[45] and by Prümm[46] in *Biblica* of 1956; and there is also an article of Prümm in the *Supplément au dictionnaire de la bible*, entitled 'Mystères.'[47] 'Mystery' means the secret counsel of a king, and it is in that sense, fundamentally, that it is employed

45 Ernst Vogt, '*Mysteria* in textibus Qumran,' *Biblica* 37 (1956) 247–57.

46 Karl Prümm, 'Zur Phänomenologie des paulinischen Mysterion und dessen seelischer Aufnahme. Eine Übersicht,' *Biblica* 37 (1956) 135–61.

47 Karl Prümm, 'Mystères,' in *Supplément au dictionnaire de la bible*, ed. L. Pirot, A. Robert, and Henri Cazelles (Paris: Librairie Letouzey et Ané, 1960) cols. 1–226.

in the New Testament. When St Paul speaks of the revelation of the mystery that is now made plain (as he does in Ephesians and 1 Corinthians, chapters 1 and 2, and in the last chapter of Romans, and in reciting the hymn in 1 Timothy 3.16), we have to do with God's counsel, God's plan, God's ideas, that is, the divine wisdom itself, 'the *polypoikilos*, the incredibly complex wisdom of God,' as it is said in Ephesians 3.10,[48] and again, 'that in Christ all the mysteries of wisdom are hidden,' in Colossians 2.3.[49]

That divine plan is presented in the New Testament in a variety of ways. It is spoken of as the kingdom of God, the kingdom of heaven, in Mark and Matthew particularly, also in Luke. And there are countless parables to illustrate what the kingdom of God is. After his baptism at the hands of John the Baptist, it is narrated in Mark 1:14–15 that Jesus came into Galilee announcing that the time is fulfilled and that the kingdom of God is at hand; repent and believe.

This theme of the kingdom of God goes back to what lies at the origins, perhaps, of Jewish messianic expectation. You know the kingdom was introduced under Samuel to end the theocracy, the direct rule of God over his people. And when the kings were introduced – Samuel the prophet did not like this, and he complained – God said to Samuel, 'It is not you they are rejecting, it is I.' Consequently to that introduction of the kings, there developed the notion of the Messiah, the anointed one of God, who was to come and be the king and establish God's own kingdom, so that the notion of the kingdom and of the theocracy would be, as it were, coincident. And when Christ announces the kingdom of God, he is drawing upon a rich background of Jewish memories and traditions. The exposition of what the kingdom is and means occupies the greater part of the synoptic Gospels – for example, the parables of the kingdom in Matthew 13. Now the same notion occurs in Colossians 1.12–13 where you have a reference to the kingdom: 'giving thanks to God our Father ... for rescuing us from the power of darkness, and transferring us to the kingdom of his beloved Son.'[50]

The same theme of the kingdom takes another form in the New Testament: of the body of Christ, which has a fundamental statement in Romans 12.4–5; a fuller statement in 1 Corinthians, chapter 12, and in Ephesians, chapter 2. And the body of Christ is also the church of Christ.

48 NRSV: 'the wisdom of God in its rich variety.'
49 NRSV: 'in whom are hidden all the treasures of wisdom and knowledge.'
50 NRSV: '... giving thanks to the Father ... He has rescued us from the power of darkness and transferred us into the kingdom of his beloved Son.'

The structure of this mystery, whether spoken of as the kingdom, the inauguration of the kingdom, the body of Christ, or the foundation of the church, is set forth in the New Testament in terms of antitheses.[51]

There is the antithesis of the old law, which is recurrent particularly in Galatians and Romans, where law and sin and wrath and death are contrasted with the promise made to Abraham and justice and grace and life. It is the presentation of our life in Christ Jesus in terms of an antithesis to the old law. It is a theme that is constant in Galatians, and particularly in the first three chapters of Romans, to some extent in the fourth, and again in chapters 6, 7, and 8. It is also set forth in the antithesis of the first and second Adam, and there the contrast is not between the kingdom of Christ, the body of Christ, and the old law, but between redeemed humanity and humanity without redemption. That you will find particularly in such passages as 1 Corinthians 15.21–22 and 45–49, and Romans 5.12–21.

The same general antithesis that St Paul expresses in terms of the first and second Adam is found in St John between the world and darkness and law and sin and, on the other hand, life and truth and grace and light. And to enlarge upon those themes would be to go through the whole New Testament.

The New Testament above all is a document of salvation. The gospel is the good news, and the good news is the kingdom of God, the body of Christ, his church, the fulfilment of the promise made to Abraham, the gift of justice and grace and life in opposition to law, sin, wrath, and death. Christ is a new Adam, and again Christ is light and truth and grace and life – that theme runs through the whole of St John. Within this general antithesis running through the whole New Testament, there is to be found its concrete illustration, application, realization, in the theme of death and

51 Lonergan here tends toward at least a partial identification of the church with the kingdom of God. Later he is concerned to distinguish them. See, for instance, the transcript by Nicholas Graham of Lonergan's lectures on Method in Theology at Boston College, 3–12 July 1968 (File no. 481 in the library of the Lonergan Research Institute, Toronto) [illegible]: 'When I was a student of theology, the kingdom of God was identified with the church, and that is something that has been eliminated by Vatican II. The church is God's instrument, one of God's instruments, in this world for promoting the kingdom of God with regard to the whole world.' See also *Method in Theology* (London: Darton, Longman & Todd, and New York: Herder and Herder, 1972; latest reprint, Toronto: University of Toronto Press, 1994) 364: 'Its [the church's] aim is the realization of the kingdom of God ... in the whole of human society ... also in this life.'

resurrection. Its illustration is in the symbolic or sacramental sense of dying in the death of Christ; its application is the admonition to mortify ourselves; and its actual aspect is that Christ really died and that we shall die and rise again.[52]

Suffering as retribution has its place in the New Testament, but retribution is far from being the only or the practical meaning of suffering. We have already read the passage from the First Epistle of St Peter, chapter 2, where he says that there is nothing to boast about when you suffer justly for your own offences; it is the innocent sufferer that means something before God. That, in the Sermon on the Mount, is the doctrine of Christ:

> You have heard that it was said, Thou shalt love thy neighbor and hate thy enemy. But I tell you, Love your enemies, do good to those who hate you, pray for those who persecute and insult you, that so you may be true sons of your Father in heaven, who makes his sun rise on the evil and equally on the good, his rain fall on the just and equally on the unjust. If you love those who love you, what title have you to a reward? Will not the publicans do as much? If you greet none but your brethren, what are you doing more than others? Will not the very heathen do as much? But you are to be perfect, as your heavenly Father is perfect. (Matthew 5.43–48)

And earlier in the same chapter, 'Blessed are you, when men revile you, and persecute you, and speak all manner of evil against you falsely, because of me. Be glad and light-hearted, for a rich reward awaits you in heaven; so they persecuted the prophets who went before you' (Matthew 5.11–12); and again, 'You have heard that it was said, An eye for an eye and a tooth for a tooth. But I tell you that you should not offer resistance to injury; if a man strikes thee on thy right cheek, turn the other cheek also towards him; if he is ready to go to law with thee over thy coat, let him have it and thy cloak with it' (Matthew 5.38–40). Again, in the fundamental passage in which Christ speaks of giving his soul in redemption for many, giving his life in redemption for many – 'giving his soul' is a Hebraism – we have to note the context. The context is when the mother of the two sons of Zebedee asked that James and John sit at the right and left hand of Jesus when he came into his kingdom. And when the other apostles heard of this, they were angry. It reads:

52 This sentence was just a series of headings; we have turned the headings into a sentence.

> The ten others were angry with the two brethren when they heard it; but Jesus called them to him, and said, You know that, among the Gentiles, those who bear rule lord it over them, and great men vaunt their power over them; with you it must be otherwise, and whoever has a mind to be first among you, must be your slave. So it is that the Son of Man did not come to have service done him; he came to serve others and to give his life as a ransom for the lives of many. (Matthew 20.24–28)

The New Testament, I think, in such a passage and in many others provides the clue to the intelligibility of the redemption. It is the victory of suffering, of accepting the consequences of sin, the evils of this world, in the spirit that animated Christ. It is the transformation of the world that arises when evil is transformed into good by the Christian spirit. Christ refused the strict justice of an eye for an eye and a tooth for a tooth. He imposed upon his followers a command of patience and submission under wrong, because impatience usually creates only more wrong. And the meaning of his own words is fundamentally the transformation of evil into good. In the words of St Paul, in chapter 12 of Romans, in the last verse, 'Do not be overcome by evil, but overcome evil with good.'[53] What was Christ doing dying and rising again? He was overcoming in himself, and also through his followers, all the evils in the world, and overcoming them to rise again, that by his resurrection we might know and realize and act upon those words of St Paul in Romans, chapter 8, verse 28, 'To those that love God, all things conspire unto the good.'[54]

I thank you.

53 Lonergan quotes from memory here, and the NRSV has exactly the same translation.

54 NRSV: '... all things work together for good for those who love God.' Alternate readings are given as well: '... God makes all things work together for good ...' and '... in all things God works for good ...'

2

Method in Catholic Theology[1]

My title has to be understood in the light of my terms of reference. The invitation so kindly extended to me was to speak on the method I happen to employ in my work as a theologian. What was desired was, not an account of methods or of their history, but rather a report on a contemporary approach.

A method, I take it, is a set of rules or directives for the advancement of a science.[2] It is concerned to tell just what is to be done and how to do it. It also is concerned to indicate what cannot be done, what need not be done, and what can or must be left to take care of itself.

1 A lecture given to the Society for Theological Studies, at Nottingham University, in April 1959. The content corresponds very closely to that of a course, *De intellectu et methodo*, that Lonergan was teaching in the Gregorian University, February to June 1959. The typescript of the lecture, found in the Lonergan Archives, shows careful preparation, with many corrections, whole sentences and paragraphs crossed out and rewritten, and occasionally slips of paper with new versions pasted over the original; some of the deletions are of special interest, and we have indicated these in the notes. Here and there are passages that are not crossed out but marked 'omit'; this we take to be for the most part a directive for delivery, and so we have included these as integral parts of the composition, but without footnote indication.

This lecture was previously published in *Method: Journal of Lonergan Studies* 10:1 (Spring 1992) 3–26. The present version shows only minor emendations of that previously published text.

2 Compare the familiar definition of *Method in Theology* (see above, chapter 1, note 51) 4: 'A method is a normative pattern of recurrent and related operations yielding cumulative and progressive results.'

Such rules can be formulated in three manners. They may regard outward acts of looking and listening, of manipulating instruments, or employing ordinary or technical language. Again, they may go behind sense, action, and language to the concepts and the judgments of the mind. Thirdly, they may turn from the mind's immanent products to the conscious, inquiring, critically reflective subject. The rules I shall outline are of the third type. At first sight, they may well appear to be very unsubstantial. But if you will consent to be very patient with me, there is, I think, some chance you will agree that this approach makes it possible to set forth certain basic issues that otherwise can hardly be raised at all.[3]

My rules, then, are five in number.[4] They are: (1) Understand. (2) Understand systematically. (3) Reverse counterpositions. (4) Develop positions. (5) Accept the responsibility of judgment.

3 The preceding paragraph was pasted over the following two paragraphs: 'Along with an array of imperatives, a method offers a promise. Do as you are told, and you will contribute to the progress, development, advancement of science. But the fulfilment of the promise is a future event that, for the time being, cannot be observed. The fulfilment is also a somewhat indeterminate event for, if we already knew the content of future science, we should have no use for the precepts of a method.

'This promise of an unknown and, at present, unverifiable event is apt to disturb even those that are not excessively cautious or suspicious. Just what, one wonders, are the grounds that justify both the precepts and the promise?'

There follows on the next page another paragraph that is marked for omission:
'But, however legitimate this question, I do not propose to meet it directly. Modern philosophy, I believe, became so totally involved in epistemological questions, because it also was interested in the theoretical basis of method. Since I think it somewhat unlikely that you care to discuss cognitional theory, I shall venture to be generous with precepts but brief with reasons.'

4 From this point to the end of the lecture whole sentences and paragraphs are the equivalent in English of scattered passages in notes on the course *De intellectu et methodo* (see note 1); the notes bear the notation, 'notae ... collectae et ordinatae ... ab aliquibus auditoribus,' but there is good reason to trust their accuracy. Further references to *De intellectu et methodo* refer to these pages of notes as these are found in the library of the Lonergan Research Institute, Toronto.

Which came first, the paper or the course? The latter ran from 12 February to 10 June inclusive, so Lonergan would hardly have come to the second part of his course (where the similarities are most evident) when he prepared the Nottingham lecture; even if he had, the student notes (supposing he saw them) would hardly have been ready in early April. Nor would his own notes for the course (supposing he had them all ready in April) have been prepared in such detail as appears in the notes taken by the students, for in his

As you will have observed, these rules are very brief; as you will fear, their explanation is apt to be very long; and compounded with this fear, which is not unjustified, there will be some alarm. For there is nothing specifically theological about the rules I have listed.

To meet this last point at once, I note that I do not believe in a multiplicity of methods. I do not think that there is one set of precepts for mathematics, another for natural science, a third for human science, a fourth for philosophy, a fifth for theology.[5] On the contrary, as human intelligence is one, so also is the grand strategy of its advance; method is concerned to implement that strategy; it undergoes adaptations to exploit the possibilities and to circumvent the difficulties proper to different fields; but the adaptations are basically a matter of acknowledging and mastering circumstance.

It follows that my exposition will fall naturally into two parts. First, I shall

---

courses he was in the habit of lecturing from headings rather than a prepared text. The paper, it seems, is first.

There may be a further clue to the order of paper and course notes in the fact that, in preparing the paper, Lonergan first typed, 'My precepts are four in number.' Was this a slip in typing? Or was he thinking it out as he typed, and decided he needed five rules instead of four? If the latter, then again the paper is first and the course notes second.

Whatever the order of the two documents, they are clearly contemporaneous with one another.

5 Compare this position with that of 'The Ongoing Genesis of Methods,' the third of Lonergan's Queen's University lectures of 1976 (*A Third Collection: Papers by Bernard Lonergan, S.J.*, ed. Frederick E. Crowe [New York: Paulist Press, 1985] 146–65); here we still have generalized empirical method (150), but the differences of the particular methods are spelled out more sharply. See especially 152: 'not all empirical methods emerge as differentiations within the basic procedures of the natural sciences. The clear-cut instance of this leap to another genre is provided by historical studies as they developed in Germany in the nineteenth century'; and 154: 'there is a profound difference between natural science and historical study.'

From his doctoral dissertation to his later writings Lonergan believed strongly that the human mind is always the human mind. In particular, the twofold way of analysis and synthesis that structured his theology at the time of this Nottingham paper was applicable also to the natural sciences. He regularly illustrated it by chemistry. But when he had worked out his theological method in terms of the eight functional specialties, he attended much more carefully to the differences in methods. Already in the lectures of this volume, Lonergan was beginning to spell out the specific differences, within a general unity, of the methods for natural science, human science, and so on. See chapters 5, 7, and 9 below.

review the five precepts in their general and basic meaning, and in this review I shall be free to draw my illustrations from any field. Secondly, I shall turn to the adaptations relevant to theology, and then I shall have in mind Catholic theology.

1 Five Precepts

1.1 Understand

My first precept is: Understand. By it I refer not to words or sentences, not to concepts or judgments, not to the data of sense, but to what is the key act or event in any discovery, to the moment when one grasps why, knows the reason, sees the point, catches on. Such moments may be epochal. They may be accompanied with the explosive delight that made Archimedes shout, 'Eureka!' They may initiate the overmastering absorption that almost without interruption kept Sir Isaac Newton at his desk for weeks. But normally they are very pedestrian affairs, occurring with the ease and frequency that save us from acquiring a reputation for stupidity. However, if the act of understanding is neither difficult nor rare, it is nonetheless fundamental. A discovery is merely the first occurrence of an act of understanding; the advance of a science is primarily an accumulation of discoveries; and a method aims at no more than encouraging, directing, and ordering such accumulations.

My first precept is illuminated not only by its direct meaning but also by what it omits. I do not say, 'Make significant acts of understanding.' It is significant acts, of course, that are wanted; but they do not form a distinct species, and they do not result from the observance of a special set of rules; they are simply the acts that happen to close one stage of development and to open another; and they derive their significance not from themselves but from their connection with antecedent and consequent acts.

Again, I do not say, 'Make correct acts of understanding.' For though correct acts are the ones that are wanted, still the difference between a correct act and an incorrect one is not intrinsic. Understanding, of itself, yields no more than ideas, definitions, hypotheses, theories. They may prove to be correct; far more commonly they prove to be incorrect; but in themselves they are neither true nor false. They are more or less helpful, more or less adequate, more or less in the direction of success and achievement. To expect them to be correct is to demand too much; and to demand too much is an extremely efficacious way of obtaining nothing at all.

Again, I do not say, 'Be impartial. Set aside all prejudice. Drop all preconceptions. Doubt everything that cannot be demonstrated.' We have to begin with ourselves as we are, and commonly that means that we have to begin with a large ignorance of ourselves. We cannot revert at will to the *tabula rasa* to which Aristotle likened the state of our intellects at our birth.[6] Nor is the real problem deliberate bias, willful narrow-mindedness, conscious excess of certitude. What has to be eliminated is the unconscious aberration that may appear to be the very soul of truth; and the one way to eradicate it is, I think, to advance in understanding.

Again, my first rule is not 'Observe. Attend to the data. Attend to them as they really are. Attend to all relevant data.' Each of these imperatives, I believe, gives excellent advice; but I also believe that both the advice and the one effective way of following the advice are contained in the more basic precept 'Understand.' If one is trying to understand, one is inquiring; if one is inquiring, one is attending to something given but not yet understood; such attention is observation. Further, observation becomes full and accurate just in the measure that one increases in understanding. A good observer has not a broader span of attention than the ordinary man, but he does possess a greater intellectual interest, a greater capacity to organize multiplicities into perceptible unities, a greater concern to note differences that are there to be seen by anyone but noticed only when developing understanding is directing and controlling the operations of sense for its own intellectual ends.[7] In similar fashion, while it is true that one should attend to all the relevant data, it is no less true that understanding itself is the measure of relevance and that only complete understanding can tell when the totality of relevant data has been taken into account.

Finally, when I say, 'Understand,' I do not mean, 'Conceive or know the necessary, the per se, the intelligible, the abstract, or the universal.' Any such substitution involves the psychological fallacy. One can attempt to describe or define such an experience as seeing or hearing. The description will be a matter of concepts and words. But seeing is neither concept nor word. Similarly, one can attempt to describe or define the experience of understanding; but it would be fallacious to confuse the experience

6 Aristotle, *De anima*, III, 4, 430a 1: 'a writing-tablet on which as yet nothing actually stands written' (J.A. Smith translation, in *The Basic Works of Aristotle*, ed. Richard McKeon [New York: Random House, 1941] 591).

7 Four lines crossed out here include the clause, 'but he does possess a greater power of giving a form or *Gestalt* to the data.'

itself with any of the concepts or words employed in the description. Indeed, from my point of view any such confusion would be disastrous, for understanding possesses a versatility that ranges over the whole conceptual field, and as well pivots between it and the world of sense.

What is understood may be expressed as necessary. But the contradictory is also true. Understanding grasps the principles and laws of natural science, but it considers them, not necessary, but only true in fact. They are empirical intelligibilities.

What is understood may be expressed as per se. But understanding also grasps the theory of probability, and such theory reveals an intelligibility in what is, not per se, but *per accidens.*

What is known precisely inasmuch as one understands offers a definition of the intelligible. But understanding can also make issue with the non-intelligible; it can take its nonintelligibility as a premise to develop techniques that master it; in this fashion I believe understanding proceeds in treating irrational numbers, probabilities, the law of inertia, sin, and the fruits of sin.

When we are able to abstract, it is because we understand. But it does not follow that, whenever we understand, we can effect a satisfactory abstraction. A conceptual account of a smile or a frown, a painting or a symphony, fails to reach the precise intelligibility that understanding grasps in the concrete presentation.

Further, while abstract concepts are related to the sensible only as the universal to the particular, the same is not true of understanding. It is in the sensible, in the concrete, that understanding grasps intelligibility. To understand a machine or an organism or a social entity is to grasp intelligible interdependence in concrete multiplicity.

Finally, similars are similarly understood, and in this sense it is true that understanding grasps the universal. It remains that understanding may or may not exploit its capacity for generalization. Aristotle credited Socrates with the invention or introduction of universal definitions.[8] But the Athenians did not like them. They considered Socrates' teaching subversive. In fact, it was only novel. Still, I suggest, the novelty consisted in far greater concern with the universal than common sense exhibits. For common sense does not seek the universal definitions and truths that must hold in every instance with an exactitude that will bear the weight of lengthy infer-

8 Aristotle, *Metaphysics,* XIII, 4, 1078b 27–29.

ences. Commonsense understanding seeks, not strict universality, but general utility. It aims at a development of intelligence that operates, not through universal principles and deductions, but through the continuous adaptations and adjustments demanded by the successive situations of concrete living.

1.2 *Understand Systematically*

It is time to turn to my second precept, Understand systematically. By it I mean, first, that one's efforts at understanding must aim at the ideal goal of understanding, and secondly, that they must make explicit the structure through which understanding naturally moves toward this goal.

The ideal goal of understanding is completeness. Common sense operates within a cultural horizon. It settles for a mode and measure of understanding that suffice to enable one to live intelligently. But human intelligence wants more; it heads for the complete explanation of all phenomena; it would understand the universe. It distinguishes endlessly; but it does so only to relate intelligibly; and ideally the network of relations is to embrace everything. It is this complete network of relations, making intelligible every aspect of the concrete universe, that is to be thought of when I say that understanding is to be systematic.

Now this ideal of the ultimate system is not just a standard by which we know how far we still have to go. It also is an operative component in our progress. Spontaneously we employ it as an implicit premise in our efforts to understand. A method makes it an explicit and consciously exploited premise.

This may seem strangely difficult, and so I offer examples that illustrate its possibility. Texts in elementary algebra abound, or at least used to abound, in mysterious problems that, soon enough, we learned to solve by writing down, 'Let the unknown number be *x*.' Once that was done, we had only to read the problem carefully again to discover that we could also write down an equation in terms of *x*. Finally, the solution of such equations was no more than the automatic application of rules with which zealous pedagogues had made us more than familiar.

What is the magic efficacy of writing down, 'Let the unknown number be *x*?' Like all magic, it is only apparent. When one writes out that sentence, one affirms that the unknown lies in the determinate category 'number.' One implies that it possesses the very definite properties possessed by numbers. One implies that it stands within the network of relations exhibited by counting and by arithmetical operations. Granted all this, one has only to advert to the data supplied in the problem to determine which of all numbers is the one required.

Such a procedure is not restricted to an a priori science such as mathematics. Physicists know that they aim to know laws; they conceive laws as functional relations; and when they set out to determine the law of a precise type of phenomenon, they can begin by writing down, 'Let the unknown law be the indeterminate function $F(x, y, z, t) = 0$.'[9] That sentence is far from a confession of complete ignorance. On the contrary, physicists can reach a solution of a large number of scientific issues without settling exactly just which function is the required law. They can argue from differential equations and from boundary conditions, and they can do so because they are in pursuit of an ideal of system.

Now I happen to believe that a similar technique can and should be employed universally. I believe it is relevant not only to the natural sciences but also to the human sciences, to philosophy, and to theology. I base this relevance on the fact that such a technique merely makes explicit what already is implicit in all intelligent and reasonable human knowing. But if you ask in what precisely such a technique consists, I can only say that you will find it illustrated by my present efforts to bracket the unknown that is the advance of science in general and of theology in particular.[10]

1.3 Reverse Counterpositions and Develop Positions

My third and fourth rules have to do with one's own personal development

9 It was later pointed out to Lonergan, in regard to a similar line in *Insight*, that he should use 'equation' here instead of 'function,' and there is evidence that he accepted the criticism; see *Insight: A Study of Human Understanding*, 5th ed., revised and augmented, ed. Frederick E. Crowe and Robert M. Doran (Toronto: University of Toronto Press, 1992) 784, editorial note *f* to chapter 2.

10 This sentence, whose meaning is difficult to decipher, was handwritten in the manuscript of the lecture. It replaces the sentence, 'But for details I must refer you to my book, *Insight*.' A clue to the meaning might be found by referring to Lonergan's use of the word 'bracket' in the introduction to *Insight*: 'The aim of the present work may be bracketed by a series of disjunctions.' Here, to bracket is to collect, set out in brief headings, and set apart for consideration, points that need special attention. In other words, the word is not used in the sense of bracketing 'out,' but of bracketing 'in.' The process toward system, briefly 'bracketed' here, is set forth at greater length in *De intellectu et methodo* 40–43 ('De secundo praecepto: intellige systematice'). The same point is made in many of Lonergan's later writings: for example, *Method in Theology* 81–83, on the systematic exigence.

and, as well, with one's learning from others. The ideal of understanding systematically becomes clear and distinct and effective only at a late stage in the development of the individual and of the race. First we understand intersubjectively, and the intelligibility we grasp is symbolic. Such is, I think, the understanding of mother and child, of Martin Buber's 'I and Thou,' of Heidegger's *Mitsein.* By it is known the person, not as object, but as another subject, transparent in smile or frown, in blush or scowl, in tone of voice, in silent gaze. Upon this base there next is grafted the understanding of common sense that organizes the world with names and collaborates towards mastering it with language. But intersubjectivity and common sense are propaedeutic to a third stage when the *logos* immanent in man comes to awareness of its potentialities and asks for a method that will lead to complete understanding.

Now the difficulty of this third stage is that it can be itself, be true to its own inner exigences, only by taking stock of its earlier history, noting the limitations of previous modes, acknowledging their opposition to the new demands of intelligence and reasonableness, and opting consciously, deliberately, coherently, and thoroughly for the new way. This new way has been given many different expressions in the history of philosophy and of science, and not all the expressions agree. Again, it comes in different guises to different individuals. Such differences have their source, I should say, in an incomplete grasp of the insufficiency of the older, more familiar ways and, as well, in an inadequate appreciation of the implications of the new.

There exists, then, I believe, a process of intellectual conversion, and my third and fourth rules regard that process. My first rule was: Understand. In virtue of that first rule I conclude that all genuine discoveries must be retained. My second rule was: Understand systematically. In virtue of that second rule I divide the formulations of discoveries into two classes: positions and counterpositions. Positions are formulations that can be retained unchanged within the new way. Counterpositions are formulations that have to be recast before they can be made coherent with the new way.

You will recognize in such rules a variant on many older themes. The Fathers of the church believed in despoiling the Egyptians, of taking their truth while disengaging it from pagan error. Descartes preached universal doubt, and Newman thought that believing everything, while absurd, nonetheless was a preferable procedure. The history of the development of science has been a continuous transmutation of notions that once seemed too evident to be controverted. In his *Phenomenology of Spirit* Hegel has many useful things to say on the coming-to-be of mind. In our own day Rudolf Bultmann has advocated a procedure to strip the New Testament of what he considers mythical elements. The problem at least exists.

But the root of the problem, I believe, its really baffling element, lies within the subject, within each one of us. For the problem is not solved merely by assenting to the propositions that are true and by rejecting the propositions that are false. It is a matter of intellectual conversion, of appropriating one's own rational self-consciousness, of finding one's way behind the *natura naturata*,[11] the *pensée pensée*, of words and books, of propositions and proofs, of concepts and judgments, to their origin and their source, to the *natura naturans*, the *pensée pensante*, that is oneself as intelligent and as reasonable. Without such self-appropriation and the critical appraisal it generates, one may repeat all that an Augustine says of *veritas*,[12] or all that an Aquinas says of being, but in doing so, I believe, one will not be raising oneself up to their level but cutting them down to one's own size.

1.4 Accept the Responsibility of Judgment

My fifth rule is: Accept the responsibility of judgment. The obvious content of this rule is negative, for it rejects the notion that there is any set of rules

11 The pair *natura naturata* ... *natura naturans* is not part of Lonergan's regular usage in this context, and it is not clear what prompted him to include it here; in *Insight* he had a triad of pairs: *noêma* ... *noêsis*, *intentio intenta* ... *intentio intendens*, and *pensée pensée* ... *pensée pensante* (*Insight* 30). Thomas Aquinas speaks of some who call God *natura naturans* (*Summa theologiae*, 1–2, q. 85, a. 6) but does not adopt the term himself; in any case, Lonergan's context is different. Modern use of the pair is due in part to Spinoza. See James Collins, *A History of Modern European Philosophy* (Milwaukee: Bruce Publishing Co., 1954) 223: 'Like Bruno, he [Spinoza] revived the medieval terms *natura naturans* and *natura naturata*' to advance his doctrine on God and world.

12 Lonergan regularly related Augustine's *veritas* to Thomas's *esse*. See *Topics in Education*, ed. Robert M. Doran and Frederick E. Crowe, revising and augmenting the unpublished text prepared by James Quinn and John Quinn (Toronto: University of Toronto Press, 1993) 172: 'St Augustine is the one who developed the notion of judgment as fundamental in knowing, the *veritas*. St Thomas added its metaphysical equivalent, the *esse*, in the composition of the finite being.' See also ibid. 170. An especially important source on this question, since it links Augustine and Aquinas with Maréchal and Bernard Leeming (Lonergan's friend and teacher at the Gregorian University in the 1930s), is the 1973 paper '*Insight* Revisited'; see *A Second Collection* (see above, chapter 1, note 26) 263–78, at 165. See also *Insight* 437 and *A Third Collection* 52 (in 'Aquinas Today: Tradition and Innovation').

that, so to speak, automatically or mechanically brings inquiry to knowledge, truth, certitude. Method is operative only through minds. Minds reach knowledge only through judgment. And there is no recipe for producing men of good judgment.

Because such a recipe does not exist, philosophic methods tend to eliminate the issue, and scientific methods to evade it. The responsibility of judging vanishes in rationalism, because there the true judgment is necessitated. It vanishes in empiricism, because there what counts is not judging but looking. It vanishes in idealism, because there truth assumes a meaning that does not demand any personal decision. It vanishes in relativism, because there a judgment that is simply true cannot be attained. Again, in natural science the individual's responsibility of judging is not acknowledged, and in its place there comes a pragmatism, an acquiescence in what works. But while this pragmatism itself seems to work well enough in natural science, in the human sciences its results are not so happy. For in the human sciences measurement is superficial and experiment is monstrous. There has resulted, according to Edmund Husserl in his *Krisis der europäischen Wissenschaften,*[13] a proliferation of specialized fields. Each of these fields is autonomous. Each tends to be ruled by its own conventionally accepted criteria. Nor does there seem to be, under present conditions, any possibility of giving unity and depth, significance and efficacy, to this many-sided activity. For any such effort would be regarded as merely the erection of just one more specialized field that merited the attention only of those actually engaged in it.

13 Edmund Husserl, *Die Krisis der europäischen Wissenschaften und die transzendentale Phänomenologie: Eine Einleitung in die phänomenologische Philosophie*, ed. Walter Biemel (The Hague: Martinus Nijhoff, 1954; 2nd printing, 1962); in English, *The Crisis of European Sciences and Transcendental Phenomenology: An Introduction to Phenomenological Philosophy*, trans. David Carr (Evanston, IL: Northwestern University Press, 1970). This work of Husserl's keeps cropping up in Lonergan's lectures at this time; for example, in both the Halifax lectures on *Insight* in 1958 (*Understanding and Being*, ed. Elizabeth A. Morelli and Mark D. Morelli, revised and augmented by Frederick E. Crowe with the collaboration of Elizabeth A. Morelli, Mark D. Morelli, Robert M. Doran, and Thomas V. Daly [Toronto: University of Toronto Press, 1990]) and the Cincinnati lectures on the philosophy of education in the summer of 1959 (*Topics in Education*). Later, his habit was to refer to Husserl on the loss of the scientific ideal, but without mention of *Krisis*; for example, *Collection*, ed. Frederick E. Crowe and Robert M. Doran (Toronto: University of Toronto Press, 1988) 228, and *A Third Collection* 121, 213, 233.

I have been indicating the dimensions of the issue, and now I must attempt to clarify my position. My first two rules – Understand, Understand systematically – yield no more than bright ideas, hypotheses, theories; and none of these is knowledge. Of themselves, they are merely sounding brass and tinkling cymbal. Only when one can go beyond them to affirm their truth, to assert that things are so, does one reach knowledge; and taking that step is a matter of good judgment. My third and fourth rules – Reverse counterpositions, Develop positions – introduce the problem of judgment, inasmuch as they are concerned not merely with the inner coherence of systematic understanding but also with a conversion of the subject that judges. It remains that the four rules together fall short of the present issue.

However, if we ask what good judgment is, I think it will appear that the four rules have a preparatory value. Whenever we understand, we feel called upon to judge; but it is only when we understand not merely the matter in hand but also its relevant context that we can judge well. Children understand many things, but we say that they reach the age of reason when they are about seven years old. A youth understands ever so much more than a child, yet he is accounted a minor in the eyes of the law until he reaches the age of twenty-one. Every cobbler is thought a fair judge, provided he sticks to his last. Finally, the universal principle of good judgment has been named wisdom; because it orders all things, it can judge all; but we must note that philosophy holds itself to be, not wisdom attained, but a love of wisdom and a movement towards it.

In each of these instances the same feature recurs. Good judgment in a given area is not attained until, within the limits of that area, a certain fulness of understanding is reached. It seems to follow that my rules urging understanding, systematic understanding, and the coherence of systematic understanding head one to the limit where good judgment becomes possible.

Still, possibility is one thing and actuality another. For judgment demands more than adequately developed understanding. It supposes a transformation of consciousness, an ascent from the eros of intellectual curiosity to the reflective and critical rationality that is the distinguishing mark of man. On that higher level, there becomes operative what Augustine named a contemplation of the eternal reasons, what Aquinas attributed to our created participation of uncreated light, what a modern thinker might designate as rational consciousness. On that level there emerges the proper content of what we mean by truth, reality, knowledge, objectivity; and by the same movement we ourselves in our own reasonableness are involved, for every judgment is at once a personal commitment, an endeavor to determine what is true, and a component in one's apprehension of reality.[14]

However, if I believe that there is no substitute for good judgment, if I believe that method, instead of seeking a substitute, has to make use of good judgment, it is not my intention to entrust the advance of science to the vagaries of individual opinion. No less than those that evade or deny the significance of good judgment, I too believe that a method has to include some technique for overcoming individual, group, and general aberration. Where I would differ is in the technique. I acknowledge the full significance of judgment and its personal element, but my third and fourth rules imply a further judgment on individual judgments. Developing positions and reversing counterpositions are equivalent to judging judgments; and the definitions of positions and counterpositions are based on ultimate philosophic alternatives, that is, on the diverse manners in which individual judgment can go wrong not merely incidentally but in the grand manner of a superficial or a mistaken philosophy.

It is true, of course, that others may and will disagree with my account of the matter. But from the nature of the case, I think that disagreement in the main will be limited to naming positions what I name counterpositions, and to naming counterpositions what I name positions. There would result a number of distinct schools, but their number could not be very large, their epistemological assumptions and implications would be in the open, and the individuals that chose between them could do so with an adequate awareness of the issues and of their own personal responsibility in judging.

Admittedly, this is not a watertight solution. But my fundamental point is that there exists no watertight solution. St Paul held that the Law was efficacious only in giving knowledge of sin. Method would do very well if it did as much. For it was not through method that God saw fit to redeem the intellect of man.[15]

14 More than half a page was written and crossed out in the middle of this paragraph. It includes a remark that puts Lonergan's work on method in perspective: 'Much modern philosophy and modern science seem to me marked by a flight from the responsibility of judging. That flight has been cloaked under the high name of method. At least in the human sciences, in philosophy, and in theology, that flight, I believe, should be repudiated.'

15 A remark that recalls Newman's quotation, on the title page of *An Essay in Aid of a Grammar of Assent*, from St Ambrose: 'Non in dialectica complacuit Deo salvum facere populum suum.'

2 Applications to Catholic Theology[16]

2.1 *Understand*

Traditionally theology has been conceived as *fides quaerens intellectum,* faith in quest of understanding. Faith is presupposed and taken for granted. But this presupposition is understood in the light of the counsel given by Augustine and Anselm, *Crede ut intelligas.*[17] We have believed. Now we would understand.

For there are many things that the believer desires to understand. Nor is the desire an individual affair, a lack of understanding that occurs in the ignorant but not in the learned. It can be quite general. Such matters

---

Lonergan's remark here on the limits of method puts his work on method into perspective. From early on the limits are clear. 'Method is a means to an end,' he said in 1949 (*Verbum: Word and Idea in Aquinas,* ed. David Burrell [Notre Dame, IN: University of Notre Dame Press, 1967] 215). In *Insight* he remarked that a 'logic or a method is not an ultimate' (405). Later he applied his method most effectively to theology, but he could say that 'the separateness of theology is a withdrawal that always intends and in its ultimate stage effects a return' (*Method in Theology* 140). In a lecture of 1976 he spoke of 'one great delusion ... the belief that there is an island of safety called "method." If you follow the method, then you will be all right ... The only solution lies in "the good man"' ('The Human Good,' *Humanitas: Journal of the Institute of Man* 15 [1979] 126; on the authenticity of the good person, see *Method in Theology* 254). There is, then, a context for his remark here that 'it was not through method that God saw fit to redeem the intellect of man,' and his remark (crossed out) earlier in the lecture, 'Much modern philosophy and modern science seem to me marked by a flight from the responsibility of judging. That flight has been cloaked under the high name of method.' See also *De intellectu et methodo* 46.

16 The transition here is from the meaning of the five rules to their relevance to theology. That is clear from a paragraph that was written, revised, then crossed out altogether. It ran as follows:

'I have attempted to indicate roughly the meaning of five methodical rules, which I believe are applicable to any subject. I must now attempt to show their relevance to theology, and I shall do so in three steps considering, first, speculative or systematic theology, secondly, positive or historical theology and, thirdly, practical or kerygmatic theology.'

The revision would have read, 'I shall do so partly by showing them to be immanent in history and partly by showing them to provide a method for the study of the history of theology.'

17 'Neque enim quaero intelligere, ut credam; sed credo, ut intelligam.' Anselm, *Proslogion* 1 (*PL,* vol. 158, col. 227). On *fides quaerens intellectum* see below, note 22.

forced themselves on the attention of the church in the patristic period through movements known as heresies: Gnosticism and Montanism, Arianism, Nestorian and Monophysite doctrines, and from the West, Pelagianism. But what earlier had consisted of an incidental set of particular issues became in the medieval period an object of systematic concern.[18]

In his *Sic et non* Peter Abelard listed 158 propositions, and to each of them he appended patristic passages that seemed to show that the proposition was to be both affirmed and denied. This work automatically established two points: negatively, it showed that to settle an issue it was not enough to quote the Fathers of the church; positively, it implied the existence of a department of inquiry in which medieval man was on his own. A slightly later writer, Gilbert de la Porrée, gave a particularly clearheaded definition of the existence of a *quaestio*: a *quaestio* exists if, and only if, there are good reasons both for affirming and for denying one and the same proposition. That definition became the basis of a technique that endured for centuries. A proposition was prefaced with the question mark *Utrum*; passages from scripture and from the Fathers were cited in favor of the affirmative and then in favor of the negative answer; to these were added any of the arguments that might be current; then the author gave his solution and closed by applying its principles to each of the quotations or arguments he had begun by citing.

What was the material basis of these questions? About the year 1150 there appeared Peter Lombard's *Quattuor libri sententiarum*. It was an ordered compilation of scriptural and patristic passages bearing on Christian doctrine; if it did not emphasize oppositions as did Abelard's less thorough and less

18 Lonergan was wont to repeat this capsule of the history of medieval theology; see, for example, *Method in Theology* 279, 280, 297, 309; *A Second Collection* 196 (in 'Philosophy and Theology'); *A Third Collection* 49–50 (in 'Aquinas Today: Tradition and Innovation'), 187 (with note 13, p. 199, in 'Theology and Praxis'), and 245 (in 'Unity and Plurality: The Coherence of Christian Truth'); the extensive treatment is, of course, *De intellectu et methodo* passim.

It is clear that he owes much to the article 'Théologie' by Yves Congar (*Dictionnaire de théologie catholique*, tome 15: 1 [Paris: Letouzey et Ané, 1946] cols. 341–502), which he often refers to; for example, in *De intellectu et methodo* 1, 6; in *De Deo trino*, vol. 1: *Pars dogmatica* (Rome: Gregorian University Press, 1964) 7, 21; vol. 2, *Pars systematica* (same press and year) 17; in *A Second Collection* 57 (in 'Theology in Its New Context'). See the English translation of Congar's article: *A History of Theology*, trans. Hunter Guthrie (Garden City, NY: Doubleday & Co., 1968), a book that 'substantially reproduces the article' in *DTC* (p. 7 in Congar's 'Preface'); the index lists all the principals that Lonergan refers to. But Lonergan had done his own homework in medieval theology, and it is difficult to estimate the extent of his debt to Congar.

learned work, neither did it conceal them. Peter Lombard was something of a positivist, setting forth the data, and repeatedly leaving to the *prudens lector* the task of reconciliation. For over three centuries commentaries were written by almost every ranking theologian on Peter's *Sentences*, and the commentaries consisted in an ever growing and changing series of *quaestiones*.

2.2 *Understand Systematically*

It would seem that my first rule, Understand, has a solid basis in theological tradition. Now, if we turn from medieval questions to medieval answers, there will emerge the traditional form of my second rule, Understand systematically. For in every field of inquiry there comes a time when a scattered set of discoveries coalesces into a rounded whole. Pythagoras established his theorem long before Euclid wrote his *Elements*. Galileo and Kepler established laws before Newtonian mechanics deduced Kepler's laws from a set of principles. Much important work was done in chemistry prior to the discovery of the periodic table. But it is only from the moment when a Euclid, a Newton, a Mendeleev comes along with a system that a subject has a well-defined existence, that it can be treated as a unity, that it can possess a method of its own.

Now there can be shown to exist in the writings of Anselm and of the twelfth-century theologians a nest of antinomies that center round the couplets 'grace and freedom,' 'faith and reason,' to make the very conception of these terms paradoxical and to render an attempt at formulating the theological enterprise either heretical or incoherent. From about the year 1230[19] these hitherto hopeless problems vanish; theology becomes able to

19 The significance of the phrase 'about the year 1230' is probably its relation to Philip the Chancellor, whose unfinished *Summa de bono* was begun at that time. Lonergan in his doctoral dissertation (see *Grace and Freedom: Operative Grace in the Thought of St. Thomas Aquinas*, ed. J. Patout Burns [London: Darton, Longman & Todd, and New York: Herder and Herder, 1971] 1–19) had made a careful study of the literature on the medieval theology of grace, referring there, and in his later writings, to the role of Philip in forming the concept of the supernatural order (ibid. 15–16, and note 73). His authority is given as Artur Landgraf's articles, 'Die Erkenntnis des Übernatürlichen,' *Scholastik* 4 (1929) 1–37, 189–220, 352–89, at 381–84; later in book form, *Dogmengeschichte der Frühscholastik*, vols. 1/1 and 1/2: *Die Gnadenlehre* (Regensburg: Friedrich Pustet, 1952, 1953); see vol. 1/1, pp. 182, 197–98. A check on his reference to Landgraf, however, suggests that Lonergan added his own clarifications to what he found there. (There is, in fact, a general question that needs further investigation, on Lonergan's 'creative' use of his sources.)

conceive itself, to distinguish its field from that of philosophy and of other disciplines, to tackle particular questions in the light of a total viewpoint. The key discovery was the recognition of what is named the supernatural order, but as the word 'supernatural' in ordinary English usage sometimes has a connotation of the irrational, I had best pause to indicate that the primary emphasis lies, not on the word 'supernatural,' but on the word 'order.'

Things are ordered when they are intelligibly related, and so there is an order inasmuch as there is a domain of intelligible relations. The discovery of a supernatural order was the discovery of a domain of intelligible relations proper to theology. Just as Newton discovered that natural laws reduced to a system of their own (mechanics) and not as Galileo had thought to a preexisting system (geometry), just as Mendeleev, by discovering an order to which chemical entities reduced, defined the field of chemistry, so too, when Aquinas was still a boy, theology found itself. The meaning of the supernatural is that Christian theology has to deal with the gift of God, where not only is the gift from God but more basically the gift is God. It is a transcendent gift, and utterly free, not only in itself, but also in its whole retinue of consequences and implications. Knowing of it is a faith that is above reason, possessing it is a grace that is above nature, acting on it is a charity that is above good will, with a merit that is above human deserts. Christian fellowship is a bond, transcending family and state, that in the fulness of time was established when God sent his Son that we might have the adoption of sons, and to show that we are sons, sent the Spirit of his Son, crying out in our hearts, 'Abba, Father.'[20]

There is a further aspect to this realization of my second rule, Understand systematically. The natural objective of our intellectual desire to know is the concrete universe. Theology can succeed as a systematic understanding only if it is assigned a determinate position in the totality of human knowledge, with determinate relations to all other branches. This further step was taken by Aquinas. Where Bonaventure had been content to think of this world and all it contains only as symbols that lead

20 Lonergan here is drawing on Galatians 4.4–6: 'But when the fullness of time had come, God sent his Son, born of a woman, born under the law, in order to redeem those who were under the law, so that we might receive adoption as children. And because you are children, God has sent the Spirit of his Son into our hearts, crying, "Abba, Father!"'

the mind ever up to God, Aquinas took over the physics, biology, psychology, and metaphysics of Aristotle to acknowledge not symbols but natural realities and corresponding departments of natural and human science.[21]

2.3 *Reverse Counterpositions*

My third rule was 'Reverse counterpositions,' and it can be illustrated theologically by adverting to the so-called Augustinian reaction against Aristotelianism. In essence, that reaction was an acceptance of Aristotelian logic but a rejection of the ancient pagan's views on science and philosophy. Theology was to be pure. In the hands of Duns Scotus and of William of Ockham it quickly became very purely logical, and while logic is a valid systematic ideal, its atmosphere is too thin to support life. The vagaries of fourteenth-century and fifteenth-century scholasticism are a long series of illustrations of the counterposition that insisted on certitude and rigor and therefore brushed aside the uncertainties and the apparently haphazard process of coming to understand.

2.4 *Develop Positions*

My fourth rule was 'Develop positions.' The achievement of the thirteenth century is not a goal but a starting point. In particular, it lacked what we call the historical sense, namely, an awareness that concepts are functions of time, that they change and develop with every advance of understanding, that they become platitudinous and insignificant by passing through minds that do not understand, and that such changes take place in a determinate manner that can be the object of a science. Not only was the sense of history missing in medieval thought, but also it happens that subsequent theology has been ever increasingly occupied with an array of questions that arise from a critique of Christian origins and of the development of Christian doctrine and Christian thought. What, it will be asked, is the relevance to historical theology of the rules I have indicated?

It is, I think, twofold. There is their adaptation to historical study in general, and on this point I shall not dwell. There is also their adaptation to

21 This contrast of Aquinas and Bonaventure is clearly traceable to Congar; see *A History of Theology* 120–21.

historical theology, and how this occurs perhaps I have already indicated. The rules seem to be immanent in history. I have illustrated the first rule from the twelfth century, the second from the thirteenth, the third from the fourteenth, the fourth from a subsequent and still expanding inquiry. At least, I suggest, this gives us a clue, and a few further considerations will help to determine its significance.

First, I would note a general fact. Historical competence does not suffice to write the history of such a subject as mathematics or physics or medicine or philosophy. If one is ignorant of these subjects, one might meet all the general requirements of historical investigation, but as soon as one turned to what is specifically mathematical or medical or philosophical, one would be at a loss. One could compile masses of data, but one could not discover, select, emphasize, evaluate, order, judge.

Secondly, from this general fact one can ascend to its ground. The history of a subject is the history of its development. The development of a subject is, so to speak, the objective process of learning by which the subject gradually took shape, progressed, suffered setbacks, underwent transformations. To be able to discern that objective process of learning, to appreciate what was known and what was lacking at each stage of the process, to determine accurately what were the strokes that moved the process forward and what were the oversights that delayed it, one has to have a thorough grasp of the subject itself.

Thirdly, general methodical rules for the advance of any subject, if valid, hold not only for the future but also for the past. For such general rules, if truly general, merely make explicit, conscious, deliberate the native process of learning of the human mind. Hence, even when they were not explicit, nonetheless they were operative. It is in this sense that the rules are immanent in history, and it is in virtue of this sense that the general rules can be assigned their concrete theological significance by appealing to significant periods in the history of theology.

Fourthly, I have appealed from explicit rules to a prior implicit operativeness. Now I have to take a parallel step from what becomes explicit in theology to what was implicit before theology. Theology is faith in quest of understanding.[22] But if the understanding that theology seeks is systematic,

22 This definition of theology, originally one of the titles Anselm gave a work of his (G. Söhngen, 'Fides quaerens intellectum,' *Lexikon für Theologie und Kirche*, vol. 4 [Freiburg: Herder, 1960] cols 119–20) dominated Lonergan's thinking at this time, when he was working to substitute Thomist emphasis

the faith that precedes theology is not without understanding. What is understood systematically in theology was in some manner understood previously. But the earlier understanding was in another mode, in the mode of intersubjectivity, of symbolic apprehension, of common sense. Nor is the theologian ignorant of those modes. He was a Christian before he was a theologian. If he teaches theology, then he is engaged in making Christians into theologians. If he preaches what he has learnt from theology, then he is engaged in transforming what he understands systematically into the more immediate modes of intersubjectivity, symbol, and common sense. Hence, just as previously I have argued that to write the history of theology one must be not only a historian but also a theologian, so now I should say that to write the history of Christian doctrine one must be not only a historian and a theologian but also a theologian familiar with the process of transformation that occurs when one moves from one mode of understanding to another.

Fifthly, how does the theologian acquire familiarity with this process? There are two steps: first, one grasps the general notion; secondly, one sees it operative in the manifest turning points in the history of Christian doctrine.

The general notion may be illustrated by our apprehension of space. For our initial apprehension of space seems to be kinesthetic; it involves a coordinate system in which up and down, front and back, right and left have felt qualitative differences; it is an apprehension that serves us well in all our bodily movements. But it is not an apprehension that can bear the weight of a theory about the universe; for it implies that, if the earth were a sphere, then people at the antipodes would fall into the sky; and so when

---

on understanding for conceptualist emphasis on certitude. It remained a key factor all his life, but in terms of the functional specialties of *Method in Theology*, it regarded only two specialties out of eight, namely, Doctrines (faith) and Systematics (understanding). In between Lonergan had progressed to what he called 'a greatly enlarged notion of theology'; see 'Bernard Lonergan Responds,' *Foundations of Theology: Papers from the International Lonergan Congress 1970*, ed. Philip McShane (Dublin: Gill and Macmillan, 1971; Notre Dame: University of Notre Dame Press, 1972) 223–34, at 224. Research, interpretation, history, which were once mere 'auxiliary disciplines,' can now claim a place with systematics as an essential part of theology, and theology as a whole is conceived in terms of its mediating function: 'A theology mediates between a cultural matrix and the significance and role of a religion in that matrix' (*Method in Theology* xi).

we attempt to think about the universe, we have to leave aside notions adapted for more immediate and quite different ends. Another illustration is supplied by the intersubjective mode of understanding: within its proper limits it is both legitimate and necessary; but to attempt to apprehend the universe through the intersubjective mode results in a mythical personification of everything, where, of course, personification means, not a figure of speech that presupposes some prior, literal mode of meaning, but rather the prior, literal mode of apprehension itself.

Once one has grasped the general nature of transformations from one mode of understanding to another, one can turn to the beginnings of speculative thought in the Christian tradition. They are not hard to find. The fourth century was in an uproar over one word, *homoousios.* The meaning of that word is not to be sought in intersubjectivity, in symbolic apprehension, in common sense. It is a technical term that, of itself, announces the emergence of some initial step towards systematic thinking. As one might expect, there were represented all shades of opinion about it. Even its most staunch defender, Athanasius, regarded it as no better than a regrettable necessity. Not only were there fifty years of controversy after Nicea, but also there had been a problem long before Nicea. One can see it take successively different forms in Justin, Tertullian, Hippolytus, Origen, Novatian, Dionysius of Alexandria, and Dionysius of Rome.

I have indicated one instance of a shift in the mode of understanding. But there are others. Something similar took place at Chalcedon with antecedents and consequents extending over centuries. Something similar began with the condemnation of Pelagius at Carthage. Something similar happened when twelfth-century theologians conceived sacraments in terms of grace, of sign, and of efficacy. In each of these instances – and there are others – one can study empirically the nature of a shift from the intersubjective and commonsense mode of understanding towards the systematic mode.

But a further and more relevant observation seems in order. Newton insisted, 'Hypotheses non fingo.' In a sense his claim was false, for the theory of universal gravitation is a theory, a hypothesis. But in another sense his claim was completely justified, for Newton's theory added to observable data nothing but their immanent intelligibility, their verifiable law. As he did not attempt to determine final causes, so he refused to assign the efficient cause that made bodies fall. He was content with an inner functional relationship that was to be verified in the observable and measurable features of any local movement and could be extrapolated successfully to the planets. That functional relationship, on the theoretical side, served to define a whole class of movements, and so it opened the way to the discovery of quite different classes; and on the practical side, it enabled man to become an efficient cause and to use natural forces for the attainment of human ends.

I think there is some similarity in the procedure I have indicated. There is not raised immediately the question of the final cause – whether systematic understanding is a good thing – or whether Nicea and Chalcedon reached truth. Such questions are not questions for understanding but for judgment, and their treatment comes under the heading of positions and counterpositions. There is not raised immediately the question of the efficient cause: sources and influences have their significance in historical investigation, but I think one first should know what is taking place in the product before one begins to inquire what causes it to take place in the precise manner that can be observed; and besides, the question of sources opens the way to an almost unending series of hypotheses that inevitably take the theologian out of the field in which he, and he alone, is competent, into the excessively large investigations concerned with the broad stream of human thought, human literature, and interacting cultures and civilizations. Similarly, there are not introduced the somewhat indeterminate entities named biblical, evangelical, Pauline, Palestinian, Johannine, Hellenistic, medieval mentality. Rather, specific manifestations of each of these would be analyzed in terms of modes of understanding. For such modes exist. Their nature and content can be illustrated in personal experience. Their functioning in the initial stages of Christian theology can be examined, not in minutiae, but in broad movements, in sharp differences, in long-sustained controversies, and to some extent in patterns that recur in different topics at different places and widely separated times.

I have been indicating that my general rules, because they are general, are no less applicable to historical than to speculative theology. But I should note as well that, because they are rules, because they are dynamic, they serve to unite historical and speculative theology as past process and present term. Historical or positive theology is concerned with the becoming of speculative; and speculative theology is the term of historical process. To add positive to speculative theology is not to add something quite extrinsic; it is not to add a new and autonomous department that goes its own independent way. Rather, I should say, historical theology is speculative theology becoming conscious of its origins and its development, and at the same time, speculative theology is just the contemporary stage of the movement that historical theology examines and analyzes. To overlook or to reject that unity has, I believe, only one result. On the one hand, historical theology becomes lost in the wilderness of universal history;[23] it ceases to be a distinct discipline with a proper field and competence of its own; for it is only from speculative theology that historical can learn just what its precise field is and what are the inner laws of that field in their enduring manifestations. On the other hand, speculative theology withers away; for its proper task is, not just understanding, but understanding the faith; its positive basis is historical, and without that basis it may retire into an ivory tower to feed itself with subtle memories, it may merge with the general stream of philosophic thought, or it may attempt to take over, modestly or despotically, the teaching office of the church, but the one thing necessary it cannot do: continue today the process begun so long ago of adding to living faith the dimension of systematic understanding.[24]

2.5 *Accept the Responsibility of Judgment*

There remains my fifth rule, Accept the responsibility of judgment. As it is the supreme rule in any science, so its adaptation in theology is the most significant. For theology presupposes faith, and for the Catholic, faith includes judgment. It is an acceptance of truths revealed by God and taught by his church, not because we see them to be true apart from that witness, but because we are ready to enlarge our notion of truth itself, because we are ready to take as the measure of truth that is truth even for us, not what we can understand in this life, but what God understands.

23 Chapter 10, § 5 of *Topics in Education* is relevant on the problem of general or universal history. The education lectures followed the present lecture by only a few months.

24 The material on speculative theology in this paragraph replaced a passage which ran as follows, beginning at 'To overlook':
'To overlook or to reject that unity has, I believe, only one result: on the one hand, historical theology becomes lost in the wilderness of universal history; it ceases to be a distinct discipline with a proper field and competence; and on the other hand speculative theology shrivels into Church Dogmatics; it gives up the effort to understand, to serve faith in its quest for understanding; and it attempts to take over some part in the teaching office of the Church, to tell the faithful what is so.'

This view of faith transforms the meaning of all my five rules. In other fields, understanding begins not from truths but from data. It is understanding that will promote data to the level of truth, and the truth to be attained is no guiding presence but an ideal whose precise features are not to be discerned. In theology, things are otherwise. There are, indeed, data that are just data as in the other sciences: most exegetical and historical questions are of that character. But there are also truths, and understanding them involves a reversal of roles; where in other fields understanding precedes and determines truth, in theology understanding follows and is determined.[25]

Now this reversal of roles gives rise to special techniques that center about the true proposition, the logic of presuppositions and implications, and the semantics or metaphysics of meaning. My one observation is that they are techniques; they serve to chart the path of efforts to understand, but they are not ends; they provide the scaffolding needed to build the theological edifice, but they are not the edifice itself, the understanding sought by faith; they serve to delimit and to define what is to be understood, but the understanding is something more. It lies in the realm of analogy and in the intelligible interlocking of the truths of faith.[26]

The adaptation of my second rule, Understand systematically, would have to do with the character of the intelligibility to be reached in theology. It too would be concerned with the definition of limits and the indication of possibilities, and while highly relevant to method, it would also prove to be of a highly technical and specialized character.

As the Catholic view of faith makes theological understanding a grasp of converging lines that focus upon uncomprehended mystery, so too it places human wisdom and judgment within a context of communicated

25 This is said of systematic understanding, Lonergan's main concern at the time of the lecture. Later, with his 'greatly enlarged notion of theology' (see note 22 above), he will find room for the understanding proper to the mediating specialties (research, interpretation, history, dialectic), an understanding that is possible to some extent without faith. See *Method in Theology* 268: 'in the phase of mediating theology, in research, interpretation, history, and dialectic ... conversion is not a prerequisite; anyone can do research, interpret, write history, line up opposed positions.'

26 This line is almost a straight translation of a passage in Vatican I that was Lonergan's authority in his lifelong pursuit of understanding. The Council spoke of a limited but most fruitful understanding of the divine mysteries, that could be gained 'tum ex eorum, quae naturaliter cognoscit, analogia, tum e mysteriorum ipsorum nexu inter se et cum fine hominis ultimo' (*DB* 1796, *DS* 3016). See above, chapter 1, note 26.

divine wisdom and divine judgment. As the Catholic theologian accepts a divine revelation, so also he believes in its providential preservation. None-theless, this does not liberate him from also accepting the responsibility of making judgments of his own. We learn from Geoffrey of Fontaines[27] that, in the 1290s, the theological students at the University of Paris believed they would be excommunicated if they read the writings of Thomas Aquinas. In 1323, forty-nine years after his death, Thomas Aquinas became St Thomas Aquinas. Two years afterwards the Archbishop of Paris officially removed the ban against him. Clearly, if today Aquinas holds a preeminent position in Catholic theology, it is because he had the daring that is needed to understand, and the courage to make far-reaching judgments on the basis of his daring understanding. Moreover, if the decisions Aquinas made were momentous, the element of decisiveness is not removed when one turns from the man of genius to the ordinary honest worker. Everyone engaged in theology as something more than an exercise in repetitiveness has to make decisions; and the point to my fifth rule is simply that he would be deceiving himself if he thought that there existed some automatic technique onto which he could shift the burden.

27 The paragraph to this point is a revision pasted over an original draft which asks how the fifth rule, with its Protestant ring, can be upheld by a Catholic; but, Lonergan says, the rule 'does possess a very definite and vitally important area of application. We learn from Geoffrey' – here the original text is resumed.

3

The Philosophy of History[1]

The subject I have tonight is on the one hand enormous and complex, and on the other hand one in which you very easily become too speculative and in which it is particularly difficult to say anything significant in an introductory lecture. I do not know whether I shall be able to present basic *questions* but I shall try to do something about basic *notions*, and I have divided what I have to say into three topics: first of all, history as a subject; secondly, philosophy of ...; and thirdly, philosophy of history.

1 History as a Subject

Two quite different things can be meant by 'history': the history that is written, and the history that is written about.[2] My first point is history that is

1 This is a lecture given at the Thomas More Institute, Montreal, 23 September 1960, being the introductory lecture in a course, 'The Philosophy of History,' offered in the fall term. A transcription from the tape recording of the lecture was made at the Institute with the notation 'not corrected by the speaker.' Two related documents are in the Archives of the Lonergan Research Institute, Toronto: one a slightly variant transcription of the lecture at Thomas More (in Lonergan's own catalogue of papers, File 205) and the other a schematic yet detailed outline of the lecture by Lonergan, six pages, single-spaced, undated (Batch IX, 7a). All three documents were used in the present editing.

2 This distinction is found already in Lonergan's unpublished writings on history, dated 1937–38, and preserved in File 713 of his Papers. See his 'Analytic Concept of History,' *Method: Journal of Lonergan Studies* 11 (1993) 5–35, at 9. The distinction remains central in the discussion of the functional specialty 'history' in *Method in Theology* (see above, chapter 1, note 51) 175.

written: history as a subject, as a specialized field of inquiry, investigation, research, marked by the product of procedures and by cumulative results (later historians using the work of the earlier ones), as a process of composition, publication, criticism, and use – doing the same thing over and over again. This is a field of knowledge that develops and is sustained by the academic process of libraries, teachers, students, classes, and degrees. Now history in that sense – history of Canada, history of England, history of Europe, history that is 'history of ...' – can be divided perhaps into three types, and the division, as we will see later, already takes us into the question of the philosophy of history. This is because the methodology of history is not quite historic; while the history of the methodology of history would be a historical question, the methodology of history itself is not historic. I will speak first very briefly of occasional history, secondly of technical history, which is the more solid of the work that is being done, and thirdly of explanatory history, which tries to get off the ground.

1.1 *Occasional History*

First, occasional history. Herodotus wrote his nine books on why the Persians fought the Greeks. Thucydides wrote to say what the Peloponnesian War was; he is supposed to have been influenced by the biological or medical concepts of his time – he was doing a report on the diagnosis. Livy asked, What was the virtue and glory of Rome? Gibbon wrote on the decline and fall of the Roman Empire. All of these are historical works bearing on particular issues.

1.2 *Technical History*

History as a scientific subject had its principal development in the nineteenth century, say, since von Ranke; and I will now try to suggest the notion of technical history.

History begins as belief; the historian is not at all places at all times. He does not see and hear everything, he needs the reports of other people, and he takes the word of others for what happened elsewhere and at other times. There can arise conflicting testimonies, and in a conflict between what the witnesses say and what the historian believes could really happen, there will arise a critique of witnesses – of what they could know, how accurate their knowledge is likely to be, how truthful they are, whether they have ulterior motives, and so forth. However, as Collingwood points out in a fable in his *The Idea of History*, the historian need not be simply a believer.

Collingwood composed a detective story in which all the witnesses were lying and all the clues were planted and yet the detective could figure out what really happened. He was not believing any of the witnesses, he was not trusting any of the clues, yet he could determine just what happened, who was the criminal.[3]

With that point reached, history turns over from a collection of beliefs to something analogous to an empirical science. It is concerned not with testimonies but, if I may use the word of Professor Renier, with 'traces.'[4] Everything that exists in the present and had its origin in the past constitutes a trace of the past. It may be a document; it may be anything else in the way of ruins, buildings, coins, inscriptions, folkways, traditions, and so forth. All that comes from the past into the present is so much raw material. To the historian it is data, it constitutes data, and as a datum it is valid. It is irrelevant as yet whether it is going to be classified as something truthful or as a lie, as a genuine moment of the past or as a fake. That will depend upon how we classify it, what period it will be attributed to, what value will be placed upon it. All of that will depend upon the judgment of the historian. Just as the physicist considers all the colors he sees in the spectroscope and all the measurements obtained, and so on, as so much data in which he seeks an understanding and as the start of the hypothetico-deductive process, so in somewhat similar fashion the historian is not simply a believer of what other people have told him, a shrewd believer sizing up, accepting some, discounting others, but something like a scientist seeking an understanding of all the traces of the past that are existing into the present.

That understanding reached by the historian is a thing that develops as do the empirical sciences. If one historian interprets the data a certain way, another, by pointing to data that have been overlooked or misinterpreted, can challenge his conclusions and set up a new view on the subject, which can be a progressively improving interpretation of what happened in the past. However, history differs from the empirical sciences in two ways. First of all, historical understanding is not of general laws. It is of the particular and the concrete. Consequently, following upon this first difference, it is not possible for the historian to check his understanding of this case by

3 R.G. Collingwood, *The Idea of History* (Oxford: Clarendon, 1946) 266–74.
4 Gustaaf Johannes Renier, *History, Its Purpose and Method* (London: Allen & Unwin, 1950); see esp. pp. 87–127.

appealing directly to other cases. If the physicist says that the ratio between the angle of incidence and the angle of refraction of a ray of light is some constant which he applies to this particular case, well, he can appeal to *all* similar cases to check his interpretation, his account of the phenomena. The historian is interpreting just this particular case; other cases may *all* differ; he does not have the type of check which the empirical scientist has. On the other hand, he does have something similar insofar as the historical interpretation of a period, of all the particular cases in a given section of space-time, has to present something of a coherent picture; an interpretation of one set of events has to be able to fit in with another closely related set of events; so there is a fair analogy between the understanding the historian seeks of the traces of the past and the procedure of the empirical scientist. That type of historical work I venture to call technical history.

It differs from the earlier history that was largely a matter of sizing up witnesses. I do not want to simplify too much what the earlier people did, but history in the nineteenth century became largely a systematic use of methods somewhat of the type I call technical. It is not possible to develop now the full consciousness of methodology, and I am giving you a schematic view only; to go through the historians of the nineteenth century and say what each one did and what the strong point of each one was would require a whole course. But I think what I have said hits it off fairly well, and I want to insist that that is a fundamental element in historical work and something of real value. It has its limitations – we will go into that later – but I want you to get the point that there is an interlocking of the traces of the past that yields an understanding; and that understanding is going to be independent of the philosophic, the religious, the national, and all the other limitations of the individual who happens to be the historian.

I will illustrate this, not from general history but from doctrinal history, by a case of my own work. I wrote a series of articles in *Theological Studies* (1941–1942) on operative grace in the writings of St Thomas Aquinas,[5] and can use it to illustrate the interlocking of the data on this subject. First of all, a German by the name of Artur Landgraf (later a bishop) investigated

5 'St. Thomas' Thought on *Gratia Operans*,' *Theological Studies* 2 (1941) 289–324; 3 (1942) 69–88, 375–402, 533–78; later published in book form as *Grace and Freedom* (see above, chapter 2, note 19).

the doctrine of grace throughout the twelfth and early thirteenth centuries. The whole movement of thought is tabulated in a long series of articles by this author.[6] There was another series of articles by Dom Lottin on the conceptions and the development of the notions of freedom from St Anselm to St Thomas,[7] and that provided me with the setup, what the situation was, when St Thomas started writing.

Now there were three places in which St Thomas explicitly discussed operative grace, and he had three different views on the subject in the three places. Successively, these were the *Scriptum super Sententias* of his youth, the *De veritate* a few years later, and the *Summa theologiae* towards the end of his life. Three entirely different views, fundamentally different views on the subject! Concomitantly with this difference in his views on operative grace, there were changes in his view of what Pelagianism consisted of. The notion of Pelagianism is very closely related to the notion of grace. There were developments in his notions on operation and on God's operation on the will, developments in his notion of the will itself, and developments in his notion of liberty; and all these developments were not just single strands, they all tied together; you could almost see him think. Now that work does not give an absolutely certain conclusion about just where St Thomas was when he finished writing on the subject, what exactly his views were, just what aspect tied them down. But the movement itself and the interlocking of the data provide an understanding of St Thomas as thinking, as developing, as changing his opinions, that is exceedingly difficult to interpret in different ways. I give that as an illustration of the meaning of what I conceive as technical history.

On the other hand, technical history has its weakness. That type of interlocking of the data is not something that can be applied along the whole historical continuum. There are points at which that technique can be applied; but there are equally the lacunae, and the lacunae can occupy many more places than the points. Consequently, there remains a permanent temptation for the historian to fill in the blanks, and there is a fundamental problem in historical method with regard to these periods in which

6 These articles, from different journals, are contained in Artur M. Landgraf, *Dogmengeschichte der Frühscholastik* (see above, chapter 2, note 19).

7 Dom Odon Lottin, 'Les définitions du libre arbitre au douzième siècle,' *Revue Thomiste* 10 (1927) 104–20, 214–30; 'La théorie du libre arbitre pendant le premier tiers du XIIIe siècle,' *Revue Thomiste* 10 (1927) 350–82; 'La traité du libre arbitre depuis le chancelier Philippe jusqu'à saint Thomas d'Aquin,' *Revue Thomiste* 10 (1927) 446–72; 12 (1929) 234–69.

there are some data but not enough to give you that interlocking of a whole series of considerations that pins down the meaning of the event. Herbert Butterfield takes the stand that history is a *limited undertaking.*[8] We do what we can; we do not undertake to answer all questions; and that is pretty much the common sense of the historian. He will indicate his various degrees of confidence in the exactitude of what he is saying, point out that he is not quite sure of that, and so forth. One does not hesitate to say one does not know, is not sure.

A second view is *relativism.* Now that is an extremely large doctrine. I will just take a single and rather simple example of it, using one of the set of papers in a Festschrift presented to Ernst Cassirer on his sixtieth birthday, about 1936, with the title *Philosophy and History.*[9] If I remember rightly, the first essay was by Johan Huizinga,[10] and his definition was that history is a people interpreting to itself its past. But the people of today who do the interpreting are not the people who did the interpreting fifty years ago, and they have quite a different slant on things. A lot of water has gone under the bridge, and consequently the interpretation of the past in the present history is not the interpretation of the past of fifty years ago, and much less of a hundred years ago, and so on. There are several histories. This relativism can come out in many ways. You can have the English history of England, the French history of England, the German history of England, and the three are not exactly the same; and similarly, you can have several other combinations. The possibility of that arises insofar as history is not simply the strict technical history, insofar as it fills in the blanks or holes, or leans rather heavily on qualities and probabilities that depend a good deal upon the subject who is writing the history.

A third view comes out in Rudolph Bultmann. He distinguishes between understanding and preunderstanding, *Verständnis* and *Vorverständnis.*[11] The understanding, the *Verständnis,* is this interlocking of the data (although he expresses himself somewhat differently). But the preunder-

8 Herbert Butterfield, *Christianity and History* (London: Collins, 1958) 21–27. Lonergan here begins a series of four responses to the problem of lacunae: Butterfield's 'limited undertaking,' relativism, Bultmann's *Vorverständnis,* and the so-called naive approach.

9 *Philosophy and History: Essays Presented to Ernst Cassirer,* ed. Raymond Klibansky and H.T. Paton (Oxford: Clarendon, 1936).

10 Johan Huizinga, 'A Definition of the Concept of History,' ibid. 1–10.

11 Rudolf Bultmann, 'Das Problem der Hermeneutik,' *Zeitschrift für Theologie und Kirche* 47 (1950) 47–69; reprinted in Bultmann, *Glauben und Verstehen,* vol. 2 (Tübingen: Mohr, 1961) 211–35.

standing, the *Vorverständnis,* is a philosophy, and his philosophy for interpreting the New Testament is Heidegger's. I think he has the better part of the argument against the less sophisticated New Testament scholars, insofar as they say he is using a philosophy to interpret the New Testament. 'But so are you,' he says, 'and I know what my philosophy is; yours is just a set of unconscious assumptions. I am making it quite plain to people what I am presuming. You are unconsciously – perhaps deliberately, but then you are just trying to fool them – passing off your assumptions without letting them know.' Again it is a case of the interlocking of the data; give one, take one, so far, but the questions that are raised about history, and especially about a history such as that of the New Testament, are not easily settled in that manner. The historian's view of human nature, of human destiny, plays a fundamental role in the selection, first of all, of the field that he studies (why is he interested in the New Testament?) as well as in the way he goes about it, the types of thought he appeals to to illuminate the New Testament, the selection of topics, and so on. (I suppose there is no element in history that has been studied with such intensity and such a terrific flow of volumes during the past century as all that is concerned with the New Testament. It is an overworked field, in many ways.) There is very clearly in the New Testament, taken as a historical document, the problem of how far does our understanding of the text take us, and how much does that understanding of the text depend upon other factors.

Finally, of course, there is the naive approach, unaware of the issue. People have their own minds, and that's good common sense; when the other fellow's assumptions begin to appear and reveal differences of interpretation, well, he's wrong. But they have not too much consciousness that they are doing the same sort of thing themselves.

So much for technical history.

1.3 Explanatory History

Next, explanatory history. Technical history, I said, had a clear assimilation to empirical science, but there is a very important and a very fundamental difference methodologically, and we have been heading to that difference in our discussion, for example, of Bultmann.

1.3.1 In Empirical Science

In empirical science, the most conspicuous part is the work of observation, of measurement, of collecting measurements, putting them on a graph, curve-fitting, finding a formula; but that is what I call insights, simply the lower blade of the method. The method is a pair of scissors, and it has not only a lower blade but also an upper blade, and the two come together. Galileo proceeded from falling bodies, bodies falling from the leaning tower of Pisa and bodies sliding down inclined planes. He also had an upper blade: the understanding of nature was going to fit into Euclidean geometry. That general assumption was just as much a determinant of his results as the observations and measurements. Newton substitutes for Euclidean geometry a similar deductive science called mechanics. It was a matter of setting down definitions and axioms and deducing things like movement of bodies in central fields of force, discovering that bodies moved just as Kepler had found the planets to move. Again, that mechanics is an upper blade that combines with the lower blade and gives you empirical science. Later, there came, in the place of Newton's mechanics, Einstein's relativity mechanics; and the quantum theory introduces notions of discontinuity and indeterminacy.

There is always operative an upper blade; and the same holds in the other empirical sciences. There is not just simply a matter of proceeding from the data; there is also always operative an upper blade, usually expressed in differential equations or something like that. Can the weakness of technical history, the problem of going beyond the sure points where the data interlock, of having a systematic type of bridgework between those strong points, those piers as it were, be met by the introduction of an upper blade into historical method?

Now in particular fields that is not only possible but achieved. If you think of such a subject as the history of mathematics, the history of physics, the history of chemistry, of astronomy, geology, biology, technology, medicine, economics, it is quite possible in such a limited field of history to write an explanatory history that goes beyond the interlocking points in the data and satisfies everyone; and that is quite possible because there is a science of mathematics, physics, chemistry, and so on, on which everyone agrees. You cannot write the history of mathematics unless you are a mathematician, you cannot write the history of medicine unless you are a medical doctor; of course, you have to be a historian and know the techniques of the historian, but you also have to have this specialized knowledge, and without it you would be lost. You would not be able to pick out what are data relevant to a history of the field unless you know the subject inside out; you would not be able to pick out what is significant, or when what is significant arose, or what section is fulfilling its promises immediately, and so on. A man who really understands his mathematics can write an extremely intelligible history of mathematics, and similarly for these other subjects. The subject can be put together as a whole, and you have operating in your method not only the lower blade that comes from the interlocking of the data but also the upper blade which is derived from the science at the present time. And that type of history, too, is subject to revision. Insofar as mathematics or physics will further develop, new points will become significant in the future that previously were not; and similarly, insofar as new data come to light, you will have fuller data to connect your history. It is a type of change; it is not falling into a relativism of any sort, but rather it is the same sort of 'subject to change' that is found in the empirical sciences themselves.

1.3.2 In Philosophy

Now we go a little further into the complexity of the problem. We ask about the history of philosophy. A philosopher from the viewpoint of *his* philosophy can write an explanatory history of philosophy, and he can fill in the lacunae. But another philosopher with a different philosophy can do the same thing, and you get different results, because any philosophy will supply an upper blade if it is sufficiently developed, and it can take on the form of a philosophy of philosophies. Also, it can take on the task of fulfilling the function of an upper blade in the history of philosophy. The trouble is that there are many philosophies, and the debate here obviously shifts. It is not to be settled so much by historical criteria as by the debate between the philosophies themselves.

1.3.3 In Art and Culture

The problem of relativism is illustrated in reduced form by the problem of the history of philosophy. A third instance,[12] where a further complication arises, occurs when you come to the history of art, the history of a literature or literatures, the history of culture, the history of religions. The further

12 The tape transcription has 'type,' but 'instance' seems to fit the context better: a third instance of the introduction of an upper blade into historical method.

complication is not only that there are many types of religious belief, many types of literature, and so on – there are many philosophies, and the multiplicity of the philosophies is also reflected in the religions and the arts and the cultures – but also that in this case there is a concreteness, and so a resistance to the systematic conceptualization which is of the essence, as it were, of such subjects as mathematics or physics.

1.3.4 In General History

Now one comes to the final question on this point of explanatory history. There can be an upper blade for things like mathematics and medicine, and to get, as it were, unambiguous results, not a multiplicity of results, you can write explanatory history, you can complement technical history with explanatory. Secondly, you can write explanatory history of philosophy and similar things, or of theology, but the trouble is that you get many histories because you have many different upper blades. History of art and culture introduces a further complexity in its concreteness. Can there be an upper blade for *general* history, history in the ordinary sense as contrasted with, say, a history of capitalism?[13]

A contender for the position is sociology. Sociology is the study of human society at a given time and place, but this sociology over time should provide history with an upper blade, should do for history what the science of mathematics does for the history of mathematics. Something along that line was attempted by a sociologist, a Russian émigré, Pitirim Sorokin. In the thirties, he published four large volumes of *Social and Cultural Dynamics.*[14] It is largely artistic but deals also with several other types of things that he was classifying. What he was proving was the existence of a cycle, and it was applied to Hellenistic and Western culture extended over 2500 years. All I know about this work is that, to do a thing like this, you have to introduce categories, such as a field, and

13 This is a point that Lonergan was clearly wrestling with in his 1959 lectures on the philosophy of education. The 'problem of general history' is there called 'the real catch,' 'the big problem.' See Bernard Lonergan, *Topics in Education* (see above, chapter 2, note 12) 236, 250.

14 Pitirim Sorokin, *Social and Cultural Dynamics*, 4 vols. (New York: American Book Company, 1937–41). Lonergan makes reference to these same ideas of Sorokin's in *Topics in Education* 42 and in *Understanding and Being* (see above, chapter 2, note 13) 221.

Sorokin's categories were not properly sociological; rather they were philosophic. His fundamental division was of cultures: were they sensate, idealistic, or ideational? These categories correspond roughly to Kierkegaard's three spheres of existential subjectivity: the aesthetic, the ethical, and the religious;[15] and again, they correspond to the three spheres you get from *Insight* according as your emphasis is on experience, understanding, or judgment.[16]

What Sorokin really was doing was using philosophic categories rather than sociological categories. Sociological categories would be something much more precise, and would find an application (say, of a cycle, if it were defined sociologically) without going over tremendous amounts of time. And, of course, in the human sciences there is quite a leap from the merely descriptive type of science to explanatory science – even greater than moving in empirical science from talking about things being heavy, hot, and so on, to talking about mass (which is something quite distinct from weight) or temperature (something quite distinct from being hot). That, perhaps, in sociology, is coming out at the present time in a work by Robert Merton, *Social Theory and Social Structure* (which the people at the Gregorian University in Rome who are teaching sociology speak of as 'the bible for sociologists').[17] Merton seems to be introducing explanatory categories. Insofar as he is successful, there perhaps will be from sociology a tool that will supply an upper blade. We will discuss that further in this course, and many questions will be raised.

Another illustration or contender as an upper blade in explanatory history is provided by Arnold Toynbee's *A Study of History*.[18] What is history

15 The three spheres of existence are so pervasive in Kierkegaard that it would be guesswork to give a specific reference as Lonergan's source; but see the index to *Concluding Unscientific Postscript*, trans. David F. Swenson, completed and provided with introduction and notes by Walter Lowrie (Princeton: Princeton University Press, 1941) under Aesthetic, Ethical, Religion.

16 Bernard Lonergan, *Insight* (see above, chapter 2, note 9). The connection between Sorokin and types of philosophy is made as well in *Understanding and Being* 221; *Topics in Education* 41–42 connects types of philosophy, Kierkegaard's categories of subjectivity, and Sorokin's types of society in the same way as appears here.

17 Robert K. Merton, *Social Theory and Social Structure* (Glencoe, IL: The Free Press, 1957).

18 Arnold J. Toynbee, *A Study of History*, 12 vols. (London: Oxford University Press, 1934–61). Toynbee is treated in similar fashion but also in greater detail in *Topics in Education* (see Index: Toynbee, Arnold).

about? Is it like the history of Canada, or the history of England, or the history of Czechoslovakia? History, says Toynbee, is history of civilizations. The unit of study is the civilization. He pins the subject down to one object, what he calls the civilization; he defines the civilization as a field of interdependence. You cannot write the history of Canada and prescind from the history of France and England. You cannot write the history of a European country and prescind from the history of the neighboring Europeans. But you *can* write the history of Modern Europe (great parts of it, anyway) and allow for merely incidental contacts between it and, say, China. Consequently, there is here a norm of what he means by civilization – the functional concept of civilization. He uses this to say that there are many civilizations, and he makes a guess at the number. Each has its origin, its development, its breakdowns, its decline, its decay. There are relations in space and time between different civilizations. Finally, in volumes 7 to 10 the push, the moving thing behind the whole business, behind the whole of history, is religion; the basic carrier wave is religion. There you have, taken out of historical study, a set of *explanatory categories* and a set of principal questions for the historian to deal with. Does that set of categories stand to explanatory history as differential equations stand to physical theory, physical explanation? That is the question. (Of course, I am not supposed to answer them all!)

Now that is not the whole of Toynbee. There is something else besides that fundamental conceptualization of what history is about (namely, about civilization's distinctive developments). This 'something else' is a set of humanistic categories. I spoke a moment ago about terms like weight, something heavy, and terms like mass, which can be defined only by relation to other masses, and ultimately by the inverse-square law of gravitation. And that is a step which is a purely theoretical type of conceptualization. Again, in scholastic philosophy the fundamental terms come out in pairs: potency and act, matter and form, substance and accident; and their meaning is contained in their relations to one another; you have a closed conceptual system. Now humanistic categories are not of that type. A large part of Toynbee's thinking is in categories drawn from the Greek tragedies, from Shakespeare and the Bible, of course, and from Goethe. It is a type of systematic conceptualization that has a meaning to the cultured Westerner, but it is not a type of systematic conceptualization that you have in explanatory science.

Another try along this line is that of Eric Voegelin. His *Order and History* has, so far – after the mid-fifties – three volumes published by the Louisiana State University Press.[19] He has since gone to Munich. Before that, in the early fifties, the University of Chicago Press published his *New Science of Politics*.[20] In these works, the upper blade is a philosophy of man, a philosophy of man of the type that is not just tied down to Heidegger, but is very much in the movement in which you find Heidegger and historians of religion of the type of Mircea Eliade and Ernst Cassirer – Cassirer's *Philosophy of Symbolic Forms*[21] – and so on.

Well, this discussion of history as a subject provides perhaps a step towards philosophy of history. I mentioned an occasional history, which we did not bother to analyze, to set up in opposition; technical history, which is very much down to earth and very solid but appeals to professors; it does not appeal so much to students and even less to the man on the street – he wants 'meaningful' answers to questions! Also, there is explanatory history, which has a great appeal and is beset with very fundamental difficulties. The difficulty that has been most conspicuous is the problem of relativism; it becomes conspicuous in dated history ('that was a fine historical work, but for 1850 or 1910; it does not count any more') or national history, or history that is acceptable to people of certain philosophic convictions or of certain religious convictions – Catholic history, Protestant history, Jewish history, history that will satisfy Arabs, and so on. That problem of relativism, and the possibility of surmounting it somewhat on the historical level, was raised in connection with the notion of explanatory history. I will now attempt to handle briefly my second topic, namely, *philosophy of …*

2 Philosophy of …[22]

I began with history as a subject, and spoke of occasional history, technical

19 Eric Voegelin, *Order and History*, vol. 1: *Israel and Revelation*; vol. 2: *The World of the Polis*; vol. 3: *Plato and Aristotle* (Baton Rouge, LA: Louisiana State University Press, 1956, 1957). The fourth volume, *The Ecumenic Age*, was published in 1974, and an incomplete fifth volume, *In Search of Order*, was published posthumously in 1987. Lonergan first refers to Voegelin, it seems, in his 1959 lectures on the philosophy of education (*Topics in Education*).

20 Eric Voegelin, *The New Science of Politics* (Chicago: University of Chicago Press, 1952).

21 Ernst Cassirer, *The Philosophy of Symbolic Forms*, 3 vols., trans. Ralph Manheim (New Haven: Yale University Press, 1953, 1955, 1957).

22 'Philosophy of …' is a category recurrent in Lonergan's thinking at this time. See *Topics in Education* 19–20, 259–61; 'Openness and Religious Experience,' in *Collection* (see above, chapter 2, note 13) 185–87.

history, explanatory history; now we will move to the topic 'philosophy of ...'

One is asked traditionally to think of philosophy *absolutely*; philosophy is *something*, it is not *of something else*; philosophy is logic or epistemology or ontology or psychology or cosmology or ethics or natural theology or preferably all put together; but it is that and nothing more nor less. What is this 'philosophy of ...'? Philosophy of history is one member of a species or genus. There is philosophy of nature, philosophy of science, philosophy of spirit, philosophy of man, philosophy of law, philosophy of religion, philosophy of education, philosophy of art, philosophy of history. What is this 'philosophy of ...'?

It is a question that can be given a general answer very easily in traditional terms. Philosophy, as one case of a very explicit and deliberate etymology, means love of wisdom. It is a modest reply to the assertiveness of the Sophists, who proposed to hand out wisdom, while the philosophers had a lot more but did not think that they had got there yet. Wisdom is the ordering of all. And because it is an apprehension of universal order, it is also a potentiality of ultimate judgment. A judgment on anything has to take into account everything that is relevant to that point; and consequently ultimate judgments have to take into account everything. Hence wisdom is a principle not only of universal order but also of ultimate judgment. But while wisdom as such is concerned with universal order and ultimate judgment, still it will, of its very nature, have application to particular fields. Precisely because it is universal and ultimate, it will have its participation in such fields as science, nature, spirit, art, law, education, religion, history; and so you have this 'philosophy of ...'

The general answer is one thing, and the technique of setting up a 'philosophy of ... ,' a philosophy that is so conceived that it automatically becomes a 'philosophy of ... ,' is quite another. Philosophy can be misconceived, I would say, as a dam across the river of life and thought, rather than the bed in which the river flows. What seems to me to have provoked that view of philosophy arises from taking the easy way of conceiving one's own intellect, one's own intelligence,[23] pretty much in the same way as one comes to know God. You know the methodological procedure in natural theology of coming to the concept of God. It begins from the effects and proceeds by a method of analogy, of affirmation, negation, and eminence,

23 On intellect and intelligence, see below, chapter 4, note 7.

to a concept of God. Man can proceed in exactly the same way to knowledge of his intelligence. There are the effects of intelligence in the sciences (sciences in the sense of written books of science), in the use of common names, in intelligent products. And from that one goes on, proceeding on the analogy that just as with our eyes we see, so there is a spiritual eye. If we use common names, this spiritual eye looks at universals. And since we have general principles, well, the spiritual eye sees the connections between these universals. When it sees those connections, you have a universal and necessary truth of which you are absolutely certain. While particular people might not be certain about it, still per se it is certain. And while these truths, since they are universal and necessary, hold for all possible worlds, still there may be very many qualifications to be added on. Yet per se they are true, and their being true is not the being true which is *formaliter in iudicio,* something that is in the mind; rather the truths are out there too. Finally, there is the notion of system as a deduction from a set of principles. What system? Well, something like Euclid's *Elements.* You lay down axioms as definitions, and then you proceed to deduce. If philosophy is conceived in that manner, it is going to be extremely difficult to get the type of wisdom that finds its applications in particular fields.

Let me handle very briefly the notion of a *system.*[24] If anyone reads St Thomas, one notices no similarity to Euclidean procedure. He does not start from a set of definitions and axioms, and he never treats any question by giving one proof and writing the matter off with *Quod erat demonstrandum.* Rather, he sets up an ordered series of questions, and in the *Summa theologiae* he subdivides the questions into articles. In a work like the *Summa contra Gentiles,* in his ordered set of topics, he brings to bear on each, not just one argument but several, and sometimes approximately twenty, and the arguments are all different; but when you move to the next question,

24 There is a good 'systematic' account of 'system' in *Philosophy of God, and Theology: The Relationship between Philosophy of God and the Functional Specialty, Systematics* (London: Darton, Longman & Todd, and Philadelphia: Westminster, 1973) 6–8 (and see the Index). There we are told that the general characteristics of a system may be found in quite different contexts. Three such contexts merit our attention: there is the Aristotelian type based on a metaphysics; there is the modern type based on empirical science; there is the transcendental type based on intentionality analysis' (6). There follows an account of the three types of system. See also 'Questionnaire on Philosophy,' where Lonergan responds to questions on 'systematic' philosophy and on pluralism in systems (*Method: Journal of Lonergan Studies* 2:2 [October 1984] 1–35, at 25–31).

well, it is pretty much the same arguments coming up again in a somewhat different application, and so on. Now St Thomas *is* systematic. Of what does his system consist? It consists of a basic set of *operations* that can be combined and recombined in various ways, and the various combinations are able to handle all the questions that arise. We have here, then, a concept, a notion, of system that is something far less static and abstract than Euclidean deduction. Moreover, it is a notion of system that can be applied to very concrete, very human developments. It is the fundamental notion of Piaget's some twenty volumes on child psychology.[25] Now, if you conceive system this way – a man has a system, he is thinking systematically, he is reaching systematic knowledge, insofar as he possesses a basic set of related operations – then, because the operations are related, the terms, the products, of the operations will be related. Because the operations are related to one another, the operations can be combined in various ways. You can have all sorts of terms, all sorts of problems, and you will know exactly what the meaning is in each term because you know exactly what the operations are and what are the relations between them. Moreover, one has, as it were, the mastery of a field in which this group of operations is more or less the principle and the intelligibility.

Now philosophy *can* be conceived as a basic group of operations; and as an insight into what that basic group of operations might be, you can take *experiencing, understanding,* and *judging.* The understanding can be differentiated, and you can get different kinds of combining of experiencing, understanding, and judging.

3 Philosophy of History

Now to the more difficult topic, philosophy of history. To bring the two together is the problem. Let us take philosophy of history as reflection on history, philosophic reflection on history, a mutual illumination of philosophy and of history. Now history has to be understood in the twofold sense of history that is written and history that is written about – the latter having to do with historical process, the totality of human action or human actions, and historicity. ('Historicity' is a rather difficult concept. The word

25 Piaget's volumes on child development, in English translations, are listed in the bibliography of John R. Phillips, *The Origins of Intellect: Piaget's Theory* (San Francisco: W.H. Freeman & Co., 1969) 139–40. Lonergan refers to many of Piaget's works in chapter 8 of *Topics in Education.*

is an attempt to translate the German *Geschichtlichkeit,* understood as a dimension of human reality.)

3.1 Philosophy and History That Is Written

Insofar as one is concerned with the relations between philosophy and the history that is written, our first topic was largely engaged in exploring this relationship. I was using my own philosophic categories to clarify notions of history as a science, its problems, and its possibilities. The indication of the distinctions among occasional, technical, and explanatory history came right out of notions of what the nature of human understanding is as developed in *Insight.* There is a further point: just as metaphysics is conceived in *Insight* as the integrating subject, just as the notion of being is conceived as the notion that underpins, penetrates, and goes beyond all other notions, so metaphysics is, as it were, the science of fundamental inquiry. This inquiry is broken up into the inquiries of the several sciences. It is an inquiry that also criticizes the inquiry of the several sciences. It is an inquiry that also criticizes the results of those inquiries and integrates them and goes beyond them. So too, there is, from that view of metaphysics, a connection with history. Insofar as the historian is operating in the light of a philosophy, he can deal with concepts, and raise questions, that people are interested in, even though those concepts and questions do not pertain to a specialized notion of history (such notions as the good, what is right, what is wrong, and so on). Again, insofar as you conceive your 'philosophy of' as the basic group of operations – experiencing, understanding, and judging – what would be true about those operations and their products will all be true of the operations conducted by the historian: his experiencing the traces now existing from the past, his understanding them, and his passing judgments.

That conception of 'philosophy of,' on the one hand, involves no intrusion into the specific procedures, the autonomy, of the historian qua historian; and at the same time it facilitates either his or his critics' discussion of the fundamental notions involved, and the valuation of his mode of conceiving them, and the relation of his work to other works. Again, that philosophic background makes it possible to relieve the historian of problems that really are not his concern qua historian. (Historians have been greatly troubled by the problem of relativism, and this has been rather pronounced since large numbers of them were expelled from Nazi Germany, and they could not say, 'Well, one opinion is just as good as another, they are all just so many opinions.' Experience was a little too deep for that. Particularly notable is Karl Mannheim, who did his work especially on the sociology of knowledge.)[26]

3.2 Philosophy and History That Is Written About

However, what I wish to communicate in the time that remains are certain fundamental notions that arise when reflection on history – on the history that is written about – occurs on the philosophic level.

3.2.1 Historicity

The first of these is the notion of historicity, of *Geschichtlichkeit.* It is said of Hegel, or he said it himself, that he transferred philosophy from the *substance* to the *subject*; Spinoza wrote about the substance, Hegel wrote about the subject.[27] The notion of the subject is a difficult notion to get hold of. One is not a subject, though one is a substance, when one is asleep and not dreaming. If one starts to dream, one becomes a subject, though a subject of

26 See Karl Mannheim, *Essays on the Sociology of Knowledge* (London: Routledge & Kegan Paul, 1952).

27 'From substance to subject' is one of a half dozen key phrases which in their extreme brevity sum up the most significant and far-reaching concerns of Lonergan's lifework: in this case, the transition from scholastic philosophy to a philosophy of the subject.

Was it from Hegel that Lonergan derived the idea? It seems likely. He speaks in a letter of 1935 (to Henry Keane, his Provincial Superior, 22 January 1935) of the enormous influence Hegel had had on him (p. 5), and though the specific reference was to a philosophy of history, the same letter goes on to speak of naive-realist views on substance (p. 6), so we may suppose a Hegelian influence there as well.

In any case the transition from substance to subject keeps surfacing in central contexts of Lonergan's thought. One instance is a passage in *Topics in Education* entitled '"We," "I": From Substance to Subject' (pp. 81–82, and see pp. 209–10). Another is the 1962 lecture on 'Time and Meaning' (see below, chapter 5, at note 20): 'The view of time in terms of "now" ... makes us move from substances to subjects.'

There is no need to multiply references, but two of the more important may be mentioned. First, there is the 'Introduction' he wrote for the book publication of his *verbum* articles (*Verbum* [see above, chapter 2, note 15] vii–xv); it is entirely on the present topic, weaving the thought of Aristotle, Augustine, and Aquinas into a pattern; further, when requested by *Philippine Studies* for an article, he offered this essay with the significant difference that the bland title 'Introduction' becomes the extremely significant 'Subject and Soul' (*Philippine Studies* 13 [1965] 576–85). Secondly, there is the application of this to the spiritual life, when in the 1965 lecture '*Existenz* and *Aggiornamento*' (*Collection* 222–31, at 230, and note *g* to chapter 15, p. 305) Lonergan developed the topic: 'being in Christ Jesus may be the being of substance or

an inferior type. But when one wakes up, one is much more of a subject, one is an *empirical* subject, a subject of acts of sense, seeing, hearing, and so on. If one inquires, understands, a new dimension emerges in consciousness; one is not only an empirical but also an *intelligent* subject. If one questions one's understanding, proceeds to judge, one becomes, one takes on the further dimension of, the *rational* subject. When one comes to making a decision or choice, the choice involves not only the chosen but also the chooser, and one is in the final level of the human subject, the *self-conscious* subject.

What is the subject? Well, the subject is what is known in consciousness. It is a term that, as it were, involves a leap from such metaphysical terms as substance and subsistence, which are defined and are verified independently of whether the subject is conscious or not. The subject is this substance inasmuch as he is known by consciousness; and not only is the subject known by consciousness, but he is also constituted qua subject by consciousness. It is when one moves from the metaphysical level of thinking to another level that there is a discontinuity, and I was talking about the notion of the subject to illustrate that discontinuity. We are always substances, but we are subjects only when we are awake, and we are subjects in different degrees according to what type of activity is going on in us.

Now just as man is a subject known and constituted by consciousness, so also man is known and constituted in his humanity by historicity, by this historical dimension of his reality. That notion of historicity is one that happens to be receiving all sorts of attention this century. From the thought of Martin Heidegger, there has radiated – often with decreasing degrees of dependence – a whole series of illuminations and transformations in previous ways of thinking of things. The notion goes back much further than Heidegger, but an illustration of it is the application of Heidegger's existentialism to depth psychology, and I will try to use a paper by Ludwig Binswanger on the dream and existence to elaborate.[28]

---

of subject' – an application made also, though only implicitly, in chapter 8 below, 'The Mediation of Christ in Prayer' (pp. 178–82).

The point is important, not only for understanding Lonergan's own developing thought, but also for relating him to Kant and Hegel. Too limited a focus on *Insight* suggests that Kant was his partner in philosophic dialogue, but the evidence keeps mounting that Kant is second to Hegel here. Lonergan did say, as if in correction of simpler views, that for him Kant was an afterthought (*Caring about Meaning: Patterns in the Life of Bernard Lonergan*, ed. Pierrot Lambert, Charlotte Tansey, and Cathleen Going [Montreal: Thomas More Institute, 1982] 10), but, dazzled by *Insight*, we tend to overlook that statement.

28 Ludwig Binswanger, 'Dream and Existence,' in *Being-in-the-World*, trans. Jacob Needleman (New York: Basic Books, 1963) 222–48.

He distinguishes two types of dreams: the dream of the night, which is more largely determined by somatic influences, and the dream of the morning, in which the existent is shaping himself and his world. Consciousness is such that there is always a subject conscious of something, and the range of things the subject is conscious of is the horizon. Now the dream of the morning is a symbolic, incipient positing of the subject and his world. That world is not just a world of objects; it is a world in which the subject is acting, and because this human acting is determined, conditioned, by the historical developments of the past and a contribution to what the history of the immediate future is to be, you also have its historicity in the very constitution of the subject.

To try to get hold of this notion from a slightly different angle, or perhaps to carry the point a step further, note that a person suffering from amnesia does not know who he is. If I were to forget that I was a Jesuit, a priest, a professor of theology, and so on, my possible activities would be entirely out of conformity with what I am. My memory of myself is constitutive, a fundamental determinant, of what I do. And to generalize, if a people were to forget themselves as a people, if all Canadians were to have amnesia insofar as they are Canadians, then Canada would no longer exist, and the same is true of any other people. There is an existential memory that is constitutive of the people qua people just as there is an existential memory constitutive of a personality qua personality.

Again, the history of a people is an account, an interpretation, of what the people were; but what the people were was their own self-interpretation. A man is not just a thing; he is what he does. What he says, what he works for, is all a function of his experience, his accumulated experience, understanding, judgment, his mentality, his way of thinking, what he approves of and disapproves of, what he wants and does not want. His mental activities are the main determinants of all his actions, and his mental activities include an interpretation, an idea, of what he himself is and what he is for – his nature and destiny. As this is true of the individual, so also it is true of the group. The historian, in writing the history of the people, in interpreting what the people were, is not the first to step into the field of interpretation. There is an understanding that was constitutive of the history that is written about, not only the understanding of the historian.

So history becomes an objectification of the existential memory of the people, of their self-interpretation. Just as drama is an objectification, a symbolization, of human life in some aspect or some situations, so, on a more fundamental level, you could say that all living is in a sense drama – people dealing with people and things. That more fundamental drama is the more fundamental objectification in civilization of what, more originally, the person is. In that way, one has a comparison between drama and history – as though drama is, as it were, a prehistorical, more simple type of history, of objectification and criticism of the way that people live, while history is a fuller, more ample, more reflective drama.

Now what I have been trying to do is to suggest this notion of historicity, but it is a very difficult notion to get hold of. On the other hand, it is a field of very fruitful reflections on the nature and significance of history. I cannot carry this notion any further here.[29]

3.2.2 Dialectic

I will now go on to another notion that emerges on the level of philosophic reflection on history. The notion is dialectic. About the beginning of the last decade, Joseph Moreau wrote a very small book on idealism and realism in Plato,[30] and its final paragraph ended up with a statement from Blondel, *L'Action* (1893), in which Blondel said that a fully coherent idealism ends by eliminating all the differences that separate it from realism.[31] It is the statement that one type of philosophy, if fully coherent, if worked out to the end, becomes another; and there you have a fundamental opposition between what I call positions and counterpositions. Positions express the dynamic structure of the subject qua intelligent and qua reasonable. Counterpositions contradict that structure. Whenever a person is explicitly affirming – presenting or affirming – a counterposition, he is involved in a queer type of contradiction. The contradiction is not between statements that he makes; the contradiction is between the statements that he makes and the subject that he is. He is intelligent and reasonable, and purports to be intelligent and reasonable, and he would not admit any fall from intelli-

29 We have added the word 'here.' For further comments, see the entry 'Historicity' in the indices to *Method in Theology* and *A Second Collection* (see above, chapter 1, note 26) as well as § 1 of 'Natural Right and Historical Mindedness' (*A Third Collection* [see above, chapter 2, note 5] 170–71) and § 9 in *Doctrinal Pluralism* (Milwaukee: Marquette University Press, 1971) 53–56.

30 Joseph Moreau, *Réalisme et idéalisme chez Platon* (Paris: Presses Universitaires de France, 1951).

31 'Une idéalisme pleinement conséquent fait s'évanouir toutes les distinctions qui le séparent du réalisme.' Maurice Blondel, *L'Action. Essai d'une critique de la vie et d'une science de la pratique* (Paris: Presses Universitaires de France, 1950) 457; originally published 1893. We are grateful to Pierre Robert of Montreal for supplying this reference and quotation.

gence or reasonableness. Yet the implications of the one, the real consequences, so to speak, of the one, and the implications of the other, which are in a field of conceptions or a field of judgments, are in conflict.

Such a conflict tends to work itself out in one way or another. It sets up a tension, and it is a principle of movement; and that, to my mind, is a fundamental instance of what is meant by dialectic. It is in the concrete, it involves tension and opposition, and it is a principle of change; and the change is not so much, not merely, in the statements; it will also be in the subject who comes to a fuller realization, a fuller appropriation, of what he himself really is. The effect of the dialectic is not simply a matter of straightening out the sentences, and affirming the ones that are true and denying the ones that are false. A person can be affirming propositions that are true, but misinterpreting them; and you cannot correct what is wrong with him by telling him the right ones, because he is always going to bring in the misinterpretation. There is a more fundamental step: the development in the subject himself through dialectic.

Now that dialectic goes on not merely within the individual. Platonic dialectic was dialogue. There was ruled out eristic dialectic, that is, argument for argument's sake: the man in Goldsmith's deserted village, though vanquished, could argue still.[32] But let the argument have its run, let it have its free course, and things will come to light that we had not thought of before. The Platonic dialogue is a concrete, group use of dialectic in that individual sense. The individual will make his statements, and another individual will state what this subject really is, in an implicit manner no doubt, but there is another example of dialectic. A third example, what Aristotle called dialectic, was reviewing the opinions of all the people that discussed the question before him; and there you have the dialogue put out into time. But what goes on in the subject, what goes on in the dialogue, what goes on in the development of opinions on a single question, that also has relevance to the total field of human development; and that is history.

Now that notion of development has come to notice today. It is a little hard to describe it; there has been both Hegelian and Marxist dialectic. Think of Hegel's account, in the *Phenomenology of Spirit*, of the master-slave

32 Oliver Goldsmith, *The Deserted Village*, line 211:
In arguing too, the parson own'd his skill,
For e'en though vanquish'd, he could argue still ...
As given in *The Oxford Dictionary of Quotations* (London: Oxford University Press, 1962).

relations.[33] It is a beautiful piece of work. It describes the initial situation, where you have a master who is really master and the slave who is really slave. But time goes on, and the master becomes more and more dependent upon the slave, and the roles become reversed. That is an illustration of the notion of development of situations working themselves out to their consequences. But that notion of dialectic has been plunged into the problem of the interpretation, the grand-scale interpretation, of history on the philosophic level, and that is very much a problem of our time. The liberals – the Enlightenment and then the liberals – had a doctrine, an interpretation, of history in terms of progress. Things were getting better and better. The Marxists had an interpretation in terms of what they call the materialistic dialectic of history, which has become the interpretation of human reality in Russia and in China; and it seems to be accepted there in all seriousness as the correct view of this world and what its meaning is, what it is about. (We had a sample today with Mr Khrushchev's speech at the United Nations.[34])

We have had others of these grand-scale interpretations of history. Another example is Rosenberg's myth of the twentieth century,[35] which is the interpretation of history behind the Nazi movement. There is very definitely a problem here. Christopher Dawson, in a recent book, *The Historic Reality of Christian Culture*,[36] speaks of these movements going on and of Christians having very little influence because of largely passive attitudes. Eric Voegelin, in his *New Science of Politics*,[37] suggests – perhaps does more than suggest – that the Christian view of this world, as waiting for the second coming of Christ, left a vacuum of meaning in that merely day-to-day aspect of human living which these modern philosophies of history are attempting to fill. When they fill it, they obtain stupendous results, stupendous influence over human life in all its aspects, as is illustrated by

33 G.W.F. Hegel, *Phänomenologie des Geistes* (Frankfurt-am-Main: Suhrkamf, 1970) 145–55; in English, *Phenomenology of Spirit*, trans. A.V. Miller (Oxford: Oxford University Press, 1977) 111–19.

34 From his arrival in the United States on 20 September 1960, Khrushchev stole the headlines (details in the Index to the *New York Times* for that year). The text of his 23 September address to the United Nations Assembly, strongly critical of that body itself, was published by the *Times* on 24 September, pp. 6–9.

35 Alfred Rosenberg, *Der Mythus des 20. Jahrhunderts* (München: Hoheneichen, 1937).

36 Christopher Dawson, *The Historic Reality of Christian Culture* (New York: Harper & Row, 1960).

37 Voegelin, *The New Science of Politics* 107–10.

nineteenth-century progressivism – it goes on well into this century – and the influence of Marx at the present time.

3.2.3 Stages

A third notion is stages. Most of you are familiar, from the study of the New Testament and the Old Testament, with the difference between the Greek and the Hebrew mentality. The difference is essentially that the Greek view of man and the Greek's apprehension of himself was more differentiated than that of the Hebrew. In the cultured Greek there was the difference between intellect and sense, between apprehension and appetition, between appetite and choice. These were differences that were very clear and explicit. The Hebrew thinks of man more compactly, as a whole. Anterior to both the Greek and the Hebrew mentality is the emergence of individualism. A primitive tribe is not a group of individuals, each of whom thinks and judges and decides. The thinking, judging, and deciding is a community operation; and Karl Jaspers, in a very stimulating book on the origin and end of history,[38] places this emergence of individualism, of individual responsibility and individual judgment, in the period between 800 and 200 B.C., in China, India, Persia, in Israel with the prophets, and in Greece with the Sophists and the philosophers and the tragedians.

In order to do the historical work of extending history back into the relatively primitive, or to understand the differences of the earlier and later civilizations, there is needed some exact knowledge of that differentiation, that movement from the undifferentiated consciousness, the primitive, to the later and fuller differentiations of consciousness (and also some understanding of the problem of the primitives in our own days, in our own mass societies, the public reversion to primitivism); and one has to draw upon philosophic concepts to understand the difference between these fuller differentiations of consciousness and the high civilizations of ancient Babylon, Egypt, China, and India, the cultures of the Cretans, the Mayas, the Incas, the Toltec. They possessed, first of all, large states; they carried on enormous engineering projects; they knew mathematics, and so on. But

38 'It would seem that this axis of history is to be found in the period around 500 B.C., in the spiritual process that occurred between 800 and 200 B.C. It is there that we meet with the most deepcut dividing line in history.' Karl Jaspers, *The Origin and Goal of History*, trans. Michael Bullock (London: Routledge & Kegan Paul, 1953) 1.

their fundamental thinking had not broken through the mythical type of consciousness, in which the simple, the naive, the name of the reality, the symbol, the exact conception, are all pretty much of a blur. The understanding of that primitive mentality, and then, in the times of troubles following those civilizations, this breaking forth of individualism, is rather convincingly put forth in that work by Jaspers. This is, again, another aspect of that notion of historicity that I was trying to communicate earlier, namely, if differentiated consciousness is itself a product of the historic process, it becomes evident in a particularly clear way that there is a dimension of human nature contained in historicity itself. Think of Heidegger's famous title, *Sein und Zeit* (*Being and Time*).[39]

3.2.4 Good and Evil

Further illuminations, further types of questions, projected into history from philosophic reflections, regard the notion of the good and the problem of evil. In a rather celebrated fantasy and satire, *1066 and All That*,[40] the history of England was recounted in terms of 108 good things. What is the good? The position of a developed philosophic notion of the good is extremely relevant to the questions historians get asked, whether they want them or not; and if you want to get into that type of question, what the philosophic notion of the good is, and also how it ties in with the notion of history, it is considered in chapter 18 of *Insight*.[41] It is the sort of thing that can be left for the discussions of the year, if anyone is interested in it. Similarly, the soteriological issue is raised in the twentieth chapter of *Insight*.

4 Theology of History

As I am a theologian, I should probably be asked, 'But what about the theology of history?' My answer very briefly would be that theology, insofar as it is a science and is systematic, follows a basic group of operations; that the

39 Martin Heidegger, *Sein und Zeit* (Tübingen: Max Niemeyer Verlag, 7th ed., 1953); in English, *Being and Time*, trans. John Macquarrie and Edward Robinson (London: SCM Press, and New York: Harper & Row, 1962).
40 Karl C. Sellar and Robert J. Yeatman, *1066 and All That: A Memorable History of England* (New York: E.P. Dutton, 1931).
41 See also *Topics in Education*, chapters 2–4. '... my notion of the human good is interconvertible with my notion of the structure of history' (ibid. 24).

basic group of operations are, again, experiencing, understanding, and judging; but that judging here is of a different type, involving beliefs; that the understanding has a new type of inverse insight because of the mysteries; but that, just as there is a basic philosophic set of operations, so it can go on to a specialization into a basic set of theological operations; and then one proceeds as before to have a mutual illumination of philosophy, theology, and history, just as one has of philosophy and history.

5 Conclusion

My illustrations have been largely one-way, the illumination of history by philosophy; but it is very important to realize that it is a two-way street. All contemporary subjects are historical. Not only is there history as a specialized subject, but also the development, the presentation, of any science or any subject at the present time has a historical dimension; we have become historicized. 'Truth is eternal in an eternal mind,'[42] according to St Thomas, and our minds are not eternal. What is defined, qua defined, is as beautiful as a Platonic Idea, but definitions arise at a determinate time. The advance of science, the development that goes on in every science, involves the seriation of the concepts and truths attained at any time over periods of time. The presentation of a subject at the present time is, briefly, four-dimensional, and philosophy is no exception. There is a terrific development within philosophy itself, and again within theology, concerned with the development of dogma and the development of theology. If I have not touched upon those points[43] – and it is not that I should in any way wish to slight them – I hope I have said something that will be of some use to this course during the coming year.

42 '... si nullus intellectus esset aeternus, nulla veritas esset aeterna. Sed quia solus intellectus divinus est aeternus, in ipso solo veritas aeternitatem habet.' Thomas Aquinas, *Summa theologiae,* 1, q. 16, a. 7.

43 Lonergan does treat these topics in the final lecture, 'History,' in *Topics in Education* (see pp. 241–50). That lecture begins and ends by referring to the history that happens, but the entire treatment is in terms of the history that is written. Further, Lonergan does not there mention the two meanings of 'history.'

4

The Origins of Christian Realism (1961)[1]

The topic I have chosen, 'The Origins of Christian Realism,' is derived directly from a set of notes I put together last year on the positive part of the treatise *De Deo trino*. If you want further details you can consult the first one hundred and sixty-five pages of that manual.[2]

1 Lectures with this title were delivered at the Irish Jesuit Theologate, Milltown Park, Dublin, 22 May 1961; at Alma College (theologate of the California Jesuits), Los Gatos, California, 5 August 1961; at Regis College, Willowdale, Ontario, to the academic community, 8 September 1961; at the Venerable English College, Rome, 3 April 1963; at Gonzaga University, Spokane, Washington, 21 July 1963; and at the North American College, Rome, 15 April 1964. A quite different lecture under the same title was given as the Seventeenth Annual Robert Cardinal Bellarmine Lecture at the Saint Louis University School of Divinity, 27 September 1972 (printed in *Theology Digest* 20 [1972] 292–305 and published again in *A Second Collection* [see above, chapter 1, note 26] 239–61). Much of the foregoing bibliographical information is supplied by Mark D. Morelli in an editorial note to the publication of the Regis College lecture in *Method: Journal of Lonergan Studies* 5:1 (1987) 1–12. What is published here is based on a transcription made by Michael G. Shields soon after the Regis College lecture. Dated 10 October 1961, the Shields transcript was retyped and mimeographed at the North American College, Rome, 15 April 1964; it was also used by Morelli in the *Method* publication. Lonergan did not have a full text but spoke from notes.

2 Bernard Lonergan, *De Deo trino: Pars analytica* (Rome: Gregorian University Press, 1961). Lonergan is probably referring to the Praemittenda (pp. 13–113) and the first thesis (pp. 114–63). The text is revised at several places in the 1964 *De Deo trino*, vol. 1: *Pars dogmatica* (see above, chapter 2, note 18).

1 Four Approaches to the Question

1.1 Christian Realism and Christian Philosophy

The question can be approached in four different ways. The title will probably suggest to many of you, if not to all, the disputed question that was raised first of all about thirty years ago in France and Belgium when, in 1928, Emile Bréhier gave a lecture in Brussels on the question of the existence of a Christian philosophy.[3] His opinion was that there is no more a Christian philosophy than there is a Christian mathematics or a Christian physics; that philosophy is philosophy, and there is nothing specifically Christian about it. In 1931 Etienne Gilson, in a paper read before the Société française de Philosophie, took issue with Bréhier.[4] He did not want any confusion whatever of philosophy and theology, any mixture of their procedures, and de jure he does not believe too much in the capacity of unaided reason to arrive at truth. But he put forward the historical point that de facto the Greek philosophers did not anticipate and did not work out the specifically Christian conception of God as Creator, and the conception of divine providence. The philosophy that arrived at God as Creator and God as Providence was something that de facto, historically, is Christian. It arose in a Christian milieu. So at least historically there is such a thing as a Christian philosophy. And most recently he has returned to the issue in his book *Le Philosophe et la théologie.*[5]

In 1932 Maurice Blondel took issue with both Bréhier and Gilson.[6] He denied that there was any parallel whatever between philosophy and math-

3 Emile Bréhier, 'Y a-t-il une philosophie chrétienne?' *Revue de Métaphysique et de Morale* 38 (1931) 133–62.

4 Etienne Gilson, 'La Notion de philosophie chrétienne,' *Bulletin de la Société française de Philosophie,* 31e année (1931) 37–93. The controversy is reviewed by Maurice Nédoncelle, *Existe-t-il une Philosophie Chrétienne?* (Paris: Librairie Arthème Fayard, 1956) 65–76; in English, *Is There a Christian Philosophy?* trans. Illtyd Trethowan (London: Burns and Oates, 1960) 85–99.

5 Etienne Gilson, *Le Philosophe et la théologie* (Paris: Librairie Arthème Fayard, 1960); in English, *The Philosopher and Theology,* trans. Cécile Gilson (New York: Random House, 1962). Lonergan added, 'I haven't read all of it myself, but I was told by a man from France that it is an extremely well written work, just the sort of work that justifies Gilson's membership in the Académie Française.'

6 Maurice Blondel, *Le Problème de la philosophie catholique* (Paris: Bloud & Gay, 1932), esp. pp. 127–77.

ematics, and that consequently there was no point in saying that there is no more a Catholic philosophy than there is a Catholic mathematics. He considered Gilson's introduction of the historical element as irrelevant; and he came to his point, namely, that philosophy is not a closed, abstract system; philosophy is worked out in the concrete, and in a Christian milieu develops differently from the way it does in a non-Christian milieu.

Now there are three opinions there, and I think a great deal can be said for each. I think that any ultimate view of the matter is going to take something from all three. This question of Christian philosophy is not the same as my question of Christian realism, but it does provide something of an antecedent for it.

1.2 The Meaning of Realism

The issue can be put in more abstract terms, in more specifically philosophic terms, namely, What precisely do you mean by a 'realism'? As I have discovered, there are people who seem to think that if you hold that intellect is intelligent,[7] then you are bound to be an idealist. And that conclusion follows if one holds certain ideas about realism. Realism is not just one type of philosophy; there is a series of different meanings of realism.

1.3 The Historical Issue

That is the point I propose to illustrate tonight by discussing an issue that is historical, namely, the origins of the Christian type of realism; that will pin down just what type of realism is specifically Christian. In its historical form – a third approach to the issue – one will ask, 'How is it that Christianity became involved in philosophic issues, that it gravitated toward a realist position, and that it gravitated toward the specific type of realism that is characteristic of Christianity?'

7 To say 'intellect is intelligent' seems redundant, but those three words state a key position of Lonergan's, namely, his stand against a conceptualism in which the operations of intellect are not intelligent at all, but are 'a matter of metaphysical mechanics' (*Verbum* [see above, chapter 2, note 15] 26, note 122), 'of some metaphysical sausage-machine, at one end slicing species off phantasm, and at the other popping out concepts' (ibid. 34). See *Understanding and Being* (see above, chapter 2, note 13), note *c* to Discussion 2, p. 425. For more on 'metaphysical mechanics,' see *Verbum* 45, *A Second Collection* 222, and *Topics in Education* (see above, chapter 2, note 12) 113 (and see 168–70).

1.4 *The Popular Approach*

There is a fourth approach to the question – and this might be called the popular approach, one that is in everyone's mind, more or less, at the present time. It is of course an old question. Blaise Pascal in his *Pensées*[8] contrasted the God of Abraham, Isaac, and Jacob, the God of our Fathers, on the one hand, and on the other, the God of the philosophers. The God of the philosophers is an *actus purus,* an *ens necessarium,* or, if you wish, 'an unrestricted act of understanding.' It is a God that is concluded to and demonstrated and proved, worked out as the conclusion to a series of theorems. On the other hand, the God of Abraham, Isaac, and Jacob, the God of our Fathers, is the God of revelation as recital. The God of Abraham is the One *who* – who did this and this and that, who said this and this and that, who promised this and this and that, who threatened this and this and that. He is conceived in what we would call the category of a person – the One who, a personal pronoun; he is characterized as a man is characterized, by his deeds, by his words, by his promises, by his threats. He is a personal force acting in and forming the Hebraic tradition. When God is so conceived, there is no attempt made to say that the symbol is merely the symbol. The one element that bears witness to that philosophic concern is the prohibition of images. Similarly, in the revelation of our Lord in the Gospels, he is set forth in exactly the same type of category. He is the one who was promised; he is the only-begotten *Son* of God. He is the one who did and said this and this and that, as narrated in the Gospels, who suffered and died and rose again, who sits at the right hand of the Father, who will come to judge the living and the dead. You have two entirely different modes of conceiving God: the one of recital of deeds about a person, in the Old Testament about God, in the New Testament about our Lord; and the other, the God of the philosophers.

But between those two conceptions of God there is a third, the God of the theologians. And it is with that conception of God that we are concerned tonight.

2 The God of the Theologians

The theologians (or the Fathers, rather) from the second to the fourth centuries were concerned with trinitarian questions, and from the fifth to

8 Blaise Pascal, *Pensées,* trans. with introduction by A.J. Krailsheimer (Markham, ON: Penguin Books, 1987) § 449.

the seventh with Christological questions. In that time they moved from the New Testament conception of God to the conception of one divine substance in three persons, and again, from the New Testament conception of our Lord to the conception of one person with two natures, two properties, two wills, and two operations. That historical process has been a subject of historical and theological discussion for a number of centuries, in fact since Petavius.[9] In *Scholastik*, 1958, Fr Grillmeier has two long articles, on the interpretation of the history of that discussion, and on contemporary efforts along that line.[10] It is within this process from the God of the New Testament to the God of the theologians, of the Fathers and theologians and councils, that I think are to be located the origins of Christian realism. In that period it was gradually discovered – and not too explicitly, but rather by results than by any reflexive and methodical formulations – that a technical development was needed to state the truths of revelation, on the one hand without departing from scripture and tradition, and on the other hand without exposing the Christian church to ridicule.

2.1 *Jewish-Christian Thinking*

The process unfolds on a rather large background. The first type (at least in, so to speak, a logical order) of Christian thinking upon the revelation concerning God and his Son was that of the Jewish Christians. And on Jewish Christianity as a specific type of thinking, Fr Daniélou has written his *Théologie du judéo-christianisme.*[11] As he shows, there are to be found traces in a series of works – in the *Ascensio Isaiae*, in *Pastor Hermae*, in Irenaeus (in the *Demonstratio evangelica*), and in Origen – of a conception, and an explicit conception, of the Son and the Holy Spirit as angels. The passage in Isaiah 6.3 in which the two seraphim with six wings continually cry, 'Holy, holy, holy, Lord God of Sabaoth,' is interpreted of the Father as God and of the Son and Holy Spirit as the two seraphim. In other words, Jewish Christianity was an attempt to understand the Christian revelation within the symbols of the Old Testament. The person who first went into this mat-

9 Denis Petau (1583–1652), whose name was latinized as Dionysius Petavius, was one of the most brilliant theologians of his time, and a pioneer in accepting the idea of doctrinal development.

10 Aloys Grillmeier, 'Hellenisierung – Judaisierung des Christentums als Deuteprinzipien der Geschichte des kirchlichen Dogmas,' *Scholastik* 33 (1958) 321–55, 528–58.

11 Jean Daniélou, *Théologie du judéo-christianisme* (Paris/Tournai: Desclée, 1958).

ter of the angelology of the Jewish Christians was Barbel in his *Christos Angelos.*[12] Werner, in his *Die Entstehung des christlichen Dogmas,*[13] held the view that for the Jewish Christians the Son and Holy Spirit were not God, were merely creatures. That, I think, has generally been rejected as imposing upon the Jewish Christians Greek categories which they simply did not have. What they were doing was conceiving the Son and Holy Spirit as persons, namely as angels, and angels of the highest possible order, with the greatest proximity to God. It was an attempt to conceive the Trinity within the symbolism of the Old Testament.

2.2 *Christian Gnosticism*

Another type of symbolic, or rather pseudosymbolic, thinking was Christian Gnosticism. As you know, there are four types of Gnosticism: pagan, Jewish, the Gnosticism (or traces of it) found in the New Testament, and finally, heretical Christian sects of maybe the second century, in which the speculative interest was dominant. As Karl Prümm says of them in his article in *Lexikon für Theologie und Kirche,*[14] the fundamental aspiration or inspiration of Christian Gnosticism is represented by a passage from the *Excerpta ex Theodoto* of Clement of Alexandria: 'Up to baptism, the Fates are true; but after baptism the astrologers no longer predict our lives. But it is not only the washing that brings us to liberty, but also knowledge (*gnôsis*) of what we were, what we have become, where we were or were cast, whither we hurry, whence we have been redeemed, what is generation and what regeneration.'[15]

The Gnostics had a speculative interest. But it was a speculative interest that was satisfied with a pseudosymbolic type of thinking. Their symbols were not properly sensible; they were using abstract terms, numerology, and so on, to cover over profundities and pseudo profundities. They had a

12 Joseph Barbel, *Christos Angelos* (Bonn: Peter Hanstein, 1941).

13 Martin Werner, *Die Entstehung des christlichen Dogmas* (Leipzig: Paul Haupt, 1941; also published by Haupt in Bern with the same date, and with a second edition there in 1954). The English translation, *The Formation of Christian Dogma: An Historical Study of Its Problem* (London: Adam & Charles Black, 1957) states on the title page, 'Rewritten in shortened form,' and refers to the second edition of the German as published by Haupt (Bern) and Katzmann (Tübingen).

14 Karl Prümm, 'Gnostizismus: im Hellenismus,' *Lexikon für Theologie und Kirche,* ed. Joseph Höfer and Karl Rahner (Freiburg: Herder, 1960), cols. 1021–24.

15 Clement of Alexandria, *Excerpta ex Theodoto* 78; *PL* 9: 694. See below, note 17.

fantastic conception of the divinity as consisting of thirty eons, with all sorts of psychological and other analogies running through it. They could prove everything in their doctrine – and did – by appealing to the spiritual sense. Take the parable of the vineyard in which the lord of the vineyard goes out at the first hour, the third, the sixth, the ninth, and the eleventh. If you add those numbers up you get thirty; therefore the Gospels testify that there are thirty eons. Not, of course, to everyone, but to those able to read the scriptures spiritually. And so on all along the line. The Ogdoad and the Decad were proved by the fact that the name 'Jesus' begins with IH, the iota standing for 10 and the êta standing for 8, making 18. They had endless proofs from scripture, and they were almost impossible to refute simply because they were fantastic. Irenaeus is full of this constantly recurring fantastic exegesis of the Gnostic sects. If he is not refuting it, at least he is reprimanding them for what they are saying.

There we have two of the types of thinking, the Jewish symbolic interpretation of the New Testament in terms of the symbols of the Old, and a Gentile Greek interpretation of the New Testament in terms of the pseudo symbolism of Gnosticism.

2.3 *Rationalistic Types*

There are also more rationalistic types. The Marcionites had no interest whatever in the emanations; but they give the impression of being anti-Semitic, and they conceived the God of the Old Testament as a fierce, repellent deity from whom we have been redeemed by the God of the New Testament. Redemption, then, is from the wicked God of the Old Testament by the good God of the New. They also practiced the Higher Criticism: they accepted Paul and Luke, no one else, and not even all of Paul and Luke. Finally, there were the obvious antitheses with regard to our Lord. The Sabellians acknowledged his divinity but denied distinction from God the Father; the Adoptionists admitted that the Son was distinct from God the Father and concluded that he was only a man.

2.4 *Mainstream Problems*

2.4.1 Stoic Categories

Now these are, as it were, background problems; they were not problems within the Greek church. They represented rather the lunatic fringe, so to speak, people that were not within the mainstream of thought of Christianity. But there also were problems within the orthodox or general stream of Christianity. Michel Spanneut published in 1957 *Le Stoicisme des pères de l'église, de Clément de Rome à Clément d'Alexandrie.*[16] He has found continuous similarities, analogies, and contacts with Stoicism in Christian writers from Clement of Rome to Clement of Alexandria. Just how much this is due to the influence of Stoicism and how much it is a matter of just ordinary human nature would be a difficult question to solve – probably much more of the latter, although they used Stoic categories.

2.4.2 Naive Realism

There was an influence of what we would call today 'naive realism.' In Irenaeus there is the traditional concept of God: God is the God of the Old Testament and of the New, against the Marcionites; the God of Abraham, Isaac, Jacob, and of the prophets; the God of our Lord and Savior Jesus Christ; the God of the apostolic preaching; the God that is believed by the church. But he also undertakes to prove that there is only one God, and his argument is largely that of the container and the contained. There must be one God that has dominion over absolutely everything, that contains everything; and it is very difficult not to find in Irenaeus a rather materialist conception behind his proof of the unity of God.

The same thing appears in Tertullian. In Tertullian the Son undoubtedly is God. Why? Because God, though he is a spirit, certainly is a body; otherwise he would not be *real.* To be real, a spirit has to have a body, has to be a substance. And out of the divine substance there proceeds a spirit informed by the divine Word, and that is the Son. This is what has been called Tertullian's organic monotheism. Father, Son, and Holy Spirit are, as it were, organic parts of one divinity. And behind that is the type of naive realism to which Tertullian perhaps did not consciously subscribe, but which de facto was the way in which he thought. Because of that, Tertullian can hold that the Son is not eternal but came forth in time. Whether he is eternal or not is of no importance in settling his divinity; he is divine if he is made of the divine matter, the divine stuff. The Son can be subordinate: the Father can give the orders and the Son execute them; and that will not

16 Michel Spanneut, *Le Stoicisme des pères de l'église, de Clément de Rome à Clément d'Alexandrie* (Paris: Editions du Seuil, 1957).

be against the divinity of the Son because it is not whether the Son is subordinate or superior that settles whether he is divine, but what he is made of. Is he made of the divine stuff or not? Now Tertullian does not put it quite so bluntly as that, but that is what his position comes to. In other words, when Tertullian makes his subordinationist utterances, for us they imply denial of the divinity, but they do not imply denial of divinity in Tertullian's mind.

In Clement of Alexandria there is a series of passages from the *Excerpta ex Theodoto*[17] that indicates, in parts that scholars attribute to Clement himself and not to quotations, that Clement is quite clearly involved in a naive realism. He speaks of the angels of the little ones, who continuously gaze upon the face of the Father;[18] and, blessed are the pure of heart because they see God. But how could there be a face of the Father to see if he has no shape? The Apostle, then, knew about celestial bodies that are beautiful and intelligent when he said, 'Other is the glory of the heavenly beings and other is that of the terrestrial, other that of the angels and other that of the archangels.'[19] Compare them with the corporeal bodies we see on earth, and of course they are invisible, far too subtle for us to see them; but they are bodies nonetheless. Similarly the demons: if they had no body, they would not be able to suffer from the fire of hell. Clement has a series of arguments – not only philosophical, but some are also from scripture – to prove that God and the angels have bodies in a sense. This is a confusion of the notion of body with the notion of reality. He argues, as also Irenaeus seems to have argued before him, from the parable of Lazarus. The rich man asks Abraham to have Lazarus dip his finger in a glass of water and place it on his tongue. Well, both Lazarus and the rich man are dead, have departed from the crass bodies of this world. But obviously Lazarus couldn't have a finger to dip in the water, and the rich man couldn't have a tongue on which to place the water, if they had no bodies at all. There is, then, a great deal of what we would call 'naive realism.' What do you mean by the 'real'? It is what you can put your hand on. And if you extend that

17 Lonergan added parenthetically, '"Excerpts from Theodotus"; Theodotus was a Gnostic, and the *Excerpta* are a notebook of Clement's in which part is Clement's own thinking and part quotations from Theodotus.'
18 For this example and for what follows, see *Excerpta ex Theodoto* 11.
19 The closest scriptural reference is 1 Corinthians 15.40: 'There are both heavenly bodies and earthly bodies, but the glory of the heavenly is one thing, and that of the earthly is another' (NRSV).

idea of the real and acknowledge the reality of God, then you have to conceive God in a manner we should reject.

Now what pulled these thinkers and what pulled the Christian tradition out of that naive realism was the exegetical problem set by the Gnostics (less by the Jewish Christians, because they received less attention). Irenaeus makes no systematic effort to get to the roots of Gnostic exegesis. He proceeds much like the boxer described by Demosthenes: the barbarian boxer puts his hand up not where the blow is coming, but where he has been hit. In a similar manner Irenaeus is meeting each objection as it arises. But Clement of Alexandria in the eighth book of his *Stromateis* begins to set up a systematic type of exegesis. He says, first of all, that if you use a name, then you should define it, and define it in terms better known than the name itself. Define it in a way that everyone will accept. And after you have agreed on its definition, ask whether anything corresponding to the name exists. When you have settled that it exists, inquire about its nature. And then he goes on giving all the precepts of Greek hermeneutics which he followed.

Now the necessity of that systematic procedure set up by Clement of Alexandria is seen when one thinks of Gnostic exegesis. If the only interpretation of scripture were symbolic, then you could never settle what the symbols are symbols of. If you are going to say that the symbols are not just symbols of more symbols, then you have to have some idea of reality. And if Clement was to contribute to defeating the Gnostic exegesis of scripture (which reduced it to nonsense, really) he had to appeal to some reality, and he had to appeal to some method that settled just what the real was. You have, in the exegetic problem, the implicit philosophic problem, What do you mean by reality?

That problem of reality implicit in the exegetic problem was met by the Alexandrians by turning to Platonism.

2.4.3 Platonism

The idea that the early Christians held a spiritualist philosophy in the contemporary sense of the term is weakened not only by the examples I have indicated but also by Origen's treatment in *De principiis*, book 1, of God the Father, God the Son, and God the Holy Spirit. His treatment of God the Father, which runs over a number of pages, is devoted entirely to proving that God the Father is a purely spiritual being, and making it absolutely clear what he meant by 'spiritual.' Moreover, Origen conceived the generation of the Son from the Father in a purely spiritual fashion. The Son proceeds from the Father by contemplation and love, an eternal contemplation and love. But Origen was involved in his Platonism – it was a Middle Platonism, pretty similar to that of Plotinus – and while he conceived the Father as the absolute good and as God *simpliciter*, he conceived the Son as good and as God by participation. The Son is Wisdom itself and Truth itself and Revelation itself and Resurrection itself, where the 'itself' refers to the Platonist abstract Idea; but the Father is something greater than these. On the other hand, the Son is not God, Divinity itself, but a participation of Divinity, not Goodness itself, but a participation of Goodness. That was Origen's Platonist solution to the problem raised by Sabellianism on the one hand and Adoptionism on the other. In Origen, naive realism has been transcended, but it has been transcended in the direction of Platonism. While Tertullian held the divinity of the Son, and truly held it, on false philosophic assumptions, Origen has a conception of the Son as a really subordinate being, not 'true God' in the sense of Nicea. We have moved to the second step in which philosophic issues were involved in Christian thinking.

2.4.4 Consubstantiality and Christian Realism

A century later the Arians had brought the question back to the Hebraic and Christian categories: 'Is the Son Creator or is he creature?' And they argued that the Son is not unbegotten. He is begotten, he is generated, he has an origin, he depends on someone else; therefore he cannot be the First Principle, he cannot be the Creator, he cannot be God in the proper sense of the term. On the other hand, in Athanasius, who represented and defended the Council of Nicea, the distinction, which had been clarified earlier and then obscured by the Arians, between *agennêtos* and *agenêtos* – the first is from *gennaô*, 'to generate,' the second from *gignomai*, 'to become' – was affirmed. What is *agenêton* is *increatum*, not created; what is *agennêton* has not been generated. In Athanasius one finds fundamental reflections on the notion of creation, on the notion of God as He who is. The Greeks – Aristotle and Plato – had spoken of *to on*, what is; but with the Old Testament, the Septuagint, Athanasius speaks of *ho ôn*, he who is, the masculine of the present participle of the verb 'to be.' From the fact that the Son is indeed not ungenerated (*agennêtos*) it does not follow that he has been created, that he is not *agenêtos*. You have fundamental reflections on the being of God in Athanasius's refutation of Arius, in his distinction between *agennêtos* and *agenêtos*, in his reflection on *ho ôn*, and most of all in his notion of the consubstantiality of the Son.

What does consubstantiality mean? Well, it has several meanings, but the meaning in Alexander of Alexandria (who condemned Arius), in Athanasius, and in the Christian tradition is put very briefly in the formula, 'The same statements are made of the Son as of the Father, apart from the name "Father".' As it is put in the Preface of the Blessed Trinity in the Mass, 'Quod enim de tua gloria, revelante te, credimus, hoc de Filio tuo, hoc de Spiritu Sancto, sine differentia discretionis sentimus' ('What we believe about your glory [the *kabôd Yahweh*], through your revelation, all that is known about the divine glory, the same of the Son, the same of the Holy Spirit, without any distinction, is what we hold').

And note the difference between that formula, which was finally crystallized in the Latin Preface of the Mass, and Tertullian's position – the difference between that naive-realist conception of the divinity of the Son and the conception implicit in Nicea and explicit in Athanasius and subsequent writers. For Tertullian (and not only Tertullian, of course; that same type of thinking, that naive realism, runs through all the writers of the Western church, and a good deal in the East too) the Son is divine if he is made of the same matter as God the Father, of the same stuff. Whether he comes out early or late, whether he is subordinate or not, makes no difference; he is still divine because he is made of the right stuff. And that is a possible meaning also of 'consubstantial.' But on the other hand, when you take the real as *what is known by a true affirmation*, then the Son is God if you affirm the same things about the Son as about the Father. The difference there is the difference between two realisms. Is a thing real because of what it is made of, its matter, its stuff – is that what constitutes it as reality, and so is it by a contact with that reality that you know the real? Or is the real *what you know when you truly affirm*? There is an antithesis here between two meanings of the word 'realism,' a fundamental antithesis, and there is a historical transition from one to the other as one follows the evolution of Christian theology in the early centuries.

2.4.5 Christian Realism and Scholastic Method

Now that same realism, the realism of judgment, of truth (where 'truth' means not the truth of saying but the truth of affirming) is at the root not only of all dogmatic definitions ('Si quis dixerit ... anathema sit,' 'If anyone says this ... let him be anathema'), but also at the root of the whole scholastic method in its fundamental conception.[20] Abelard in his *Sic et non* with regard to, I think, 158 topics quoted the Fathers and the scriptures both for and against these propositions: 'Yes, that is so; no, it is not.' Exactly the same procedure had been used by the canon lawyer Gratian in his *Concordantia discordantium canonum.* Gilbert de la Porrée defines the question. He says there is a question if, and only if, sound authorities and good reasons can be given for and against both sides of a contradiction. The question is the fundamental tool of medieval thought. It has become somewhat formalized and dead, at least it seems dead, for example, in the *Summa theologiae* of St Thomas, where automatically there is the *Videtur quod non* with usually two or three reasons on one side, the *Sed contra* with usually one, sometimes two, reasons for the other side, then the response, and then the solutions. But if you want to see St Thomas using the *quaestio* as a tool that is fully alive, take *De veritate,* question 24, article 12, where he is contradicting the position he had held in the *Sentences* (*Scriptum super sententias magistri Petri Lombardi*). You will find that in the *Videtur quod non* there are twenty-four authorities; they are all authorities, and they are all against what he held in the *Sentences*; and then eleven more are cited on the other side. His solution runs through about nine columns in the Vivès edition.[21] But implicit in that method of the question, the issue always is *affirming what is true.* It is the same type of thinking as you have in the dogmas: 'Si quis dixerit ... anathema sit.' It is the same type of thinking as you have in the meaning of *homoousion,* when *homoousion* is taken not as identity of matter but identity of predication.

20 See chapter 2 above, note 18, for more data on Lonergan's survey of scholastic method. On the truth of saying and the truth of affirming, the following may be said. The word 'say' is used twice in the same sentence here, but in different contexts and with different meanings. In 'not the truth of saying' the context is the question of lying or being truthful; see § 1.1.1 of chapter 5, below: 'a smile can be true or mendacious; one can smile and smile and be a villain'; the point is set forth more fully in *Insight* (see above, chapter 2, note 9), chapter 17, § 2.4, 'Truth and Expression' (pp. 576–81). But in 'If anyone says this ... let him be anathema,' the context is that of the true or false content of a judgment, in the sense of truth or error, which is the context also of the phrase 'truth of affirming.'

21 The two standard editions of Thomas Aquinas's works available to Lonergan (both gradually superseded by the authoritative Leonine edition) were regularly referred to as the 'Parma' (so named from the place of publication), 25 vols., 1852–73, and the 'Vivès' (from the name of the Paris publisher), 32 vols., 1871–80.

3 Christian Realism and the Word of God

Now what is the origin of that Christian realism, the realism of the true affirmation? Clearly, it is the scriptural word of God. It is the word of God as a command in the Law; it is the word of God as a correction in the prophets; it is the precept of our Lord to the apostles in the Sermon on the Mount, 'Let your speech be "Yea, yea; nay, nay"' (Matthew 5.37).[22] It is the word of God as conceived by St Paul in Galatians 1: 'If an angel from heaven should preach to you a gospel different from the one I have preached to you, let him be anathema.'[23] The word of God! To say it is not true would be a blasphemy; to say it does not regard reality would be an impious trifling. And those implications of the word of God as received by the Christian communion are the real foundations and origins, I would suggest, of Christian realism.

I thank you for your very kind attention.

22 NRSV: 'Let your word be "Yes, Yes" or "No, No."'
23 Galatians 1. 9. NRSV: '... if anyone proclaims to you a gospel contrary to what you received, let that one be accursed!'

5

Time and Meaning[1]

I wish in this lecture to speak of the realm of meaning and, in the second place, of an apprehension of the kind of time that is relevant to meaning. Ordinarily one thinks of mechanical time, but here we are concerned with time in terms of meaning. I want particularly to offer a sketch of the way in which meaning develops.

The study of literatures, of cultures, of philosophy, of religion can become simply an archipelago of islands with no relations between them. The 'Semitic mentality' becomes something that is simply irreducible to

1 A lecture given in Montreal, 25 September 1962, to begin the Thomas More Institute course 'To Be a Philosopher.' The same lecture was given earlier, on 13 September, at Regis College, Toronto, and later, on 28 September, at Collège de l'Immaculée-Conception, Montreal. A transcription from tape of the lecture at the Thomas More Institute was made by Philip McShane in April 1973, a copy of which is in the Lonergan Research Institute Library, Toronto (File 343). Another transcription was made by the Thomas More Institute, and was edited and published by R. Eric O'Connor in *Bernard Lonergan: 3 Lectures* (see above, chapter 1, note 1) 29–54. This transcription was checked by Lonergan himself in 1975 (ibid. 48, note). In the present editing we made our own literal transcription of the taped lecture (Lonergan Research Institute Library, TC 343, 344), but relied also on the two previous transcriptions for the final product.

'Time and Meaning' was as much a milestone in 1962 as 'Theology in Its New Context' (*A Second Collection* [see above, chapter 1, note 26] 55–67) was in 1967. Fr Eric O'Connor once remarked in conversation that three of Lonergan's talks on meaning form a series: 'Time and Meaning,' 'The Analogy of Meaning' (below, chapter 9), and 'Dimensions of Meaning' (*Collection* [see above, chapter 2, note 13] 232–45).

anything else; there is no comparison with it – or again, the 'Buddhist mentality' or the 'Japanese mentality.' When I speak of a sketch of the way in which meaning develops, I mean some sort of thread or highway that will perhaps be of some use in relating what appear, at first sight at least, to be totally unrelated ways of understanding human life and its significance.

The interest of the talk may also be taken in opposition to other things. It is in opposition to a provincialism for which the rest of the world is made up of strangers and the strangers are totally strange, totally odd. One reads frequently, at least in the old-time novel, about the 'inscrutable Oriental.' 'Inscrutable' means something one cannot penetrate. The study of meaning, of time and meaning, hopes to break that down in a way. Again, in opposition to classicism, to what is expressed in Molière's phrase, 'Plus ça change, plus c'est la même chose,' it draws attention to differences in detail. While human nature may be always the same in certain fairly broad aspects, still there are differences, and the differences are interesting. Again, as it is opposed to a classicism, so also it is opposed to a romanticism which knows the concrete, the singular, the individual, the personal, the historical, but does so at the expense of any overall view and results in a sort of fragmentation, compensated by enthusiasm, that is lost in detail. Finally, it is opposed to an abstraction, to a cult of the universal, the ideal, the norm, the exemplar, with the result that one never really apprehends things that exist in their particularity.

Perhaps a further utility to the lecture is that it offers some introduction to the main German contribution to thought, the contribution worked out in the nineteenth century by German philosophers, German historians, German students of languages, German students of literatures. This has been the main influence on my own thinking on this issue. The Germans did a tremendous amount of work, and they had in mind fundamental ideas that are totally different from what I believe are called currently in America the 'behavioral sciences.' In America, one is apt to study behavioral sciences; in other countries, one studies the human sciences, what the Germans call *Geisteswissenschaften*, the 'sciences of the spirit,' and in those sciences – that is, all the sciences that regard man – the fundamental category is meaning.

So much, then, for a general statement of what may be the possible utility in what I am going to talk about. The talk falls into three main parts: the first on meaning, the second on time, and the third on the development of meaning.

1 Meaning

1.1 Varieties of Meaning[2]

1.1.1 Intersubjective Meaning

On meaning, my first topic is the varieties of meaning, and I distinguish five: intersubjective, symbolic, incarnate, artistic, and linguistic. When one thinks of meaning one is apt to think immediately of words and only of words. The first point will be to break away from too narrow a view of the word 'meaning.'

In the field of intersubjective meaning the first if not the principal or sole investigator was Max Scheler in his book *The Nature of Sympathy.*[3] There is such a thing as intersubjectivity. There is a unity of human persons that antedates, precedes, the distinction between 'I' and 'thou.' To give you a concrete instance, I will call upon my own experience. Leading up to the Borghese Gardens in Rome, where I usually go for my favorite walk, there is a ramp. Coming down the ramp was a small child running ahead of its mother. He started to trip and tumbled; I was a good twenty feet away but spontaneously I moved forward before taking any thought at all, as if to pick up the child. There is an intersubjectivity, there is a sense in which we are all members of one another before we think about it. A shriek frightens us; it does not merely startle us but also frightens us.

To narrow down, to grasp a more particular form of intersubjectivity,

2 What here are called 'varieties of meaning' – and there is later use in this lecture of the expression 'type of meaning' and at the end of § 1.7 of chapter 9, below, of 'forms of human communication' – are in *Method in Theology* (see above, chapter 1, note 51) called 'carriers of meaning.' See his mention there on p. 57 of the way meaning 'is embodied or carried.' In *Method in Theology* Lonergan, drawing on and expanding the discussion of meaning in chapters 18 and 17 of *Insight*, added a greatly enlarged analysis of meaning under the headings Elements of Meaning, Functions of Meaning, Realms of Meaning, and Stages of Meaning. What he there calls the constitutive function of meaning begins to be spoken of in the present chapter, § 1.1.3; and see § 1.2 below; but it is quite fully analyzed in chapter 9 below.

3 Max Scheler, *The Nature of Sympathy*, trans. Peter Heath (New Haven: Yale University Press, 1954). Lonergan gave the title in German, *Wesen und Formen der Sympathie*, and added that it 'has been translated certainly into French and probably into English, *The Forms of Sympathy*.'

we will consider briefly what may be called the phenomenology of a smile.[4]

A smile is perceived on the countenance of a person, in the movements of eyes, lips, facial muscles, head; and it has a meaning. It is not simply the movements of the lips or the eyes. There is a meaning added to it; and because there is a meaning, we do not walk about the streets smiling at everyone we meet; we would be misunderstood if we did. Because it has a meaning, a smile is very easily apprehended. Apprehension, human perception, is not simply a function of light waves, sound waves, and the rest. Walking along the street talking with another person, one can pick out of the racket made by passing cars and riveters putting up buildings a small weak flow of vocal sounds. And one *can* pick them out because they have a meaning. Similarly a smile is something that can be very easily perceived precisely because it has a meaning. One can notice the slightest trace or beginning of a smile on a person's face. The meaning of a smile is natural, spontaneous. We have to learn to walk, to talk, to swim; we do not have to learn to smile. Again, we have to learn the meaning of words but we do not have to be taught the meaning of a smile; either you get it or you do not. If you do not, you are lost; you have to figure it out for yourself. That meaning of a smile is not something that can be transposed into words or concepts or some other mode

4 This is an example that Lonergan used several times: in his 1959 course at the Gregorian University, *De intellectu et methodo* (p. 31 of the student notes [see above, chapter 2, note 1]), in the 1959 summer institute on education (*Topics in Education* [see above, chapter 2, note 12] 166–67), in the Thomas More Institute interview of 30 March 1971 (*Curiosity at the Center of One's Life: Statements and Questions of R. Eric O'Connor*, ed. J. Martin O'Hara [Montreal: Thomas More Institute Papers, 1984] 388–89), and in *Method in Theology* 59–61, where he states (59) that he has lost the source of the notes he was using. Later, however, he made a marginal note on his own copy of *Method*: 'F.J.J. Buytendijk.' An editorial note in *Topics in Education* (p. 166, note 8) suggests that this might refer to *Phénomenologie de la rencontre*, but adds '... if this was Lonergan's source, he elaborated most of the details himself.' Now, through the kindness of Richard Liddy, we are able to take the matter a step further. In *Feelings and Emotions: The Mooseheart Symposium in Cooperation with The University of Chicago*, ed. Martin L. Reymert (New York: McGraw-Hill, 1950), F.J.J. Buytendijk contributes 'The Phenomenological Approach to the Problem of Feelings and Emotions' (pp. 127–41), and on pp. 134–35 discusses the phenomenology of the smile; further, in regard to the first smile of the child, he tells us in his note, 'Amply discussed in F.J.J. Buytendijk, *De eerste glimlach von het kind*,' Nijmegen, 1947. This does not determine just how Lonergan came to know Buytendijk, but confirms the latter as his source.

of communication. It is irreducible; it is something that is found in its own order and not elsewhere. It is one incarnate intelligence making itself known to another.

If one compares the type of meaning in a smile with that in words or concepts, one finds that one's words try to be univocal, to have a single meaning, but a smile can have all sorts of meanings; it has no univocity. There is a smile of recognition, a smile of welcome, a smile of friendship, a smile of love, a smile of joy, a smile of pleasure, a smile of satisfaction, a peaceful smile, a derisive smile, an ironic smile, a resigned smile, a tired smile, a sad smile, a sardonic and enigmatic smile. It has not some single meaning; it is capable of all sorts of different meanings.

Again, any conceptual or verbal meaning is true or false. It states things as they are or it does not. But a smile can be true or mendacious; one can smile and smile and be a villain; one's smile does not mean what it seems to mean; it is something like a lie, not something like a mistake.

Again, the conceptual or verbal meaning is able to draw all sorts of distinctions between feelings and desires, fears, thoughts, knowledge, will, orders, intentions, and so on. But intersubjective meaning is undifferentiated. It belongs to a level of meaning in which the further differentiations, the distinctions and divisions, the subdivisions, and sub-subdivisions that can be communicated by words simply do not occur. The meaning of a smile is, as it were, a meaning that presupposes a situation, a meeting, an encounter, a set of previous personal relationships. It acknowledges the interpersonal situation and adds a further determination, a further constituent, to the present situation. It does not so much describe the subject as reveal him, betray him. There is no deduction from the smile to the person, but by the smile the person becomes, as it were, transparent. He is *in communication with* another, and that communication is something that antedates the distinction between sign and what is signified, the distinction between the soul that means and the body by which the meaning is expressed. The person is revealed in his smile, and the same is true – with all sorts of variations – of intersubjective meaning in general. The fact of meaning on that intersubjective, immediate level of relationship with persons is merely illustrated by the example of the smile; there are countless other examples.

1.1.2 Symbolic Meaning

Now briefly consider symbolic meaning. It is the meaning of affect in the most elementary form. By affects and our affections – affections are something more elaborate than affects – we have our orientation in life, in the world. They reveal the direction of our living, our attitudes to the world, to other persons, to things. A symbol is an image that either induces an affect, causes the affect to arise, or on the other hand expresses an affect – one has the affect first and the image emerges. Further, images that are symbols, that is, expressions or causes of affects, also reveal the attitude and the orientation of a person in the world and towards other persons.

Now such affects, such symbols, have been studied very thoroughly in this century. The Freudian study of symbols, particularly of dream symbols, is based largely on interpersonal relations, and interpersonal relations gone wrong. The Greek cycle of *Seven against Thebes*,[5] in which the family centering around Oedipus was involved in all sorts of crimes and hatreds, provides the fundamental nucleus of the description. There is an entirely different analysis worked out by Jung. But I would like to mention a recent study by Gilbert Durand, *Les Structures anthropologiques de l'imaginaire.*[6] There are some thirty-five pages of bibliography, so he has been over a fair amount of material.

Durand sets aside all the Freudian analysis of symbols as pertaining to a certain type of civilization, a certain type of family problem, and he does not go on to the higher dynamics of Jungian psychology, but he connects symbols, images that express affects, with three fundamental dominant reflexes. There is the reflex by which we maintain our balance: if one is going to fall, one's reflex interrupts everything else until one recovers one's equilibrium. It is a dominant reflex: it operates spontaneously,

5 Aeschylus, *Seven against Thebes*, trans. Anthony Hecht and Helen Bacon (New York and London: Oxford University Press, 1973). Actually, Freud's references, when he speaks of the origin of his theory, are to Sophocles' *Oedipus Rex.* See, for example, his letter of 15 October 1897 to Wilhelm Fliess, in *The Origins of Psycho-Analysis. Letters to Wilhelm Fliess, Drafts and Notes: 1887–1902*, ed. Marie Bonaparte, Anna Freud, and Ernst Kris; authorized translation by Eric Mosbacher and James Strachey (London: Imago Books, 1954) 223.

6 Gilbert Durand, *Les Structures anthropologiques de l'imaginaire: Introduction à l'archétypologie générale* (Paris: Presses Universitaires de France, 1963). This is the second edition, mentioned in *Method in Theology* 69; Lonergan here had to be working from the first edition, which he indicated as having been published in 'Grenoble, 1960.' Durand says in his preface to the second edition that there are hardly any differences between the two editions.

masterfully; it cuts out everything else (as do the other dominant reflexes: swallowing and mating).[7]

Connected with maintaining one's equilibrium, there are what Durand calls the ascensional symbols: rising, standing, being upright, exercising control, manipulation, power, the sceptre, the sword, going up the ladder, the bird that flies, the tree that rises from the earth, all the symbols that express uprightness in the moral connotation of the word – something a child develops very strong feelings about in learning to walk, in learning to maintain its balance.

Opposed to these ascensional symbols there are all the symbols of fear, and you get the whole combined in, for example, the image of St George and the dragon. The dragon combines in one monster all the symbols of fear or a vast number of them. On the other hand, St George destroying the dark dragon is mastering the object of fear; he is upright, he is riding, he holds the spear. A whole affective orientation is expressed in that symbol.

The second dominant reflex is swallowing. You get an entirely different attitude from St George and the dragon when you take Jonah and the whale. The whale is just as much a monster as the dragon, but it is not terrifying. The object of terror is euphemized; it is not so bad after all. Jonah went down into the whale but he came out three days later and was just as well off as ever. Instead of mastering the object of fear, controlling it, dominating it, there is resignation, quietness, peace, and not the *fall* from the upright position but the *descent*, improving the descent when one is falling.[8]

You can see how Durand's analysis of symbols is connected with very fundamental physiological, psychic facts, and how it enables him to put together vast arrays of symbols. In the symbol there is a meaning, not on the conceptual level but still on a very real level; it has a meaning for people, all the meaning, for example, in the word 'upright'; it has connected with it all sorts of meanings, all sorts of feelings and suggestions, that are fundamentally affective and symbolic; the affective is directed toward something, and the meaning of the symbol is the meaning of the affect; or there can be a combination of affects, an interplay between affects as, for example, with courage overcoming fear, and so on.

7 The words enclosed in brackets are not spoken on the tape, but they appear in the O'Connor edition (*Bernard Lonergan: 3 Lectures*), which was approved by Lonergan; and they are helpful here, since this is the only spot in this lecture where all three dominant reflexes are mentioned.

8 For more on Durand's description of this dominant reflex, see below, chapter 9, § 1.4.

1.1.3 Incarnate Meaning

A third type of meaning I call incarnate meaning. On this subject I must be very brief. The young French thinker Georges Morel published three volumes in 1960 and 1961 on *Le Sens de l'existence selon s. Jean de la Croix*.[9] Where Heidegger from the viewpoint of an agnostic or atheist has worked out an account of human existence as the meaning of human life, Morel worked out John of the Cross's idea of the meaning of human existence and has written a penetrating, profound account of what he calls the symbol; and to distinguish it from symbols as considered by Durand or Jung or Freud, one can call it incarnate meaning, namely, meaning in the sense of the meaning of a man's life, the meaning of a decisive gesture in a person's life. The meaning resides *in* the person, in everything he has done leading up to this moment. Let me merely suggest some of the points that Morel has made, and leave it there; it is very theological.

'Perhaps one could now understand why the best definition of a symbol, it seems to us, is the following: a real evocation of God which, taking its departure from within the world of nature or man, reaches its term necessarily in prayer.'[10] Again, 'the symbol is not just *one* possible manner of speech among others, but the Logos in its plenitude. It is human existence in its phenomenal manifestation ... Man is essentially a symbol; that is his definition.'[11] What is a man? Well, you will see a little more fully later that meaning plays a constitutive part in human living.[12] The meaning of one's

9 Georges Morel, *Le Sens de l'existence selon s. Jean de la Croix* (Paris: Aubier, 1960–61). Lonergan discusses Morel's work again in chapter 9 below, § 1.3.

10 'Peut-être pourra-t-on maintenant comprendre pourquoi la meilleure définition du symbole nous semble être la suivante: une évocation réelle de Dieu qui, partant de l'intérieur du monde naturel ou humain, s'achève nécessairement en invocation.' Georges Morel, 'La nature du symbole,' *La Maison-Dieu* 42 (1955) 102.

11 'Le symbole n'est donc pas *une* manière de parler possible parmi d'autres, mais le logos dans sa plénitude. Il est l'exister même en sa manifestation phénoménale. C'est pourquoi avant d'évoquer le langage symbolique il convient de rappeler que l'être humain est lui-même de nature symbolique. L'homme est essentiellement symbole: telle est sa définition.' Morel, *Le Sens de l'existence*, vol. 3, p. 39. We are grateful to Pierre Robert of Montreal for drawing attention to the importance of the complete quotation here.

12 Here, in this lecture of 1962, is found the first occurrence we have noticed of 'meaning as constitutive.' Lonergan's promise to return to the question 'later' is fulfilled in § 1.2, 'What Meaning Constitutes,' where he takes up 'the ontology ... of meaning.' It is also in 1962 that Lonergan begins to refer to Dilthey (the 'Hermeneutics' lecture in the Regis College institute 'The

life – the meaning that one lives in one's life and manifests in one's activity – is what constitutes one as a man, as the man that one is. Again for Morel, mystical experience is experience of reality in its totality. The metaphysician thinks of reality in its totality; the mystic *experiences* it. And a person such as St John of the Cross is a manifestation, a symbolic manifestation, of that experience of reality in its totality.

I must stop there; I can treat only briefly these different varieties of meaning, but I think you see that there are some very profound thoughts involved in Morel's approach to the symbol, an approach which I take under the different name of incarnate meaning.

1.1.4 Artistic Meaning

Next there is artistic meaning. In this I follow Susanne Langer's *Feeling and Form,*[13] which I found very illuminating on the nature of art. I shall put very briefly her thought on the subject.

I have already stated that our perceiving, our experiencing, is never just the chaos that would be produced if we attended to all the impressions made by all the light waves and sound waves that fall upon us. There is a construction, a selection, of meaning. Now that selection of meaning can occur in different ways. One can be the person well-adapted to the modern city, providing the automatic behavior required in a ready-made world. The simplest example: the light goes red, and you put your foot on the brake; the light goes green, and you put your foot on the accelerator. You are not looking at the red light or the green light; it is just a signal to which you automatically respond. One's sensitive life can be simply such a set of automatic responses to sensible signals.

Again, one's sensitive life can be entirely at the disposal of some higher purpose; one is a scientist, and one sees things simply and entirely from the

Method of Theology'); it was from Dilthey that he took the idea of meaning as constitutive (see § 6 of chapter 9 below). This year, then, marks a major advance in Lonergan's thinking; from now on meaning as constitutive of human reality will be an important part of his thinking (see, for example, chapter 8, § 3.3, below).

13 Susanne K. Langer, *Feeling and Form: A Theory of Art Developed from 'Philosophy in a New Key'* (New York: Charles Scribner's Sons, 1953). In chapter 9 of *Topics in Education,* Lonergan draws much more extensively on Langer's work in presenting his own understanding of artistic meaning.

scientific viewpoint. One's sensitivity is simply an instrument serving the purposes of inquiring or verifying intelligence.

Besides such subservience of sensitivity to alien purposes, sensitivity can be allowed to develop its own meaning, its own structures, to be on its own, to work out its own forms; and that, according to Langer, is the fundamental moment in the work of the artist. The meaning of these spontaneous vital patterns into which sensitivity can spontaneously flow is a meaning of what it is to be alive, both in the generic sense and as able to have further determinations. She describes how a person looking at a picture of a room with a stove in it by some modern painter responds, 'It's alive!'[14] – it is the way in which the artist expresses just what that meaning is that is conveyed in the art. An artistic activity – whether artistic creativity or artistic appreciation – is a liberation of one's sensitive life, one's sensitivity, from all instrumentalization, all subservience to further ends. At the same time, it is a transformation of one's world: the world of art may seem to be far more real, or totally illusory, but it is totally different from the everyday world. And as there is a transformation of the world, so also there is a transformation of the subject. He ceases to be the well-adapted automaton or the purely inquiring scientist or some other form of human activity. He allows his sensitivity to assume its own form, to unfold in its own fashion.

1.1.5 Linguistic Meaning

I have been attempting to broaden the meaning of meaning by appealing to the meaning contained in intersubjectivity, in symbolism, in the incarnate meaning spoken of by Morel, in the meaning of art. There remains, finally, linguistic meaning, which is of course the most precise and the most varied form in which human meanings are expressed. In connection with linguistic meaning, you find that primitive people have enormous appreciation of the *name*: the name of something seems to be almost as big as its reality. If you want to understand that, read the passage in the life of Helen Keller,[15] a blind deaf-mute, when first she understood a name. The

14 This same point was made in *Topics in Education* 224, where the editors lacked the reference to Langer, and read 'stone' on the tapes instead of 'stove': 'Artists talk constantly about the picture's being "alive" – even things that have no life at all, like a stone.' The reference in this lecture to Langer on a 'modern painter' reveals our mistake. She asked, 'In what sense can one possibly say that Van Gogh's yellow chair or a studio stove is alive?' (*Feeling and Form* 81).

15 Helen A. Keller, *The Story of My Life* (New York: Doubleday & Co., 1954). For the passage on 'water,' see pp. 36–37.

person trying to teach her took her out into the yard and started working a pump. The cold water poured over Helen Keller's arm, and there was a notable reaction when the person instructing her wrote on her arm the word 'water.' It was the first time she caught the significance of this writing done on her skin, understood it as the sign, the way of identifying the object she had just experienced. One could tell from her facial expression that it was a terrific experience. After she calmed down a bit, she knelt down and touched the earth; she felt it all over and held up her arm to have the name of the earth written on it. And in the first half hour she learned about ten words. The significance of the name is the significance of linguistic meaning in the structuring of human life.

1.2 What Meaning Constitutes

Our first point was the varieties of meanings – intersubjective, symbolic, incarnate, artistic, linguistic. The second point is *what meaning constitutes.* If we eliminated meaning from human life, would there be any family? There would not. Family is something that we mean and that we realize. Would there be any society if there were not any meaning? Not in any normal sense. There might be a herd or a drove; there could hardly be a society. There could be no education, no morals. Morals lie in the field of meaning; they are impossible without meaning. There would be neither state nor law, neither economics nor technics. To eliminate meaning is to eliminate all human institutions. Again, to eliminate meaning would be to eliminate interpersonal relations, symbols, art, language, literature, religion, science, history, philosophy, theology. There still would be human beings in the sense of the definition 'rational animal'; but it would always be the rational animal that had not yet reached the point where it had learned any language or been able to signify anything. Human living, then, is something to which meaning is essential; it is incomplete without meaning; it has a constituent in the realm of meaning. Not only is human living constituted by meaning – it isn't constituted *solely* by meaning, we have bodies, we have physiological processes, and they are all real – but human living would not be what we mean by human living if meaning were eliminated.

What is true of the natural order is also true of the supernatural order. The word of God, the revelation God makes to man, is a matter of meaning. Similarly the church, the body of Christ, is the realization of an order, and an order is something that is meant. As in the natural order, so in the supernatural: there are graces of God, entities of various kinds, supernatural habits, that are more than and distinct from meaning, but still that revelation and that order would not be at all what they are without meaning.

Further, perhaps we had best say a few words on the ontology, the reality, of meaning. One is apt to say that on the one hand there are things that are real and on the other there is 'mere meaning' – as though meaning were not a reality. The proper division is that *esse reale*, the real, divides into the 'natural' and the 'intentional'; the intentional order is the order of meaning. Now in God the natural and intentional reality are identical. For that reason, the procession of the Word is not simply the procession of the meaning of God, but also the procession of God himself, because in God the *esse intentionale* and the *esse naturale* are one and the same; and so when God utters himself, conceives himself, not only is there a concept of God but the reality of God too. There is the identity of the intentional and the natural. In us there is not that identity. We are ourselves even when we are asleep and having no dreams. Our unconscious is as much a part of us as our conscious living, and the two interpenetrate in a very complex fashion (into which we need not go). But it would be a mistake to think that a meaning is not a reality. Our conscious living and the meaning that it carries are just as real as the realities of the spirit, and they do not belong to some shadowy world that really does not count. One mistakes the whole significance of meaning if one does not get that point correct: 'intentional' is not opposed to 'real'; it is opposed to 'natural.'[16]

Besides speaking of the ontology of meaning one might say a few words about the ethics of meaning. What exists by being willed is something that is meant. And of course what exists by being willed is something whose existence can be completely rational because the will is a rational appetite.

16 There is a difficulty in translating *esse naturale* and *esse intentionale*, and in Lonergan's own use here of the words 'natural' and 'intentional' (especially 'natural.') *Esse reale* translates well enough as 'real being.' But *esse naturale* means real being when we prescind from its meaning, and *esse intentionale* means real being when we include the meaning that is constitutive of its reality.

Thomas Aquinas used these terms in the sense that a stone has its *esse reale* in itself and in the realm of nature, but has its *esse intentionale* in the mind that conceives the stone (or in the medium between stone and mind); see *Summa theologiae*, 1, q. 44, a. 3, ad 3m; q. 56, a. 2, ad 3m; Supplementum, q. 82, a. 3, ad 2m. But this is not Lonergan's point; he refers to the difference in being that, say, a law court has when we prescind from its meaning, and the being it has when we include its meaning; for meaning is constitutive of the law court, that is, pertains to its real being.

Also pertinent here is § 6 of chapter 9, below.

And in us there is a spiraling upwards: we develop mentally and morally, we reach fuller and fuller meaning, and we realize those meanings in ourselves and in our environment by our willing. It is through this world, this intentional order, that human will has its creative opportunity, and it is within the intentional order that will is effective. Similarly, when I speak about what exists because it is willed, I mean what exists because it is loved, and love is just one instance of this creativity of the will.

Opposed to what I was saying about meaning is what is called nihilism, the negation of any meaning to human life. Take the often repeated statement of Nietzsche that God is dead. What he meant was that the atheism, the agnosticism, the religious indifference, of the nineteenth century destroyed the meaning of all the cultural tradition on which the century was actually living. What he concluded was the necessity of recreating the whole of culture. The point there is that when you remove the fundamental element in the meaning of life, you have to find a new meaning or people are desperate. A recent book has been published with the title *The Struggle for Meaning.*[17] Human living really is a struggle for meaning, an effort, because meaning is constituent of human living. The effort to live is fundamentally the struggle for meaning.

I have spoken a little too long on this topic of meaning; I want to say a few words on time.

2 Time

Time, in the Aristotelian definition, is the number and measure of movement according to the before and after.[18] It is the number of movement

17 We presume that Lonergan is referring to Victor E. Frankl, *Man's Search for Meaning,* trans. Ilse Lasch (New York: Washington Square Press, 1969) – first published in 1959. Lonergan said in the lecture, 'I haven't got the author's name correctly. It was mentioned to me.'

18 'It is clear, then, that time is "number of movement in respect of the before and after."' Aristotle, *Physics,* IV, 11, 220a 25; trans. R.P. Hardie and R.K. Gaye, in *The Basic Works of Aristotle,* ed. Richard McKeon (New York: Random House, 1941) 293. 'Just as motion is a perpetual succession, so also is time. But every simultaneous time is self-identical, but it accepts different attributes. The "now" measures time, in so far as time involves the "before and after"' (ibid. 219b 9–11, p. 292).

Thomas Aquinas, *In Aristotelis libros Physicorum,* 4, lect. 17, §1110 (see note 19 below): 'tempus nihil aliud est quam *numerus motus secundum prius et posterius*'; ibid., lect. 18, §1119: 'id quod distinguit prius et posterius temporis est *ipsum nunc,* quod est *terminus* praeteriti et *principium* futuri.

(nine hours or nine o'clock; the number 9) and the measure of movement (nine hours since noon; the movement of the hands around the face of a clock) according to the before and after (it goes through the one before the two, and the two before the three, and so forth).

That definition of time is in terms of objective, material, local movement, and it offers no problems. The problems arise when one asks, 'There are many movements; are there therefore many times?' And that question has received three different answers. St Thomas says that there is one time because there is one *primum mobile*, one outer sphere that provides a standard time for the universe; Newton went to an abstract mathematical time; and Einstein worked out a system recognizing the many movements and correlating them.

But besides that objectified clock time that is a matter of material movement, there is in Aquinas another definition of the temporal and the eternal. The temporal is the *nunc*, the 'now,' of a being that changes; the eternal is the 'now' of a being that does not change, that is immutable.[19] And that 'now' is not the mathematical point, the limit to the continuum of a local motion. It is what lies between what is remembered and what is anticipated. It is the psychological present, and the psychological present is not a mathematical limit. *Now* is within the order of *mean-er*, *meaning* and *meant*.

The view of time in terms of now, the psychological now, makes us move from substances to subjects.[20] To think of the subject, think of the three meanings of the word 'presence.'[21] The chairs and the lights are present in this room; this is physical presence. You are present to me, I am present to you, and it is the presence of an object; but unless I were here in a third type of presence, you could not be present to me. Similarly, for anything to be present to each of you, *you* have to be there; you have to be awake, or at least you have to be dreaming. That third presence is the presence of the subject.

The subject is identical through time. I am the same person today as I

19 Thomas Aquinas, *In Aristotelis libros Physicorum*, 4, lect. 18; specifically on the 'now' of eternity ('nunc aeternitatis'): §1121 in the Angeli-Pirotta edition (Naples: D'Auria, 1953).

20 See above, chapter 3, note 27.

21 Lonergan's developing thought on 'presence' can be tracked through previous volumes of the Collected Works. See, for example, *Collection*, note *n* to chapter 11, p. 293; note *i* to chapter 14, p. 302; note *d* to chapter 15, p. 305; also *Understanding and Being* (see above, chapter 2, note 13), note *g* to lecture 1, p. 401; and the index to *Topics in Education*.

was yesterday, and if I am tomorrow I will still be the same person, the same subject. The subject is intermittent. Throughout intermittence, throughout the eclipse of sleep, throughout development, the subject remains the same through time. The acts of the subject occur in time; as acts they occur now, and once they have occurred they are irrevocable. Still, they are intentional acts. They need not regard merely the present; they can regard the past, for which I have happy or repentant memories; they can regard the future, which I anticipate. By their intentionality, by the fact that they are that by which objects are present to the subject – and those objects may be not merely present but past and future – there is a second transcendence of time in that psychological *now.*[22]

Finally, objects may be timeless by abstraction: two and two; which two? this one now, or the one yesterday? it makes no difference; the two is timeless, it is outside time. Or again: the objects may be placed concretely in the temporal continuum with successor relations. The time of meaning is not a succession of mathematical points such as is the time of mechanics. It is a now of a subject that is identical through time and of a subject that is not, in his considerations, confined to meaning things that are present; he means equally well the things that are past and future.

3 The Development of Meaning

We shall go on to some account of the development of meaning. There are five elementary types of meaning of which the predominant one is linguistic meaning. One finds them in all sorts of combinations. (I have treated them very briefly; to know what they are one has to study them more fully.) The point to distinguishing them is that from them one can put together in one's own experience some approximation to the combinations that have existed at different times in the course of human development. But to do that there is a further element needed, and that is some analysis of what

22 Lonergan means to affirm two basic steps in transcending time. First, the many times of objective, local movement are transcended in three different ways: the *primum mobile* of Aquinas, Newton's abstract time, and Einstein's system that correlates different times. The second way is the time of meaning, introduced by 'another definition' in Aquinas, that of the eternal 'now,' and this is the topic down to 'there is a second transcendence of time in that psychological *now.*' The sequence is slowed down by the two paragraphs on presence. The 'Finally' paragraph seems a kind of unimportant addition of two more ways, somewhat related to Newton and Einstein, that also are contrasted with the 'time of meaning.'

precisely happens when a development occurs. Because there is human development there is temporality – the historicity, as it is called, of human living – and because that development occurs principally in the field of meaning, the development of man is principally the development of meaning.

3.1 Piaget's Analysis of Development

The analysis of development can be attempted in many different ways. In a chapter in *Insight* on the elements of metaphysics[23] there is something of an ontological analysis of development. That ontological analysis, of course, treats things just in the grand blocks of main differences and interconnections. To outline a more detailed account of what occurs in a development, I shall go to Jean Piaget, Swiss scientist, philosopher, and psychologist, who has worked out a beautiful account of the development of the child from the day of birth to about the age of sixteen.[24] Piaget is able to do this in a most illuminating fashion because he has a theory of what happens in a development, the way a development goes. Beginning from a study of biology he found that in every adaptation in the purely biological order there were two elements, *assimilation et accommodation* – in English, assimilation and adjustment. By assimilation is meant the use of an operation, of an action, that the subject already is familiar with, already can perform with ease, facility, promptitude. Adjustment is the change, the modification, of that already acquired capacity to act, so that it fits – exactly, economically, efficiently – in dealing with the object that the operation is upon. Piaget starts from what may be called natural operations, spontaneous operations that the baby is able to perform from the moment of birth. And such operations not only are spontaneous, they are approximate; they have a very low efficiency, a great lack of economy. But very rapidly that operation is differentiated into a set of quite different operations, each of which is adapted to a particular object, or to a particular object in certain determinate circumstances. The first movement in a development is the differentiation of the natural, spontaneous, poorly adapted operation into several distinct, exactly adapted operations. For his account of the

23 Bernard Lonergan, *Insight* (see above, chapter 2, note 9) 456–511.

24 On Piaget, see above, chapter 3, note 25. The relevant volume of his for the present context is *The Origins of Intelligence in Children*, trans. Margaret Cook (New York: International Universities Press, 1952).

first two years of a child's life, Piaget studied his own three children, and he noted that in the course of the first two days they became much more proficient at feeding from the breast; and he goes through details on all that.

A second point is that the person learning will not only differentiate the spontaneous operation into distinct operations but will *combine* the distinct operations. Such combinations move off into a group, namely, the totality of combinations of the differentiated operations. 'Group' is a technical term from mathematical group theory but we can be content with a simple illustration of it: the sort of idea that enabled Piaget to think out his experiment, the problems he set the children, and his ability to determine what the course of the development was. He took the example of a toddler that wanders from his mother's knee over to his father and then back again. He does not know he is coming back. He does not have spatial operations combined into an organized group so that he is able to move about anywhere in the space and know just what he is doing in all these movements. First the operations occur, and later there follows the organization, the grouping, or the combination of differentiated operations.

Then there is also a grouping of groups. The child acquires proficiency first of all in oral operations, and gradually acquires a certain amount of proficiency in moving the arm and the hand; becoming master is quite a slow process. First the infant just sees light, then it begins to distinguish objects, and it gets towards the grouping of groups when everything it sees it reaches for and, if it gets hold of it, puts it in its mouth. Here you have a combination of manual, ocular, and oral operations, and the whole builds up. Piaget is able to use this same analysis for the entire process of learning up to the age of sixteen. He has about twenty books on the subject, if not more. Now that is a very detailed analysis of the process of development.

Further, he distinguishes between operations on sensible objects – things you see, things you feel, things you can grasp, things you can put in your mouth – and operations on images. When children play 'Let's imagine this' or 'I'll be the king' or 'I'll be the robber' or 'I'll be the policeman' or 'I'll be a cowboy,' the operations are with respect to imagined operations, the world of make-believe. Similarly there are operations upon words, upon symbols, upon sentences, upon propositions – that use of language. And there is a final stage when one operates with respect to the operations themselves; then one is studying method or development, as Piaget is doing.

That highly detailed analysis could be extended. One could think of an economy, the economy of a country, as a grouping of groups of differentiated operations that are linked together according to certain laws, each person's skills being complemented by the skills of another – taking as one's unit not the developing individual but the developing economy. Still, the analysis is so fine, so exact, goes so far into detail, that it is not much help to us.

However, it is helpful insofar as this idea of the grouping of groups, the ascending to ever higher groups, has its limitations. The fundamental principle in science is that when you run up against a limit you have a new basis for thought, a new basis for arranging the material. I propose to show that there are distinct fields that do not group together.[25] And because these distinct fields do not group together, we get fundamental terms of reference from which we can study human development generally, the developments of meaning.

3.2 Distinct Types of Development

3.2.1 Common Sense and Theory

Our first example of a radical opposition is the opposition between the world of community, of common sense, the external world, the visible world – and by those four terms I mean exactly the same thing: the world that is familiar to all of us – and on the other hand the world of theory.

25 A pivotal idea emerged the year of this lecture: that of blocks between worlds or spheres, between 'fields that do not group together,' namely, common sense and theory, interior and exterior, and the sacred and the profane. It was pivotal in that Lonergan's development of theological method hinged to a large extent on his overcoming these blocks.

The theme occupied Lonergan in the course *De methodo theologiae* that he taught in the spring semester, 1962, February to June, at the Gregorian University. In the Latin notes provided, the relevant heading is 'Quaedam antitheses,' the worlds are 'Mundus sacer et profanus,' 'Mundus interior et exterior,' and 'Mundus aspectabilis et intelligibilis' (pp. 7–11), and Lonergan struggles with the problem of their integration (pp. 13–14). The same theme occupied him again in the institute 'The Method of Theology' that he conducted at Regis College in the summer of 1962, which in at least one important aspect went beyond the Roman course: the idea of mediation comes into play for the integration of the worlds. The present lecture followed directly on those two series of lectures. Note 1 of chapter 8 below provides some details on an important file in the Archives of the Lonergan Research Institute, Toronto ('Various Papers'); the last item in this file treats mediation and the integration of the worlds.

The two are related but still they do not admit this grouping of two lower groups into one single higher group. One has to shift from one to the other. There are fundamental oppositions between these two worlds, and by illustrating that, we will have a first fundamental division of fields of distinct types of development.

As the first illustration of this opposition, we will take as our object the giraffe. From the viewpoint of the world of common sense, the world of community, suppose a father and his son go to the zoo; they take a look at the giraffe and decide that it is a giraffe because it is mostly neck. They see the head, the neck, the trunk, the legs, and the tail, and say, 'That's a giraffe.' A biologist looks at the same animal; he thinks of it as a unity of systems. There is a locomotive system, a digestive system, a vascular system, a nervous system, and so on. These systems have as their implements organs, parts of the body. The systems unify the organs in their operations, bring them together; and the systems are interdependent. Without the digestive system, the vascular system lacks blood; without the respiratory system, the blood lacks oxygen; and so on. The biologist examines the organs more closely and finds that they are composed of cells, and the cells are centers of enormous numbers of chemical processes, and the chemical processes reduce, according to physics, to subatomic processes, and these cannot be imagined. What is the giraffe? The giraffe is a unity of systems that regard immediately organs, but the organs reduce to cells, the cells to chemical processes, the chemical processes to subatomic processes, and the whole is something that cannot be imagined. The world of theory considers things, not in relation to our senses, not the giraffe as he is presented to our sight or our hands, but the giraffe as reduced to theoretically determined entities. Eddington (I believe it was) distinguished between two tables.[26] There was one table that was brown, six feet by four by three, and so on. And the other table was mostly a vacuum, with electrons moving about here and there in it, in that vacuum. There are two entirely different views of exactly the same table. There is an opposition between the objects in the world of theory and the objects in the world of common sense. They are the same objects, but the mode of consideration is opposed.

They differ also in their techniques. In the world of common sense one uses what we call ordinary language, but one moves into the world of theory insofar as one plays the role of Socrates with the Athenians. Socrates

26 Sir Arthur Eddington, *The Nature of the Physical World* (Cambridge: Cambridge University Press, 1928) xi–xv.

would stop the Athenians and ask them, What is temperance? What is justice? What is fortitude?[27] They knew perfectly well how to tell a brave man from a coward, a temperate man from a drunk, and so on; but their knowledge belonged to the world of common sense; it was not the sort of knowledge that enabled them to define things exactly and stand up against all the deductions and objections that could be made about the definition. By asking for the definition, Socrates was asking them to move from the world of common sense to the world of theory, and they did not like it. When the relevant world of theory *was* reached, it was the Aristotelian theory of the virtues in terms of potencies and habits.

There is, then, an opposition in the ways in which objects are considered and an opposition between languages employed. This business of seeking definitions runs off automatically to technical terms employed in an exactly defined sense.

There is also an opposition between the two modes of the subject. In the world of theory, intelligence is dominant; anything that occurs, that is permitted to occur, regards a purely intellectual end, an aim of understanding, an aim to arrive at truth. One wills to exclude other considerations which would be irrelevant to the purpose. The theorist is not the whole man functioning, but the rest of the man subordinated to his intelligence, like Thales so intent upon the stars that he tumbled into the well. That is not the way in which the man of common sense lives; he is intelligent, he is rational, he means to be both, but he does not live for *them*; they are just a part of him, one part of total living.

That difference in the subject appropriate to operating in the world of theory is the difference illustrated by the opposition between Thales and the milkmaid. She might perhaps have been interested in the stars, but she certainly could not miss the well. It was in front of her feet. And Thales was so intent upon the stars that he could not attend to the well. This opposition between the world of theory and the world of common sense is the sort that excludes grouping the two – the operations of the two kinds, appropriate to the two worlds – into a single homogeneous group. One can have what Toynbee calls withdrawal and return.[28] One can be a scien-

27 See *Topics in Education* 118, where Lonergan referred to Aristotle as crediting Socrates with introducing universal definitions; Aristotle, *Metaphysics*, XIII, 4, 1078b, 27–29.

28 Arnold J. Toynbee, *A Study of History*, 12 vols. (see above, chapter 3, note 18); for his treatment of withdrawal and return, see the indices in vol. 3, *The Growth of Civilizations* (1934), vol. 6, *The Disintegration of Civilizations, Part Two* (1939), and vol. 10, *The Inspiration of Historians* (1954).

tist during one's working hours and live with one's family the rest of the day. One can move from one to the other world but one *cannot* be in the two worlds at the same time. There is a difference in subjectivity, a difference in the techniques employed, and a difference in the mode in which the objects are considered.

3.2.2 Interiority

As there is an opposition between the world of common sense and the world of theory, so there is another opposition. Besides the world of community and the world of theory, there is what may be called interiority. Thomas à Kempis said that he would sooner feel compunction than define it.[29] To define compunction is an operation in the world of theory. To feel compunction is something that occurs within one whether one can define it or not. Similarly, the aim in *Insight,* self-appropriation, is a movement to the world of interiority. One wants to know just what it is that happens when one understands, and all the different ways in which one understands. The exigence of critical philosophy is this: one should not talk about what one does not know, and still less should one talk about what one cannot know. It raises the questions, What can one know? What are the operations that are performed when one does know? It is a turn from the world of theory to its basis in the world of interiority. Again, the questions raised by the existentialists are questions that regard interiority: Do you know what that means? Do you know what it means to have a mind of your own? Is that just a phrase? Do you know what it means to respect others? or to be in love with them? Do you know what it is to suffer? Do you really know? Do you know what it is to pray? Do you know what it is to die? Do you know what it is to live in the presence of God? These are questions about interiority.

Interiority is not something that you can talk about in ordinary common-sense conversation. It is not something that you can handle adequately by any amount of theory. It regards immediate internal experience. And that interiority forms a third field in which developments occur. Those developments – while they are related to, and important for, and connected with

29 Thomas à Kempis, *The Imitation of Christ.* A modern version based on the English translation of Richard Whitford was edited with introduction by Harold C. Gardiner for Image Books (New York: Doubleday & Co., 1955); on compunction, see book 1, chapter 1, p. 32.

developments in the world of community or developments in the world of theory – are, as it were, a distinct world of their own.

3.2.3 Mediation[30]

We have distinguished three worlds, and I want to say something further about their relationships. A useful word in this connection is the word 'mediate.' What do we mean by mediation? What comes in between; what somehow helps something else that is distinct. It is a vague word, but it is perhaps the most useful word for bringing to light the relationships between these different worlds. For example, in writing a history of the Second World War, Sir Winston Churchill had a considerable advantage; he had all his firsthand experience as Prime Minister of England throughout the war. His history of the war is mediated by his personal experience of what went on. In writing the history of a period, one man may have a rather good understanding of art or of science; and such scientific knowledge as he has, while it is in the world of theory, will have its influence – and it can be a very important or a very decisive influence – on the way he writes his history. Yet history, since it deals with the concrete and particular, is the type of operation that belongs to the world of community, the world of common sense. Again, the world of common sense can be said to be mediated by interiority. There is that much more meaning to one's speaking in the measure that one's interiority has developed. A person who talks without any interiority at all is 'sounding brass and tinkling cymbal' (1 Corinthians 13.1).[31] There are, then, *relationships*: while these different fields do not form a single group, while one has to oscillate from one to

30 This crucial idea is just beginning to emerge in Lonergan's thinking. See above, note 25. It will be greatly developed by the time he gives the lecture published here as chapter 8, one year later. A certain coincidence should be mentioned. Just at the time of the present lecture, Lonergan was in communication with Henri Niel (letter of 11 December 1962); in chapter 8 of this volume he refers to Niel's work on Hegel and mediation, and we have a note on Niel there (note 3). The term and the idea were on Lonergan's mind a year before the lecture on 'The Mediation of Christ in Prayer' (and the Gonzaga lectures on which, as we state below in note 1 of chapter 8, this lecture depends), and Niel might be the first to influence him in this area. Notes that Jean-Marc Laporte took at Gonzaga in 1963 have remarks (pp. 24–25) on different mediations of, or approaches to, God: in the world of theory (proof), the world of community (church, liturgy, lives of saints), the world of interiority (personal prayer); but the beatific vision is immediate.

31 NRSV: 'A noisy gong or a clanging cymbal.'

one to the other – one's time of prayer is not one's time of business, and one's time of working out the theory of something is neither business nor prayer – one can move from one to the other; they are interdependent, one helps the other; still, they are distinct fields.

3.2.4 Religion

A fourth field is religion. We do not know God immediately in this life. We know God through creatures, through the creature that each one of us is, through all the rest of creation; or we know God through revelation and the teaching of the church. Our knowledge of God is *mediated.* It can be mediated by the world of community insofar as we belong to a community in which there is teaching and there are practices of religion. It can be mediated by theory insofar as one's philosophic thought leads one to prove the existence of God, to determine the attributes of God. It can be mediated by one's interiority, and the outstanding example in that field is of course the life of the mystic, in which interiority develops and constitutes, as it were, a means through which God's presence ceases to be an unidentified undertow in one's living.[32]

3.2.5 Differentiations

Now the four spheres, the four types of world, may be differentiated in consciousness. A person may be quite aware of the differences between them. In a fully developed consciousness all four will exist and function. There will be oscillations from one to the other, and the meaning of each will be clear. But in the primitive or in the child, the potentiality for the four is there but not the development that permits their differentiation. In the primitive there is no lack of theoretical problems; what is lacking are the theoretical techniques, and because the theoretical problems are met by commonsense procedures, the result is myth. There is no lack of practical knowledge, but insofar as religious procedures are employed for practical ends, the result is magic. The lack of development means not only

32 Lonergan had said, '... a means through which God is present to one in an exceptional manner.' When checking the transcript for publication in *Bernard Lonergan: 3 Lectures* (1975) he changed the wording to what we have here, in order to remove the impression that such development is a rare happening. See the note of Fr Eric O'Connor on p. 48 of *Bernard Lonergan: 3 Lectures.*

that the different spheres have not been distinguished one from the other but also that there is a possibility of aberration, an aberration that in its way – by the evils it creates – adds a further force, a further determinant to lead on the development.

Now, if we think of the differentiation of the four spheres of development as a sort of goal, we can see that, once the differentiation is reached – it remains possible, of course, to have still further development in each one of the four spheres – difficulties of determining meaning are fairly easily solved simply because the differentiation makes it possible for a person to pin down his meaning with greater exactitude. It is in the *earlier* stages, or in the stages of distortion, of aberration, where one of the fields is blocked out or disregarded or despised, that the problems of determining meaning arise. So one can think, as it were, of a basic line from the undifferentiated to the differentiated consciousness and, as well, of various types of aberration, of distortion, resultant when certain elements are not sufficiently developed or others are overdeveloped.

To illustrate this, let us go back to the distinction we have already drawn between symbolic and linguistic meaning.

Linguistic meaning, according to an ideal developed by the Greeks, is ruled by logic. But a great deal of human speech, and particularly a great deal of human literature, does not flow in any simple, straightforward, logical mode. To understand the language that is employed, the meaning that is communicated, under such circumstances, one has to be aware of the fact that besides the rules of logic governing conceptual meaning, there are also the laws of affect, which follow different principles of construction and procedure. Insofar as affective influence manifests itself in speech, there are certain well-marked tendencies that arise. In place of the universal concept, the class concept, one finds the representative figure. In place of terms, words, with a single meaning, one finds words employed with several simultaneous meanings. 'Which do you mean?' 'I mean both – or all three.' Logical proof gives way to repetition, variation on the same theme, and other rhetorical devices. What is called 'rhetoric' is a reflection, a systematization, of this more elementary thing: when the principle of the excluded middle – either *A* or not *A*; there is no third – gives way to overdetermination, to conjoined opposites. There is not only love but *also* hatred, and both at the same time. Instead of there being a simple negation, the object is posited to be overcome. Having a single theme that is developed gives way to a simultaneous occurrence of many disparate themes.

One can take as illustration the way in which the poet negates, by positing to overcome. Susanne Langer quotes Swinburne's verse:

> Then star nor sun shall waken,
> Nor any change of light:
> Nor sound of waters shaken
> Nor any sound or sight:
> Nor wintry leaves nor vernal;
> Nor days nor things diurnal;
> Only the sleep eternal
> In an eternal night.[33]

The whole meaning of the thing is negative: eternal sleep, eternal night. But there is speech of the sun and the stars, the change of light, the sound of waters, the wintry leaves, the leaves of spring; they are posited to be set aside. In affective negation – not the truly logical 'This is not that' – there is a way in which the influence of affectivity on meaning manifests itself.

Langer gives also an example of condensation, the combination of several themes, in the lines from Shakespeare's *Macbeth*:

> And Pity, like a naked newborn babe,
> Striding the blast, or Heaven's Cherubin, hors'd
> Upon the sightless couriers of the air,
> Shall blow the horrid deed in every eye
> That tears shall drown the wind.[34]

Quite different expressions, quite different themes, are there combined into a single statement, and that type of condensation of combined different things reveals affectivity at work bringing out something that is quite different from the logical rules of meaning. That is an incidental illustration of the way in which affective meaning differs from logical meaning.

But take things that are more relevant to our spheres. Take the distinction between the profane and the sacred. For the primitive, for undifferentiated consciousness, there is not a distinction between the world of the profane and the world of the sacred. There is the sacralization of the pro-

33 Algernon Charles Swinburne, 'The Garden of Proserpine,' quoted in Langer, *Feeling and Form* 243.

34 Quoted in Langer, *Feeling and Form* 244.

fane and the profanation of the sacred, so to speak, and it is spontaneous. A spade is not just a spade. Everything is open to the divine, a manifestation of the divine. And that same type of undifferentiated consciousness is predominant in symbolic processes, with the consequence that there is commonly attached to such processes a profound religious feeling. For undifferentiated consciousness, there are not separate worlds of the profane and the sacred. The two interpenetrate, and that interpenetration is something like what is described by Wordsworth in his 'Intimations of Immortality':

> There was a time when meadow, grove, and stream
> The earth, and every common sight,
> To me did seem
> Apparelled in celestial light,
> The glory and the freshness of a dream.[35]

When the differentiation occurs, one can have a distortion, namely, a separation between the two: a secularism that excludes religion and disregards it entirely, and on the other hand a pure religiosity, religion as founded on sentiment. Take such a view of religion as developed in the nineteenth century, under the influence of Schleiermacher: the religion of the heart. If your heart is all right, your religion is all right; that is the only thing you need bother your head about. As further illustration of where the differentiation is not quite made: when Yves Congar, in his article 'Théologie' in *Dictionnaire de théologie catholique,* is comparing St Bonaventure and St Thomas, he points out that for Bonaventure there is not properly any field of natural knowledge. Knowing this world is not knowing something that stands by itself; it is not a type of knowledge that has a right of its own. It has a purely ancillary function, namely, enabling us to find further analogies, further manifestations, further revelations, of what God is. Everything natural is further open to the divine; that seems historically to have been the original meaning of 'philosophy, the handmaiden of theology.' In St Thomas, there is recognized a field of natural knowledge that has its own principles, its own criteria, and stands on its own feet. There is in St Thomas a clear, cool, and systematic acknowledgment of the distinc-

35 William Wordsworth, 'Ode: Intimations of Immortality from Early Childhood,' *The Poetical Works of William Wordsworth,* ed. William Michael Rossetti (London: Ward, Lock & Bowden, 1870) 357–58.

tion between the sacred and profane in a manner that apparently is lacking in St Bonaventure.[36]

Again, one can draw a line between inner and outer, the world of interiority and the external world. Without the distinction between the two, there is not what we call individualism. In the primitive community, it is not the individual but rather the community, through individuals, that thinks, deliberates, decides, acts. In the medicine man, the shaman, you have emergence of individuality (particularly as perceived by Eliade in his fundamental work, *Le Chamanisme et les techniques archaïques de l'extase*[37] – the medicine man and his archaic techniques of mysticism). Karl Jaspers, in his book on the origin and end of history,[38] places what he calls the 'axis' of history between the years 800 and 200 before Christ. What he means by the axis of history is the emergence of individualism, the emergence of individuals who think for themselves, decide for themselves, lead their own lives. The occasion or ground of that emergence, which was connected in Israel with the appearance of the prophets and in other countries with the emergence of philosophies (in China, India, Greece, Iran), was the breakdown of the old empires which were in solidarity with their political, cosmological, and religious myths. The elimination of this whole superstructure left individuals with a highly developed technical society, yet on their own. The distinction emerges of interiority and the external world: Who am I? What am I making? What am I to do to make my way in this world or in the next? An emergence of the individual is not something native to Homo sapiens as such; it is something that develops. Present-day totalitarianism, with its tendency to the elimination of the individual, is the opposite of that emergence of individualism.

One can note also the opposition between common sense and theory. 'What on earth is the good of theory? Aren't all these theorists just nuts?' This emphasis on the world of community and common sense to the disregard of the world of theory is a very spontaneous, often widespread attitude. The opposite emphasis also occurs. In Platonism, the world of common sense is the world of appearances. The things that really are are the eternal objects of understanding. While in Platonism you have a deval-

36 See above, chapter 2, note 21, on Congar and the difference between Bonaventure and Aquinas.

37 Mircea Eliade, *Le Chamanisme et les techniques archaïques de l'extase* (Paris: Librairie Payot, 1951); in English, *Shamanism: Archaic Techniques of Ecstasy*, trans. Willard R. Trask (Princeton: Princeton University Press, 1972).

38 Karl Jaspers, *The Origin and Goal of History* (see above, chapter 3, note 38).

uation of the world of community and common sense, and an emphasis upon eternal objects, in Brahmanism there is a similar phenomenon, in which the world of common sense is also the world of appearances, but the emphasis is not upon eternal objects but upon the absolute subject, the Atman, an emphasis from the side of the subject. And, though it is not too clear, there seems to be in Plotinus's 'One' the contribution not only from Plato on the side of the object but also from the side of the subject.[39]

Again, there can be acknowledged both theory and common sense but the acknowledgment of theory is a devalued acknowledgment. It is simply through what the French call 'haute vulgarisation.' People have great respect for the great theoretical names – Newton and Einstein, Aristotle and Aquinas, weren't they wonderful people! – but they have no personal experience of the intellectual pattern of living, of what it is to live the way a theorist lives, to have that pure domination of intellect as a part-time mode of one's subjectivity. They do not know by experience what that is, they are not familiar, strictly and accurately, with any field of theoretical objects. They have a very inadequate notion of what theory is, yet at the same time they really are not in the world of community, they do not apprehend the concrete, the individual, the particular, as they really are; their apprehension is mediated by universal norms, laws, criteria, classifications, serial types, and so on, so that they do not know what the concrete is. They are lost in some no man's land between the world of theory and the world of common sense.

It is now time to end, and I have covered most of the ground I intended to. What I have had to say has been, unfortunately, either suggestive or fragmentary. Perhaps in the course of the year you may find some help from it: on the one hand, by going to elementary types of meaning, which I tried to illustrate and communicate if not define (the intersubjective, artistic, symbolic, incarnate, and linguistic) and on the other hand, by seeing in the different spheres that do not integrate (that do not mix with one another but are under the law of a withdrawal and return: a time for this and a time for that) a limitation to the possibility of the grouping of groups – this is Piaget's analysis of development – and a sort of scale on which one can fit, at least in some rough fashion, the different modes of thinking that one meets in an exploration of the realm of meaning, which is a fundamental realm in the existence, the living, of man.

39 Lonergan may be referring here to the interpretation of Plotinus given by Henry Duméry, to whom he refers in his 1959 lectures on the philosophy of education; see *Topics in Education* 191–92; see also below, chapter 6, note 8.

6

Consciousness and the Trinity[1]

1 A Contemporary Context

I would like to take as my point of departure the book by Claude Welch, *The Trinity in Contemporary Theology*.[2] Welch is concerned with the relevance of the traditional trinitarian formulae to the modern world. His position is that, even if the traditional philosophic language is thrown out when speaking about the Trinity, we must and can speak intelligently of God's unity as one being, one essence, one substance (in conformity with the ancient, traditional formulae of *mia ousia, una substantia, homoousios*), but

1 A lecture given at the North American College, Rome, 20 January 1963, followed by a question period. The tape recording of the lecture was not available for this editing, but we are indebted to Joseph Komonchak, at that time a student at the College and now Professor of Theology at The Catholic University of America, for valuable information regarding the transcription: 'A tape was made by one of the students who then typed it out ... I went over it, inserting punctuation, etc., paragraph divisions, eliminating colloquial "ands," and so on. Fr Lonergan read over this version and made some corrections and gave his permission to mimeograph it. Added to the lecture itself are a few pages of questions and answers, which Fr Lonergan also read and approved for copying' (Letter, Joseph Komonchak to Frederick Crowe, 14 September 1966, Lonergan Research Institute Archives, Toronto).

In the present edition we worked from the transcription made at the North American College. An earlier edited version was published in *Philosophy & Theology* 7:1 (Autumn 1992) 3–22.

2 Claude Welch, *The Trinity in Contemporary Theology* (London: SCM Press, 1953).

also of one person. The question whether there is one person in God or three is a question to which he has devoted a considerable amount of attention in the course of his book.

Now, when Welch speaks of one person in God, he does not do so in a Sabellian sense. He acknowledges some real threefoldness in God, but that threefoldness is not one of persons. Consequently, his position is not strictly heretical. In fact, he believes he is holding exactly what Penido holds in his book on analogy, where it is explained in what sense a Catholic holds three persons in God.[3] Welch admits that a Catholic cannot avoid speaking of three persons; but what he means, he thinks, is the same as what Penido means. Other Catholic authors he has studied are Pohle-Preuss[4] and another author named Klein.[5]

Welch recognizes that objections will be brought against his position: for example, that we should keep the traditional formula of three persons in God but explain that it is used in a noncontemporary sense. Two reasons, he admits, may be given against using the formula 'one person in God': first, that we must maintain continuity with the Christian tradition of speaking of three persons; and secondly, that we must retain in our thinking the preciseness and clarity that has been attained in the course of the seventeen centuries during which the Trinity has been discussed by Christian theologians.

In answer to the objections to speaking of one person in God, Welch questions whether enough clarity about the meaning of 'person' has been attained by theologians of the past for there to be any great advantage in retaining the formula 'three persons.' He discusses what Augustine has to say about three persons and Boethius's definition of a person, and concludes that there is really not a great amount of clarity to be preserved as a heritage from the past. As for maintaining continuity with Christian tradition, he is sceptical that the continuity is more than verbal. We use the words of the past, but we do so at the expense of the possibility of communication, of saying what we mean, and of saying what will have a meaning for other people. In this connection he quotes Gustaf Aulén, the famous author of the

3 Maurilio T.-L. Penido, *Le Rôle de l'analogie en théologie dogmatique* (Paris: J. Vrin, 1931).
4 Joseph Pohle, *The Divine Trinity*, adapted and edited by Arthur Preuss (St Louis: B. Herder, 1919); commonly referred to as 'Pohle-Preuss.'
5 Felix Klein, *The Doctrine of the Trinity*, trans. Daniel J. Sullivan (New York: P.J. Kenedy & Sons, 1940).

book on redemption, *Christus Victor*.[6] Aulén's statement is that, with the development of the notion of personality that has occurred in contemporary thought, to speak of three persons would run the danger of seeing the Trinity not in the traditional sense but in a tritheist fashion – as though there were three Gods. Tendencies toward tritheism become stronger as the concept of person becomes more definite and elaborate. Under these circumstances, to repeat verbatim the trinitarian confession of the ancient church is contrary to the original intention of maintaining the unity of being in God and leads to conclusions which the trinitarian formula was intended to guard against. Faithfulness to the letter in that case becomes faithlessness toward the spirit and purpose of the ancient confession.

Finally, Welch argues, we cannot avoid using the term 'person' at the present time. We must say either one or three. If there is one thing that has been established by biblical scholarship, especially in the Old Testament, it is that fundamentally and characteristically (and, one might add, almost exclusively) the Hebrew conception of God was the concept of a person. We cannot disassociate ourselves from that result of biblical scholarship. God was a person for the Hebrews in a sense that was not attained in any other religion, and that personal concept of God remains in Christianity. On the other hand, at the present time there are philosophic tendencies that would deny God to be a person. At the present time the Christian is called to take a stand on the question of the personality of God. Welch, then, following Karl Barth (who has done more than anyone else to reestablish interest in the Trinity in Protestant circles), wants to conceive of God, not as three persons, but as three modes of being or three modes of existence.

All this puts the question of consciousness in the Trinity in its contemporary context.

2 Consciousness in the Divine Persons

As it is presented in *Divinarum personarum*,[7] this question comes up as a

6 Gustaf Aulén, *Christus Victor*, trans. A.G. Hebert (London: Society for Promoting Christian Knowledge, 1950). Despite this reference, the summary of Aulén which follows is from his *The Faith of the Christian Church*, trans. Eric H. Wahlstrom and G.E. Arden (Philadelphia: Muhlenberg, 1948); see Welch, *The Trinity in Contemporary Theology* 60–62.

7 *Divinarum personarum conceptionem analogicam evolvit Bernardus Lonergan, S.I.* (Rome: Gregorian University Press, 1957; 2nd ed., 1959); a later edition (1964) appears as the *Pars systematica* in Lonergan's *De Deo trino* (see above, chapter 2, note 18). The questions raised by Barth and Welch are treated there as well; see *De Deo trino: Pars systematica* 193–96.

technical problem: How are we to conceive the divine processions? The position is taken there that, unless we conceive the processions in terms of consciousness, we can have no analogy at all. For the Son and the Holy Spirit are not caused, they are not created, they are not made. Of the Son we believe, *non creatus, non factus, sed genitus*; and of the Holy Spirit, *non creatus, non factus, non genitus, sed procedens*; to have an analogy, then, we have to find an instance in which there is not merely causality, but also that different type of dependence which we – and St Thomas, I believe – called *emanatio intelligibilis*.

However, we ask exactly the same question when we ask, 'Is God a person?' And when we affirm in answer that there are three persons in God, we really mean 'persons.' But what is this modern attention to the notion of personality that Welch talks about? It is a thematizing of an aspect of the person that is not explicit in earlier doctrine, though it may be implicit. It is implicit in some philosophical approaches but not in others; it is implicit in the definition of person as *subsistens distinctum in natura intellectuali*.

But what do we mean by a person, what does everyone understand by a person? We mean *somebody*, someone, not something; a conscious subject, and not just a known object, not just a force that produces effects, not just a law that is effective in the universe as was the *Anankê* of the Greek tragedians, not just a Platonic Idea of the Good – an ultimate object whence all objects derive their order and their reality – and not a Platonic One beyond the multiplicity of intelligence. (That idea of the Platonic One beyond the multiplicity of intelligence has, through a Husserlian type of philosophy, profoundly influenced Trouillard and Duméry.)[8]

When we ask, then, whether there are three persons in God, is it three cases of 'somebody' we are asking about, or three cases of 'something'? By person we mean a subject that not merely knows, but in knowing is aware that he is knowing; that wills, and in willing is aware of his willing; that chooses, and in choosing is aware of himself choosing; that speaks, and in speaking is aware that he is speaking; that promises and threatens, and in promising and threatening is aware that he is doing so; that is faithful and just and merciful, and in being so is aware of his own fidelity, his own jus-

8 Jean Trouillard, *La Procession plotinienne* (Paris: Presses Universitaires de France, 1955); Henry Duméry, *Le Problème de Dieu en philosophie de la religion* (Paris: Desclée de Brouwer, 1957), in English, *The Problem of God in Philosophy of Religion*, trans. with introduction by Charles Courtenay (Evanston, IL: Northwestern University Press, 1964). On Duméry, see above, chapter 5, note 39.

tice, his own mercy. This is the person as a subject; but, on the other hand, there is the person as a subject with whom another subject deals. We do not adore something, but we do adore somebody. We do not offend something, but we do offend somebody. We cannot repent before something, but we do repent before somebody. The one to whom we pray, to whom we make our promises, in whom we believe and hope, whom we love – it is always somebody. The question is, Are there three in God who are somebody; are there three in God who are conscious subjects?

I do not think the answer to that question is difficult. Was the God who was revealed in the Old Testament a person, was he somebody, or not? I think there can be no doubt about the answer: he was somebody. God in the Old Testament is identical with God the Father in the New Testament: that is the continuity between the Old Testament and the New. God did not change from somebody to something in the New Testament. On the contrary, the New Testament reveals that the Father was most emphatically somebody, a conscious subject. Jesus Christ is certainly a person distinct from the Father. Did he become a person when he became a man, or was he a person from all eternity? One cannot hold the doctrine of Chalcedon – one person in two natures – in the sense of Chalcedon without saying that Jesus was a person from all eternity, that he did not acquire personality through his human nature. And to say that the Father and Son are persons but that the Holy Spirit is not a person cannot be reconciled with Catholic doctrine on the Trinity.

Contemporary advertence to and thematization of the personal character of God merely makes explicit, I believe, what has always been taken for granted in Catholic religious experience. In the spiritual life of Catholics, in their prayer and penance, in their faith and hope and charity, in their sorrow for sin and their purpose of amendment, they are concerned with persons. The notion that the Father, Son, and Holy Spirit are not persons in the ordinary sense of the word 'person' would be extremely difficult for them to conceive, something they would not attempt. As far as the ordinary Catholic is concerned, there is no doubt that God is a person: that the Father is God and so a person, that the Son is God and so a person, that the Holy Spirit is God and so a person. There is a difficulty in Catholic thought, but it is not a difficulty on the level of religion, of the spiritual life, of the way ordinary Catholics think about God or the divine persons. The only difficulty lies in theoretical theology. It is the question of integrating into systematic thought something that has always belonged to the *sensus fidelium.*

3 Consciousness and the Psychological Analogy: Integration

There arises the question of how it can be integrated. The first point to be noted is that if it is to be integrated at all, it must be integrated all along the line. The course I have given on the systematic part of the treatise on the Trinity has included that integration. If you were to eliminate every reference to consciousness in *Divinarum personarum*, you would be left with a framework that could be found in every Catholic manual of theology. Consciousness can be added to that framework, but it cannot be added piecemeal. Either consciousness is brought in all along the line or it is not brought in at all. Starting from an account of the psychological analogy that is strictly psychological, we have processions that pertain to the field of consciousness, and relations that pertain to the field of consciousness; and because the relations pertain to the field of consciousness, subsistent relations will be conscious subjects. What we saw before as relations will now be the personal properties; what before were considered as processions will now be the notional acts; the notional acts plus the *terminus ad extra* give us the missions. It is always the same thing occurring under slightly different aspects from the beginning to the end of the treatise on the Trinity. Thus the whole treatise on the Trinity is something compact, simple, and coherent.

Moreover, that integration all along the line is had when the psychological analogy is taken in a genuinely psychological sense. Now just when the psychological analogy began in Catholic thought is not altogether clear and certain. One can start with Origen, who spoke of the Son as will proceeding from mind. The Father was *nous*, the Son was *thelêma*. Or you can start with Marius Victorinus – see the long and useful article on him in the *Dictionnaire de théologie catholique*, under 'Victorinus Afer.'[9] There is no critical edition of his work yet. He was a neo-Platonic philosopher who entered the church and seems to have had considerable influence on St Ambrose and, through St Ambrose, on St Augustine. In St Augustine himself, any trinitarian analogy – in the sense of analogy: not just a vestige, but an image – is certainly psychological and not at all metaphysical, for while Augustine was a magnificent psychologist, he did not work out a theoretical metaphysics in any notable way. I believe that St Thomas's analogy is

9 P. Séjourné, 'Victorinus Afer,' *Dictionnaire de théologie catholique* 15:2 (Paris: Librairie Letouzey et Ané, 1950), cols. 2887–2954.

strictly and properly psychological, as I tried to show in the *verbum* articles in *Theological Studies* from 1946 to 1949.[10]

If that is so, the question arises, How did the psychological content get lost? For example, Welch has no doubt whatever that, according to Penido and other Catholic authors he has read, there is no psychological content in the Catholic theological notion of the person; it is all a matter of distinct, incommunicable substance, and the incommunicability is not of the same kind as in persons here on earth. It is an incommunicability, not in the absolute order but in the relative order. No manual of theology you may read will speak of the divine persons as conscious subjects. They do speak of *subsistens distinctum in natura intellectuali* but they do not go on to the further aspect of person as conscious subject.

How did the psychological content got lost? Well, in a sense it was not lost, and in a sense it was. In a sense it was not lost, because in medieval thought psychological introspection did not exist as a specific technique. I believe St Thomas practiced psychological introspection. This is a conclusion deduced from the sort of things he says, from the sort of arguments he employs. But his use of introspection was private; it was not the sort of thing a modern psychologist does to explain how he goes about things, what he observes, what he finds, how it may be found in one's own experience, and so forth. Psychological introspection was not a thematized technique in Aristotle and St Thomas, although I believe they got too many things right not to have practiced it.[11] The point is, however, that because psychological introspection did not exist as a technique, there is a sense in which there was nothing to be lost.

4 Block to Integration: Notion of Reality

On the other hand, there did arise blocks which prevented attention to the results of psychological introspection and acknowledgment of their relevance. The root of those blocks is, in my opinion, twofold: a notion of reality and a notion of knowledge. We all spend approximately seven years before reaching the age of reason, but before reaching it we have some notion, some developed sense, of reality. We all possess a prerational feel-

10 Bernard Lonergan, 'The Concept of *Verbum* in the Writings of St. Thomas Aquinas,' *Theological Studies* 7 (1946) 349–92; 8 (1947) 35–79, 404–44; 10 (1949) 3–40, 359–93; in book form, *Verbum* (see above, chapter 2, note 15).

11 Lonergan makes the same point in a somewhat more detailed fashion, in the introduction to *Verbum*, p. ix. See also ibid., Index: Introspection.

ing, sense, conviction, about what is real and what is not. That prerational conviction about what is real and what is not is not exactly the same as the distinction between *id quod est* and *id quod non est.* Indeed, it is so totally different that, when we first hear about *ens,* we wonder what on earth people are talking about.

There are two ways of conceiving reality, of judging what is real and what is not. One is an appeal to a sense of reality that is prerational. It is never eliminated; if it were, we would not function properly, we would become a psychological case. The other is in terms of *ens cui suo modo competit esse.* The two notions do not sound the same and are not the same.

The difference may be illustrated by contrasting Tertullian and the Council of Nicea on the divinity of the Son. Tertullian never denied the divinity of the Son, but he did not attribute the same properties to the Son that he attributed to the Father. The Father is eternal; the Son is temporal. The Father gives orders; the Son carries them out. Perhaps – for the exegetes are uncertain of the meaning of the passage[12] – the Father is the whole and the Son is the derivative part. Now the fact that the same predicates are not attributed to the Son as to the Father caused Tertullian no difficulty for, in his opinion, the Son was divine because he was made of the same stuff as the Father. Divinity depends on what sort of stuff you are made of. This is a notion of divinity that fits in perfectly with the first sense of reality. According to the *homoousios* formula of Nicea, however, the Son is divine because the same predicates are to be attributed to him as to the Father, with one exception, the name 'Father.'[13] This notion of divinity fits in with the notion of reality in

12 The reference is to John 14.28: 'If you loved me, you would rejoice that I am going to the Father, because the Father is greater than I.' See Bernard Lonergan, *De Deo trino,* vol. 1: *Pars dogmatica* (Rome: Gregorian University, 1964) 48–49.

13 This is not explicit in the Nicene formula; it is rather the Nicene formula as explained by Athanasius: 'What *homoousios* meant exactly, was formulated by Athanasius thus: *eadem de Filio quae de Patre dicuntur, excepto Patris nomine*' (Bernard Lonergan, 'The Dehellenization of Dogma,' in *A Second Collection* [see above, chapter 1, note 26] 23). Again, '... it was the Council of Nicea and the ensuing controversies that provoked from Athanasius, along with his other clarifications, the fundamental little rule that all that is said of the Father also is to be said of the Son except that the Son is Son and not Father' (Bernard Lonergan, 'The Origins of Christian Realism,' in *A Second Collection* 250). Also, see above, chapter 4, § 2.4.4. The whole question is studied in great detail in Bernard Lonergan, *The Way to Nicea: The Dialectical Development of Trinitarian Theology,* trans. Conn O'Donovan (London: Darton, Longman & Todd, and Philadelphia: Westminster, 1976).

terms of *id quod est* and *id quod non est. Homoousios* is conceived in terms of *ens*, of *id quod est*, of identity of predicates. By that standard, Tertullian did not properly acknowledge the divinity of the Son. And the difference between Tertullian and Nicea on this point is the difference between the two notions of reality we outlined.

Unfortunately, some people have the impression that, while Tertullian and others of his time may have made such a mistake, no one repeats it today. Nothing could be further from the truth. For until a person has made the personal discovery that he is making Tertullian's mistake all along the line, until he has gone through the crisis involved in overcoming the spontaneous estimate of the real, and the fear of idealism involved in this crisis, he is still thinking just as Tertullian did. It is not a sign that one is dumb or backward. St Augustine was one of the most intelligent men in the whole Western tradition, and one of the best proofs of his intelligence is the fact that he himself discovered that for years he was unable to distinguish between what is a body and what is real.

However, the notion of reality is only one part of the problem. The other is the notion of knowledge.

5 Block to Integration: Notion of Knowledge

Now in this new block to integration ocular vision is a perfect symbol for knowing. When do you know? When you perform an act that is like an act of seeing. If you perform such an act, it is self-evident, unquestionable, beyond any possible rational doubt, that the object of that act is really and truly known, that it is valid, that it is objective. On the other hand, if a cognitional act is not like seeing, it is equally self-evident, unquestionable, and beyond possible doubt that its object is not really and truly known, that it really is not valid knowledge. That symbol, because it is symbolic, is absolutely convincing. Myths are not mere funny stories; a myth is something you are absolutely certain of. People who hold the earth is flat do not hold that view as a theory or hypothesis or possibility; they hold it as something which simply must be so. Similarly, one can be absolutely convinced that a cognitional act can be cognitional only if it resembles ocular vision. Of course, if it is like ocular vision, it does not need explanation but is self-evident.

Ocular vision here is ocular vision as popularly imagined. As scientifically studied, ocular vision demands distinction between 'real' color and visible color, between 'real' shapes and visible shapes. The 'real' color of the cassocks worn by the seminarians at the German College[14] is always the same no matter what the age of the cassock, the lighting of the room, and so forth. The visible color varies with the age of the cassock, the number of times it has been washed, the light in which you see it. This is the visible color, unseen by most people. Again, artists see things in their perspective, but the rest of us see things the way in which they are built, the way in which they are not visible. We see everything in straight lines, in rectangles, and so forth; but that is not the way they are in fact visible.[15]

Now, if human knowing is to be conceived exclusively, by an epistemological necessity, as similar to ocular vision, it follows as a first consequence that human understanding must be excluded from human knowledge. For understanding is not like seeing. Understanding grows with time: you understand one point, then another, and a third, a fourth, a fifth, a sixth, and your understanding changes several times until you have things right. Seeing is not like that, so to say that knowing is like seeing is to disregard understanding as a constitutive element in human knowledge.

A further consequence of conceiving knowing on the analogy of the popular notion of vision is the exclusion of the conscious subject. Objects are paraded before spectators, and if the spectator wants to know himself, he must get out in the parade to be looked at. There are no subjects anywhere, for being a subject is not being something that is being looked at; it is being the one who is looking; it is not what is understood, but the one who is understanding; it is not what is being questioned, but the one asking the questions; and by the very fact that he is asking them, he is aware of himself asking the questions. And if the conscious subject has been excluded, it is not surprising that three conscious subjects are also excluded or at least omitted in the Trinity.

When understanding is excluded from knowledge, not on the grounds that we do not have intellects (for we are not materialists), but on the grounds that we do not have intelligence,[16] then we may have spiritual eyes that look at universals, compare universals, see the possible nexus, and see

14 Students at the various national colleges in Rome wore variously colored cassocks, and when several nations were represented in one classroom, as they were in Lonergan's, the display was striking; the bright red of the German College was especially noticeable.

15 Philip McShane advises us that the issue here regards mediations of seeing, and refers us to the rule of explanatory formulation (*Insight* 528–29). McShane also points out that the second sentence of the paragraph is a bit loose: the real color changes with age, washing, etc.

16 On intellect and intelligence, see above, chapter 4, note 7.

the necessary nexus, and we may bow our heads in assent; but we are not understanding in the ordinary meaning of the word. And if understanding is excluded from conscious knowledge, there is no possibility of one's defining or clarifying because one understands. To speak of judging because one has understood, grasped, the unconditioned, will have no meaning. Without a notion of the conscious subject or of the intelligible emanation, the process from the judgment of value to the act of choice will also be overlooked.

For some twenty-three years now, I have been examining in theology. Jesuit students must take an examination which, besides the hundred theses on theology, includes all of philosophy. When a student is asked for a philosophical proof of human liberty, he is likely to appeal to consciousness. If it is objected that, in consciousness of a free act, we are conscious only of the fact that we chose one part or the other, but not of the possibility of choosing the opposite, most students are stumped. For the appeal to consciousness must be an appeal to the conscious subject who is principle of this act or that act and is aware of the fact that he is principle of either. The appeal must be to the conscious subject and to intelligible emanations.

The notions of knowledge and of reality which we have outlined, although distinct, still reinforce one another. Reality is what is known by an act much like an act of seeing, and not at all what is known by understanding and judging. A neat, closed-in world is built up in which there is no room for three conscious subjects in the Trinity.

There is, then, a problem for Catholic thinkers in the field of trinitarian theory. We must use the word 'person' in speaking of God, and in its traditional sense; we are bound to the formula 'three persons in God.' But we can say 'three persons' and mean three conscious subjects, that is, use the word in the sense of three who are somebody although there is one consciousness for the three subjects. There is no major difficulty in integrating the notion of person as 'conscious subject' with the whole tradition of systematic theology on the Trinity; it simply is a matter of understanding what St Thomas said. One may understand what he said or merely repeat his formula, and that is the difference between having three conscious subjects and not having them in the Trinity. The real difficulty lies elsewhere. It lies in philosophic problems and their carry-over into theology. Theology is reason illuminated by faith. And should reason limp, well, limping reason illuminated by faith will not give perfect results.

Now I think I've spoken enough. Are there any questions?

Question: Perhaps you could sketch out a little more particularly where you feel you are at variance with Gilson and Maritain in your theory of knowledge and reality.

Response: I know Gilson better than Maritain. Gilson is an extremely intelligent man, in contact with first-class philosophic thinkers. His basic objection to Maréchal is given in his work *Réalisme thomiste et critique de la connaissance.*[17] The stages in the development of his thought are studied in van Riet's book *Thomistic Epistemology.*[18] Gilson holds that being can be known only through a perception of being. This perception is not sense perception but intellectual perception. Now intellects abstract from things, but he feels that there is some sort of osmosis between the two – the human subject operating on both the sensitive and the intellectual levels; and some combination of sense and intellect amounts to a perception of the reality of being. This perception he proceeds to integrate into a Thomist exposition of intellectual operations. For him being must be perceived, and if it is not perceived you must be an idealist. Idealism does not involve an internal contradiction, so that the disproof of idealism must be the fact that we actually do 'see' being. Similarly, he has a theory about the judgment of perception.

This position of Gilson's is in complete agreement with the fundamental principle in Kant's *Critique of Pure Reason.*[19] In the opening section on the Transcendental Aesthetic, Kant lays it down that the only way in which our knowing can be related immediately to objects is through *Anschauung.* And Kant holds to that position rigorously. The operations of understanding are knowledge of objects only mediately. Unless *Anschauung* is added, they are no better than dreams or imagination. To know something, to get into the category of objects, *Anschauung* is needed. Similarly the categories of reason – the ideas of reason – are at a second remove: they guide the use of the categories of understanding, and the categories of understanding come into contact with objects insofar as there is added on an *Anschauung.*

17 Etienne Gilson, *Réalisme thomiste et critique de la connaissance* (Paris: J. Vrin, 1939) 130–55; in English, *Thomistic Realism and the Critique of Knowledge,* trans. Mark A. Wauck (San Francisco: Ignatius Press, 1986) 129–48.

18 Georges van Riet, *L'Epistémologie thomiste* (Louvain: Institut Supérieur de Philosophie, 1946) 495–517; in English, *Thomistic Epistemology,* two vols., trans. Gabriel Franks (St Louis: B. Herder, 1963) vol. 2, pp. 153–74.

19 Immanuel Kant, *Critique of Pure Reason,* trans. Norman Kemp Smith (New York: St Martin's Press, 1965).

But, as Kant holds it, *Anschauung* is only of phenomena. This is the key to his whole philosophy. With the principle of perceptionism Gilson is in complete agreement.

Why, then, does he not agree with the rest of Kant?[20]

Our intellects are not a second sense, they do not look. They are intelligent; when they know, they understand. They are faculties for understanding. Further, to say that reality is what's out there is a childish myth; it is all right for the child, but the child should grow up. What is being? Being is everything, what is not confined to a genus, what goes beyond all genera, what includes *omnia simpliciter* – and you don't take a look at *omnia simpliciter.* What is the basis of the objectivity of our knowledge, what is its first contact with the objective? It occurs after you have a sense experience – when you ask, 'What is it?' and when you know what the answer to that is; and when you ask, 'Is it so?' *An sit?*

What is this *sit?* It is the objective of the pure desire to know being. Questions are unlimited; you can't draw a line and say, 'So far and no further, no further questions.' The potency for asking questions is unlimited. And the object of that potency is unlimited. In that way our knowledge ties up with an unlimited objective that is being; such is our notion of being.

The notion of being is distinct from the concept of being; the notion and concept of being are different from knowledge of being; and the notion, concept, and knowledge of being are distinct from the idea of being. The idea of being is God's essence. To understand God's essence is to understand God and everything else, which is what God's knowledge of himself and everything else is. The idea of being is the *species intelligibilis* that is the essence of God. Knowledge of being is had through judgment. The concept of being is had when you conceive anything; any concept is always a concept of being. For any concept is ordered to a judgment: Is it so? By the mere fact that it is ordered to a judgment, it is a concept of something ordered to *esse.* And what is being? *Ens est id cui suo modo competit esse.* So any concept is a concept of being. The notion of being is the desire to understand, which is prior to understanding anything. It is the wonder that is the beginning of all science and philosophy, but also the wonder

20 The close similarity of this treatment of Gilson with that of the review article 'Metaphysics as Horizon' (*Collection* [see above, chapter 2, note 13] at 193–97) is probably explained in part by the fact that this lecture followed only a month after Lonergan had completed writing that article (letter of Lonergan to F.E. Crowe, 11 December 1962).

that makes two-year-old children plague their parents with the number of questions they ask.[21]

There's a bit of a difference there, isn't there?

Question: The next question concerned the fact that the judgment of identity in the person is made because of, and in, a multiplicity of acts.
Response: We think of our identity in relation with a multiplicity of acts because it is the multiplicity of acts that causes the problem. So the problem of identity in the Trinity will not be the same. There is only one act, but there is a distinction because the three persons have the same consciousness differently: the Father is God in a manner analogous to the grasp of sufficient evidence that necessitates one to judge; the Son is God in the same consciousness but now a consciousness analogous to that of the dependence of the judgment on the grasp of sufficient evidence; the Holy Spirit is the same consciousness in a third manner, namely, as the dependence of the act of love on the grasp of sufficient evidence and the rational affirmation. The same consciousness is had differently by three persons.

Question: What is the meaning of the term *intelligibile* as applied to acts of understanding, as distinct from the way it is applied to natural causes?
Response: The difference is clear enough in St Thomas, where he says that sensible things are not *in genere intelligibilium*, that our intellects are *in genere intelligibilium ut potentia tantum*, that to be *in genere intelligibilium ut actus* is to be infinite – that is a use of *intelligibile* that does not apply to natural objects: human intelligence is at the bottom of the ladder.[22] The *intelligibile* is the sort of thing that for it to be in full act is to be infinite. It is in a category that moves off to infinity. It makes no sense to talk about the infinitely hot, but it does make sense to talk of the infinitely intelligible. That's with regard to usage.

21 On the distinct terms 'notion of being,' 'concept of being,' 'knowledge of being,' and 'idea of being,' see *Insight* (see above, chapter 2, note 9) 804, note *b* to chapter 19; also *Topics in Education* (see above, chapter 2, note 12) 173–75.

22 Thomas Aquinas, *Summa theologiae*, 1, q. 87, a. 1. Here St Thomas gives the three levels of intellect as divine, angelic, and human. The latter is therefore 'at the bottom of the ladder.' (See ibid. q. 79, a. 2: human intellect 'est infimus in ordine intellectuum.') But St Thomas does not say, except by implication, that sensible things are not in this genus.

With regard to meaning, a learned book in Akkadian[23] may inspire your admiration for its beautiful printing but you won't know what it means. It's intelligible but I don't understand anything. That is not the sense in which 'intelligible' is used when we speak of an intelligible emanation. When we speak of an intelligible emanation, we refer to the intelligible that can be only in an intelligent subject as intelligence in act. A city plan, a parish church or hall, may be very intelligently worked out but the plan itself is not intelligent at all; it is an effect of intelligence. But what goes on in a man's mind when he thinks of the plan? It is not merely an object that can be studied and admired as neatly contrived; it is not the contrived but the contriver – namely, the intelligent. People judge because of sufficient reason. And you may say that I am here tonight because of a sufficient reason; or that something happens and there is a sufficient reason for it. But the sufficient reason is not rational in itself; it is the grounded: what results from following reason. But what occurs in virtue of reason itself is the sort of thing that is moved because it is rational, by the reason itself. As in the expressions, 'It stands to reason,' 'If you had an ounce of gumption, you'd say yes,' and so on. We become impatient when addressed in that way. But what is being appealed to? The speaker is appealing to our rationality, to our ability to be moved by reason as distinct from any other type of pressure or threat. In that ability to be moved by reason, at its center – in the intellect itself, in the rational appetite that is the will – the place where theory counts and where, if we are rational, it should 'cut some ice' (even if it doesn't in practical affairs) there is to be located the field of intellectual emanations. (A book on logic is logical, but when the Greeks called man a *zôon logikon* – a logical animal – they were talking about him as rational. The Latins did not make a mistake in translating it *animal rationale* – a rational animal. The question is, What is *rationale*?)

Question: Is it true to say then that intelligible and intelligent mean the same thing?
Response: No. In general you can say that everything is intelligible: even prime matter, though not in itself but in its form, and the social surd but only within the dialectic. Everything is intelligible but only intelligent

23 We have no tape recording to check whether this is what Lonergan said. The North American College transcription has 'Arkadian.' For 'Arcadian' Webster's gives as one meaning 'The dialect of ancient Greek used in Arcadia.' But we think it more likely that Lonergan said 'Akkadian.'

beings are intelligent. They are the only beings that understand. What is understanding? It is like seeing in this sense: that just as, if you are blind, you don't know what seeing is (you may figure out a theory about what it must mean but it is not something immediately evident to you, and can be evident only to someone who can open and close his eyes and see), so too unless you understand, you can't know what understanding means. The function of the earlier chapters of *Insight* is to stimulate the occurrence and experience of understanding. People object, 'The examples aren't familiar.' That is the point. If they were familiar, the act of understanding would occur so easily that it wouldn't be noticed. You have to work for it, and at long last it comes: 'I've got it!'

Question: To return to the philosophical basis of an understanding of consciousness in the Trinity, would you comment on the relevance, or lack of it, of the epistemological basis as worked out at Louvain by Noël and van Steenberghen.[24]
Response: I'm not certain about them. To know where a man stands, you have to get down and study him at some length. However, my impression is that Gilson had the better of the argument in his objections.[25] Gilson is quite dogmatic in his stand. He wants no truck with a pretense of a critical philosophy. I think Gilson was pushing their position to its logical conclusion. What Noël at least wants (I'm not sure about van Steenberghen) is some sort of critical method.

Question: The next questioner asked the meaning of the dictum, *Intelligibile in actu est intellectus in actu.*
Response: That's St Thomas and Aristotle. The intelligent in act and the intelligible in act are identical. The intelligible in potency and the intelligent in potency are distinct. The intelligible in potency can be understood, the intelligent in potency can understand. It depends on Aristotle's analysis of action and passion. Aristotle, and St Thomas commenting on the *Physics*, distinguish the *mobile*, the *motivum*, the *motum*, and the *movens*; these are the

24 Léon Noël, *Notes d'épistémologie thomiste* (Louvain: Institut Supérieur de Philosophie; and Paris: Alcan, 1925), and *Le Réalisme immédiat* (Louvain: Institut Supérieur de Philosophie, 1938); and Ferdinand van Steenberghen, *Epistémologie* (Louvain: Institut Supérieur de Philosophie, 1945); in English, *Epistemology*, trans. Martin J. Flynn (New York: Joseph F. Wagner, 1949).

25 For Gilson's critique of Noël, see his *Réalisme thomiste* 41–79; *Thomist Realism* 55–85.

elements distinguished in *motus*, motion.[26] Now is the motion in the mover or in the moved? Are there two motions or only one? Aristotle shows that there is only one and that it is in the moved. Then, in the third book of the *De anima* (*lectio secunda* of St Thomas's Commentary), he applies this analysis to sensation. Hearing – your ear – and the bell are distinct; what sounds in potency and what hears in potency are distinct. But the hearing in act and the sounding in act are one and the same. The bell rings in the desert – does it sound? Not in Aristotle's view. There is no sounding act unless there is an ear hearing in act. He applied the same thing to the intellectual order. *Intellectus in actu* and *intelligibile in actu* are identical, but in potency they are distinct. Because of this analysis Aristotle can conclude to what you could never arrive at in a Platonic philosophy: a prime mover that is intelligent. Aristotle's prime mover is not an object but an identity of subject and object. *In his quae sunt sine materia idem est intelligens et intellectum.*[27] Now that is a basic analysis of knowledge, but it doesn't deal with the problem of objectivity. Analysis of the judgment has to be added.

Question: The next question concerned the relation between the rational necessity of an intelligible emanation and the causal relation.

26 Thomas Aquinas, *In Aristotelis libros Physicorum*, 3, lect. 4, §§595–99.

27 An Aristotelian principle (*De anima*, III, 4, 430a 3–5; *Metaphysics*, XII, 9, 1075a 3–4) which Lonergan appealed to over and over to set a theory of knowing by identity in opposition to one of knowing by confrontation; see, for example, *Verbum* 183–84; *Understanding and Being* (see above, chapter 2, note 13) 238, 241; *Topics in Education* 215–16. It is important to note that this identity obtains only in the first stage of knowing; as Lonergan goes on to say very briefly in this lecture, '... that is a basic analysis of knowledge, but it does not deal with the problem of objectivity. Analysis of the judgment has to be added.' More fully, in *Topics in Education* 215–16: 'According to the Aristotelian axiom, sense in act is the sensible in act, and intellect in act is the intelligible in act. But a full theory of knowledge cannot be formulated simply on that basis. According to Aristotle, knowledge is rooted in an identity, an identity of the sensible and the sense in act, and of the intellect and the intelligible in act. But if knowledge is merely identity, you are never knowing anything. You have to go beyond that initial identity to reach a knowledge that is *of* something, to reach a meaning that means some "meant." This occurs through the pattern of true judgments.' See also *Method in Theology* (see above, chapter 1, note 51) 74.

For the meaning in modern psychology of this identity, set in the context of the identity of Christ, see Lonergan's 'Christology Today: Methodological Reflections,' *A Third Collection* 74–99, at 91–92. For a long lining up of the various forms the confrontation theory has taken in history, see the notes for Lonergan's unpublished lectures, Intelligence and Reality (lectures at the Thomas More Institute, Montreal, March-May 1951) 19–21, 'Confrontationism.'

Response: Two terminologies are possible. According to the first, there is causality if, and only if, cause and effect are absolute and really distinct. You have a cause (my hand, a book) and the effect (falling). You let the book go and it falls. Two absolutes, really distinct. Now a judgment is an absolute, and grasp of the sufficient evidence is an absolute, and one really depends on the other. Therefore, there is causality. But you can eliminate the real distinction between the two absolutes and retain the dependence. The intelligible emanation separated from causality is the basis of the analogy for the Trinity; it is a case where there is no distinction in the absolute order, but still a real dependence.

According to the second view, distinguish with the Germans (from Hegel on) between *Geist* and *Natur*, between the *Geisteswissenschaften* or the sciences of man and the *Naturwissenschaften* or the natural sciences. In the intentional order, the nature (what I'd call the heuristic structure) of these two cases is quite different. They are radically different in their whole build-up. When you are concerned with the intentional order on the intellectual level, you discover a sufficiency of reason that functions as a causality, but a causality that can't be compared with a definition of causality in the natural order, the definition a physicist might give you, for instance. That difference is the difference between intelligible emanation and causality.[28]

28 The difference to which Lonergan is referring here is not between *Naturwissenschaften* and *Geisteswissenschaften* but between *Natur* and *Geist* in regard to causality. The difference between intelligible emanation (the procession of an inner word) and the causality of natural process had been a major theme in Lonergan's study in the 1940s of the Thomist *verbum*. See *Verbum* on 'Emanatio intelligibilis' (the index gives references under that heading), and see especially pp. 33–34, 199–200. To put it in a sentence, 'The inner word of defining not only is *caused by* but also is *because of* the act of understanding' (p. 199).

On causality itself and its relation to modern science, Lonergan's thought was still developing. In *Insight* the focus was on the intelligibility immanent in data, that is, on what for Aristotle was formal causality and what modern science studies as correlations: 'the intelligibility that is neither final nor material nor instrumental nor efficient causality is, of course, formal causality,' though, Lonergan adds, the term is easily and generally misunderstood (*Insight* 101). In that work, except for chapter 19 (see pp. 674–80), where we go beyond science to speak of God, Aristotle's efficient causality is marginal; thus, on the question of dramatic bias, Lonergan proposes 'to prescind from all questions of causal origins and to view our account of dramatic bias simply as a functional correlation' (223). Some years later he says very simply, 'For the Aristotelian, causality was material, formal, efficient, exemplary, or final; for the modern, causality is correlation' (Bernard Lonergan, 'The Future of Thomism' [1968], in *A Second Collection* 51). See *Method in Theology* 315: '... modern science ... speaks of causes but it means correlations.'

According to the first terminology, there is cause and effect where there are two absolutes, one of which is really dependent on the other. According to this view, even in our intellect and will there is true causality. But this causality is not the causality the physicist knows about, which grounds the second terminology. Depending on the terminology employed, you could say that an intelligible emanation in us is causality or that it is not. But because in God there is no distinction of absolute being, in neither terminology could you speak of causality in God.

Question: The next question was obscure.
Response: The infinite act of understanding grasps that infinite perfection is love, rational love. This necessitates the judgment: there must be love. This judgment occurs within the consciousness of the infinite act. Because it occurs within God, it must be infinite. If it were finite, it would be outside God. But there is only one infinite and consequently it must be identified with it. The difficulty is not with explaining an emanation in the infinite, but in having simultaneously the emanation and the identity of principle and term. We can't get that in clear consciousness.[29]

Question: The next question was about Karl Barth's trinitarian position.
Response: Barth is not a modalist. In other words, he does not hold a doctrine that is Sabellian, Patripassian, or Monarchian. Barth holds that there are three really distinct in God. What is doubtful about Barth's position is whether his three really distinct in God are persons. That is the point that

29 In this difficult matter Lonergan appealed to Thomas Aquinas: 'In the *Contra Gentiles* Aquinas considered in turn minerals, plants, animals, men, angels, and God to show that in perfect intellectual reflection principle and term are identical without an elimination of the reflection and so without an elimination of the procession' (*Verbum* 199). One needs to read this in the *Summa contra Gentiles* itself (4, c. 11, §§1–7), where Thomas traces the trajectory of procession or emanation, from its lowest form (say, two material bodies colliding) where principle and term are quite distinct, through the intermediate forms where principle and term draw closer and closer together without the procession ever ceasing to be real, and so to point at last beyond human understanding to the mystery where Principle and Term are identical in their absolute reality, where, however, the procession remains real, giving us the distinction of the Persons. 'We can't get that in clear consciousness,' Lonergan says; indeed, it is the mystery of mysteries, but Thomas leads us higher and higher to extrapolate beyond human consciousness to what we know by faith.

is disputed. As for his own statements, he says that only one subsists. If he knows what 'subsists' means, he is acknowledging three modes of existence (*Seinsweisen*); this, he maintains, was the position of the Cappadocians. If his explicit statements were taken in the sense obvious to a Catholic, he would not be holding three persons but three modes. The only reason for doubting this is the opinion of Volk, who maintains that what Barth means by a mode of existence is *Existenz* in the sense of some German existentialists.[30] There is no doubt about Claude Welch; he holds three modes of being and means by that three modes of existence.

30 Hermann Volk, 'Die Christologie bei Karl Barth und Emil Brunner,' in *Das Konzil von Chalkedon* 3, ed. Aloys Grillmeier and Heinrich Bacht (Würzburg: Echter-Verlag, 1954); see p. 634, n. 9.

7

Exegesis and Dogma[1]

The topic for tonight's talk was not of my choosing. I was asked for a lecture, and I inquired, 'What on?' and was told that the burning interest of the theologians was the relation between exegesis and dogmatic theology. I tried to simplify that a bit by eliminating dogmatic theology, which adds on unnecessary complexities, and speaking simply of dogma. We will mean by 'exegesis' exegesis of scripture, the interpretation of scripture, and by 'dogma' what the Vatican Council calls objects of divine and Catholic faith, namely, what has been revealed by God and proposed by the church to be believed by all.[2] Consequently, matters that not only are revealed but also strictly of faith are the dogmas.

1 Three Exegetical Ideals

I shall begin by sketching three different exegetical ideals. The exegete explains the meaning of a text. And we can ask why it is that the exegete is more comprehensible than the text itself. Why is the text not enough? Why do you need something else to know what the meaning of the text is? What

1 A lecture given at Regis College, Willowdale, Ontario, 3 September 1963. A transcription of the tape recording of the lecture (File 371, Lonergan Research Institute Library, Toronto) has the notation, '... completed on October 7, 1978, by Jacqueline Sheehy, with some revisions by Fred Crowe.' We made our own literal transcription of the taped lecture (TC 371, Lonergan Research Institute Library), and our editing is based on that.

2 *DB* 1792; *DS* 3011.

is the function of exegesis? That function can be conceived in three quite different ways, and you get three quite different results.

First of all, it may be that the exegete fulfils a function because he thinks and talks the way we do. Isaiah, St Paul, and St John are a bit strange to us; they don't talk the way we do when there is *Deo gratias*[3] at table or during recreation. And if someone will transpose their thought and their expressions into our modes of thought and expression, then we will understand what is meant. The difficulty with this approach is that it leads to as many different interpretations as there are different audiences or different sets of readers inquiring into the meaning of the text. There is a different exegesis for every nationality, every culture, every school of thought, every religious affiliation, every historical period, and this multiplicity ends up with a greater problem than the problem one started from. There is an exegesis for Catholics and an exegesis for Protestants and one for Jews and one for Mohammedans and one for Communists, and so on. Each finds a different meaning in the text, and these differences go right through everything. One is confronted with a problem of relativism. It makes the meaning very accessible, but perhaps it makes it a little too accessible.

A second approach is that the exegete makes you think and talk the way the original author did, and that is a much more laborious procedure. One has to feel one's way into the author's soul, into his imagination, his mind, his emotions, his will, his mode of speech. After years of study,[4] one knows exactly what the authors meant because their manner of thought and speech has become one's own. This type of exegesis has been called romantic. The first approach, the relative exegesis, makes Isaiah talk like us. Romantic exegesis means being able to talk like Isaiah. The relative leads to an unrelated multiplicity of accounts of the meaning of the text, and the romantic arrives at some one unique mode of thought and speech which, however, is not accessible to any of us who have not spent a lifetime in scriptural scholarship. After all, if someone talks to you the way Isaiah did, you will not understand him any better than you understand Isaiah.

There is a third approach. The exegete conveys a meaning that is more intelligible, more accessible, than that of the original text, because he transposes the original text to a mode of thought and speech common to

3 In religious communities, normal silence while eating gave way to conversation when the Superior declared, 'Deo gratias.'

4 Lonergan continued, 'one arrives at the point where one is able ...' The tape is inaudible for the completion of this part of the sentence.

all men insofar as they are rational. Now all men are rational animals, but no man is *merely* rational. Besides being governed by the laws of the mind, thought and speech are governed also by the laws of the psyche. Susanne Langer has set forth in her *Feeling and Form*[5] an interesting use of Freud's analysis of what he called the dream work – the way in which the dream is built up – and its mode of meaning; and she contrasts this with the mode of discursive reason or logical thought, along a series of points. What according to the law of the mind is affirming is feeling intensely for the psyche. If I say, 'This is a lamp,' I am talking logically; but if I feel intensely about the existence of the lamp – why, really, the lamp is something real for me! Similarly, from the viewpoint of discursive reason one simply negates: it is not so, and that is all there is about it. But to convey a meaning to the psyche, you posit the object, and then you overcome it, overwhelm it, extirpate it, obliterate it. Swinburne is rather fond of this long series of not and nor – not this nor that, and so on indefinitely.[6] The object has to be obliterated somehow, to be negated. Mere logical negation does not convey anything 'real.' Similarly, according to the laws of discursive thought, there is a principle of noncontradiction: *A* is not both *B* and not-*B*. But for the psyche nothing is more common than what is called ambivalence: you love him, but also you loathe him. And while that may appear a logical contradiction, still it is the reality of the psyche: both love and hate. Similarly for other contraries that seem incompatible.

Again, logical thought uses class names, universals, but what the psyche wants is a representative figure. St Paul speaks about Adam and Christ as figures that represent all humanity, the old man and the new. Again, the laws of the mind want univocity. Each term is to have, insofar as possible, one single meaning, and if you use it in another meaning you give notice of the change. But for the psyche words are, as it were, the portmanteau words of Humpty-Dumpty: I pay 'em double and make 'em mean what I please.[7] They have multiple meanings, and one meaning does not exclude the other. St Paul uses some words like death and life in all sorts of senses, and all the senses can be present more or less at the same time. Again, the aim of discursive reason is to put a proof in the clearest and most objective

5 Susanne K. Langer, *Feeling and Form* (see above, chapter 5, note 13) 239–43.
6 Quoted in ibid. 243.
7 'When I use a word,' Humpty-Dumpty said, 'it means just what I choose it to mean – neither more nor less.' Charles L. Dodgson ('Lewis Carroll'), *Through the Looking-Glass and What Alice Found There,* chapter 6 (as in Bartlett's *Familiar Quotations* [Garden City, NY: Garden City Publishing Co., 1944]).

fashion possible, to pick out the nerve of the matter and not try to force the other person's mind in any way – just let him see exactly what the point is as clearly and exactly as is possible. But for the psyche, you say it and then you repeat it, you repeat it with variations, you build up an accumulation of variations and you arrange them into a climax. This follows the general rule attributed to Hilaire Belloc, 'If I say it three times it's true.'[8]

Finally, for discursive reason there is a single theme that is under consideration, and everything bears upon that theme, and a number of themes are not condensed together. But for the psyche it is just the opposite. There is the work of condensation. Several things appear at the same time. Shakespeare is the master of this condensation. In an early scene in *Macbeth,* Macbeth describes the effects, what would follow, if he were to kill the king. He says:

> And Pity, like a naked new-born babe,
> Striding the blast, or Heaven's cherubin, hors'd
> Upon the sightless couriers of the air,
> Shall blow the horrid deed in every eye,
> That tears shall drown the wind.[9]

You have there a series of themes that are quite incompatible. You have Pity like a new-born babe, and was it Pity or the babe that is striding the blast? – it is a little hard to imagine the babe striding the blast. And he shifts off to Heaven's cherubin: they are horsed upon the sightless couriers of the air, and they blow the horrid deed in every eye until tears shall drown – how tears shall drown the wind is not too clear. But it is wonderful poetry and extremely effective, and it is right in accord with the way the psyche proceeds.

Now the laws of the psyche have their pure form in dreams. They function there in more or less uninhibited fashion. But they are dominant in myth, in the religious, cosmic, and political systems – and all three were one – of the ancient high civilizations, that is, of the civilizations that developed in ancient Egypt and Babylon, the Minoan civilization, the civilizations on the banks of the Indus and the Hwang Ho, and in America the civilizations of the Mayas, and in Peru the Incas. They had everything,

8 Lonergan was probably thinking of Lewis Carroll, who is credited with the same remark below in chapter 9. See note 21 to that chapter.

9 Quoted in Langer, *Feeling and Form* 244.

except a capacity for fundamental critical thought. At the top, their thinking was myth. On that subject, you can see Karl Jaspers on the origin and goal of history,[10] and also Henri Frankfort, *Kingship and the Gods*, on Egyptian and Babylonian thought;[11] and that has been taken further in Eric Voegelin's *Israel and Revelation*, the first volume of his *Order and History*.[12]

Moreover, the influence of the psyche is marked in art, in poetry, in what used to be called rhetoric and now is known as effective communication. What are the *genera litteraria*, the literary genres? They are more or less stereotyped blends of both the laws of the psyche and the laws of the mind. And of course, besides the *genera litteraria*, you have to acknowledge as well the *species exegeticae*: not only is there this mixture on the side of the original author; there also very easily is a similar mixture of a different kind on the side of the exegete, the interpreter; consequently, you have a double problem. Then we come to a third level, where the exegetes criticize one another, or later exegetes criticize earlier exegetes, or where there is the higher-level criticism of all exegetes – a history of the study of, say, scripture or any other field.

From the classical viewpoint, it is precisely here, in the influence of the psyche, that there lies the root of the exegetical problem. Insofar as a statement is simply in accord with the laws of the mind, exegetical problems do not exist. Thus, over the past twenty-five years there has been a nearly endless bibliography on St John's Gospel, and perhaps a dozen full-scale commentaries on St John, and they do not all just repeat one another. But Euclid's *Elements* in geometry have always been understood the same way for over 2300 years. Questions can be raised about the relations between Euclid and the *n*-dimensional, curved-space geometries, or the relations between Euclid and logic. But what Euclid meant is not a matter of any exegetical problem whatever. You have to study to find out what he meant, but, no matter how different the people are that study, whether they

10 Karl Jaspers, *The Origin and Goal of History* (see above, chapter 3, note 38). On what Jaspers calls 'the ancient historical civilizations' see chapter 4 (pp. 44–50). Lonergan's expression 'At the top' refers to the identification of the king as divine and as ruler of the cosmos. See below, chapter 9, at note 27.

11 Henri Frankfort, *Kingship and the Gods: A Study of Ancient Near Eastern Religion as the Integration of Society and Nature* (Chicago: University of Chicago Press, 1948).

12 Eric Voegelin, *Israel and Revelation*, vol. 1 of *Order and History* (see above, chapter 3, note 19). See part 1, 'The Cosmological Order of the Ancient Near East,' pp. 13–110.

belong to an Eastern culture, to India or China or Japan or Africa or Europe or America, they all arrive at exactly the same thing, they understand him in exactly the same way. There is no exegetical problem once it is simply the purely discursive reason that is talking. You can agree or disagree. You will have to study before you will understand it. But the study results in a single view. What gives rise to the problem of exegesis are the innumerable blends that are possible when one departs from the pure laws of reason, the pure laws of rational processes – it is or it is not, it is the same or it is different, it is the same in one respect and different in another, and so forth – and wants to communicate one's message effectively. Then one calls upon all the resources of the psyche, and one says something with a meaning that has a further effect upon other people. Classical exegesis, then, divests the text of the psychic component, what the ancients called the figures of speech, to arrive at what they called the literal meaning; and the literal meaning is the purely rational, logical, metaphysical statement, stripped of all the arts of communication.

These three quite different exegetical ideals result in different methods, different approaches, and different results. Perhaps I had best illustrate the sense in which I am using the word 'ideal' by mentioning a book by Pierre Boutroux, *L'Idéal scientifique des mathématiciens.*[13] He describes first of all the Greek type of mathematics with its aesthetic limitations. To solve a problem by Euclidean methods you can use only a compass and a ruler; trisecting an angle is no great problem if you are not restricted to Euclidean methods, but when you are restricted to Euclidean methods, there is a lot of money offered for it if you can get it done. There is an aesthetic limitation on Greek mathematics. The type of mathematics that began with Descartes and Leibniz and culminated in the present efforts in symbolic logic, a purely logical approach to mathematics, has no aesthetic limitations whatever. And then the third type of mathematics, the one that is dominant since the beginning of the nineteenth century – which, like symbolic logic, represents an older tradition – is the type that deals with the intractable mathematical object. Take the ellipse: you can consider it by the Greek method, you can also consider it in projective geometry, you can use Carte-

13 Pierre Boutroux, *L'Idéal scientifique des mathématiciens dans l'antiquité et dans les temps modernes* (Paris: Alcan, 1920). Lonergan mentioned a reprint 'around 1949,' which we have not located; but there was a *nouvelle édition* in 1955 published by Presses Universitaires de France (Paris). Lonergan refers to Boutroux's book in *Topics in Education* (see above, chapter 2, note 12) 127–28.

sian coordinates, or polar coordinates, and there will be many things that you will not be able to satisfy. You will go on to elliptic functions and so on, and still there are problems that are not satisfied. What does the mathematician do? He builds up technique after technique after technique, circles around the object, and tries to exhaust it. Now those are three different types of ideals in mathematics,[14] and the differences that I have been pointing out also give you three different kinds of ideals in exegesis.

2 Dogmas and Classical Exegesis

Now the dogmas come out of the scriptures somehow, and the way they come out of scripture is by classical exegesis. The first Christian scholar, in the proper sense of the word 'scholarship,' was Clement of Alexandria. And in his *Stromateis* or Books – several books – he is engaged in establishing his point that symbols occur in all languages and literatures. They also occur in scripture, but, though they occur in scripture, they are not to be taken literally. Scripture will talk about God the Father sitting down and rising up, about his right hand and presumably a left, and so on. But, as Clement said, even though this is written, it is not so. For a Christian in the beginning of the third century to tell the Christian world that what is written in scripture is not so was quite a step. Moreover, in the last book, book 8, of the *Stromateis,* he has a method that is a method of classical exegesis, and it was particularly relevant to dealing with the Gnostics, who interpreted the scriptures in the light of the ancient wisdom of the Egyptians, in terms of the Ogdoad, and so forth. His first step is 'Define your term,' and your definition has to be clearer than the term you are defining; and he illustrates it, he drives the point home. Next, does the referent, what your term refers to, exist or does it not? And if it does exist, show us that it exists – a point a little difficult for the Gnostics to meet. And thirdly, 'Describe it.' After you have found its existence, describe it. What are its qualities, its properties? Go on to explain it; tell us about its causes and its effects. Merely by setting this series of questions, he was forcing interpretation of the text into the classical mold.

14 We call attention – without comment except to indicate a possible source of research – to other loci in which Lonergan has spoken of ideals in mathematics. Obviously, there are pertinent materials in his as yet unpublished lectures of 1957 on Mathematical Logic. See also *Understanding and Being* (see above, chapter 2, note 13) 254–56 and *Topics in Education* 127–28 and 187.

The dogmas of the church from Nicea to the Third Council of Constantinople, from 325 to 681, are dealing with the question raised in the synoptics, What think you of the Son of Man? And some say he was Elias, and others John the Baptist, and others a prophet. But the questions that were met in the councils were in an entirely different mode. Is he God or is he not? Yes or no? That is the Council of Nicea. The Council of Ephesus: Is one and the same, not somebody else, both God and man? The Council of Chalcedon: Does that mean that he has two natures, a human nature and a divine? and two sets of properties, divine properties and human properties? And the Third Council of Constantinople: Does that mean that he has two natural wills? and two natural operations? – and the whole emphasis falls on the word 'natural.' The councils were asking questions.

What were the questions? They were not the questions of New Testament times but of later times, and the questions were entirely in the mode of rational discourse. Dogmatic theology, as developed in the Middle Ages, continues exactly in the same line. It starts from Abelard's *Sic et non*, in which 158 propositions are both proved and refuted by appealing to scripture and the Fathers. From that there came the *quaestio*: Abelard's *non* is the *Videtur quod non* of the *quaestio* and the series of authorities on the negative side. The *Sed contra est* is Abelard's *sic* and the series of authorities on the positive side. The *quaestio* goes on to give a solution and to offer interpretations, in the light of the solution, of the various authorities. Every *quaestio* will make some distinctions, but you are getting nowhere if you have different distinctions for every *quaestio*. So theologians started writing *summae* that commonly treat fundamental notions on every question. These all held together, and finally the exegesis was simply an application of the theological categories to the text that was being interpreted. Theologians were transposing scripture into the purely discursive mode.

3 Limitations and Value of Classical Exegesis

We can pause for a moment to say something on the limitations and value of classical exegesis. First of all, it is selective. It does not give an account of the whole text, but of a purely intellectual content or component: is or is not, is the same or is different, is the same in one respect and different in another, and so on.

Secondly, it demythologizes. It eliminates the psychic component. It does so not in Bultmann's sense: his sense of myth is anything that is objectified; any *Weltanschauung*, any metaphysics, any theology is objectification and myth. Classical exegesis is not demythologization in that sense, but it is in the sense that the psychic component is dropped, the figures of speech are dropped, and the literal sense is paramount.

Thirdly, it sterilizes. The psychic component – imagination and feeling – is the vital, dynamic element in the text. It is what excites interest, what moves, what attracts, what fascinates, what wins man as he exists in the concrete; and all of that is dropped. Consequently, this sterilization creates a need for spiritual exercises. You have to meditate and contemplate and apply the senses to add on once more this psychic element that has been dropped out by classical exegesis. There is, of course, a great tendency that what is added on is what *you* imagine and what *you* feel, without any reference to what *was* imagined and *was* felt. Classical exegesis leaves a great part of the text unexplained, and so it creates a large and generous *libertas errandi*, because you know only that Christ is God and man, and has two natures and two wills and two operations, and so on, but there are endless other questions that can be raised, and because they are not dealt with in any systematic and orderly fashion, one has an open field to think pretty much as one pleases.

Further, it is not historical. There is nothing historical about the purely discursive approach, and that vacuum created by the omission of the historical dimension is easily filled in by anachronism. Although it is true that Matthew, Mark, Luke, and John were rational animals, still it does not follow that they thought and wrote in the manner of the Greek councils. Anachronism is precisely the attributing of later modes of thought to earlier writers.

That is on the negative side of the ledger. All the same, the classical is a species of exegesis. It is making explicit what is implicit in the text. The scriptures are not dream work constituted solely by the psychic element; not even myth is that. There is a certain measure of rationality to them; and that can and should be made explicit in exegetical work, to some extent – it depends on the type of exegesis. Consequently, classical exegesis is a partial exegesis of the text. Further, its basis is the fact that truth is an unconditioned. What once is true always is true, and what is expressed in one way can be transposed into another; that possibility of the same truth being expressed in many different ways is the fundamental justification of this classical exegesis. Finally, it is catholic. It is something that is accessible to all men of all times and places, provided they have a modicum of education. It is something that is necessary if there is to be a catholic church, in the sense of a church for all nations, all cultures, all times.

4 Romantic Exegesis

We turn next to romantic exegesis. Romantic exegesis is the natural complement of classical exegesis. It does for the psychic component in the text what the classical does for the rational. There are whole ranges of meaning on the preconceptual, preintellectual level: intersubjective, symbolic, incarnate, artistic. I think I said something about them to you last year.[15] To grasp them, to appreciate them, we have to feel our way into them, enter into them as it were, reenact them in ourselves. It is in the concrete, by some type of reproduction in ourselves, that meaning on the psychic level can be attained. No conceptual account of a Bach sonata, a Beethoven quartet, a Brahms symphony is the equivalent of the sonata or the quartet or the symphony. And what is true of music is true on the level of depth psychology, of all art, of all meaning on the psychic level.

According to Bultmann and others writing on the topic at the present time, such romantic exegesis springs from Winckelmann's studies of art criticism.[16] It received a very special application to exegesis in Schleiermacher's work on hermeneutics.[17] For Schleiermacher, religion was essentially a matter of feeling, and consequently, romantic exegesis for him would have to be the *one* exegesis that was relevant. Finally, Dilthey aimed at a *Lebensphilosophie,* a philosophy of life, that is, a philosophy of man insofar as he is spontaneous, insofar as all rationalism is eliminated.[18] In this aim, the fundamental difficulty with Dilthey's thought is precisely that he did not

15 'Time and Meaning,' lecture at Regis College, Willowdale, Ontario, 16 September 1962 (above, chapter 5).

16 Johann Joachim Winckelmann, *Geschichte der Kunst des Altertums* (Dresden, 1764); in English, *The History of Ancient Art,* trans. G. Henry Lodge (Boston: Houghton Mifflin, 1872).

17 Friedrich D.E. Schleiermacher, *Hermeneutik, nach den Handschriften,* ed. with introduction by Heinz Kimmerle (Heidelberg: Carl Winter, Universitätsverlag, 1959); in English, *Hermeneutics: The Handwritten Manuscripts,* trans. James Duke and Jack Forstman (Missoula, MT: Scholars Press, 1977).

18 Wilhelm Dilthey's *Lebensphilosophie* is presented in vols. 5 and 6 of his 12-volume *Gesammelte Schriften* (Leipzig and Berlin, 1914–36; 2nd ed., Stuttgart and Göttingen, 1957–60); the section 'Das Wesen der Philosophie' from vol. 5 has been translated by S.A. Emery and W.T. Emery as *The Essence of Philosophy* (Chapel Hill: University of North Carolina Press, 1954).

accept all the implications of this idea of a *Lebensphilosophie*, and retained elements of science, the ideals of science, and even of Cartesianism. When Karl Barth insists that the theologian think and speak the word of God as did the apostles and the prophets, he does not want the theologian to think that *he* really is an apostle or a prophet, but perhaps he *does* want the theologian to feel and speak as though he donned the prophet's mantle, as though he stood in the apostle's shoes or his sandals; there is a sort of romantic identification with the prophets and the apostles, and that identification, that entering into the mind and soul of the original writer, putting on his modes and thoughts and speech, is essential, is the key idea, in this romantic exegesis. The full psychology of it would take rather long to evaluate.

5 Value and Limitations of Romantic Exegesis

As I spoke about the value and limitations of classical exegesis, I can do the same for romantic exegesis. First of all, it goes back to the text as it is, and it brings the text to life; it reads the text aloud, as it were, adding a tone of voice, an accent, an emphasis, a modulation, as if Isaiah or Paul or John were speaking to you. Romantic exegesis, then, stresses real apprehension, real reentry into the mind of the original writer. It seeks to realize the ideal of what the Germans call *Philologie,* which was introduced and launched with great success at the end of the eighteenth century by Friedrich Wolf, the man who worked on Homer.[19] This *Philologie* starts from a mastery of grammar and language, comparative grammar and comparative linguistics, literary study, historical documents; and later, archeological remains were added on. Its aim is a total restoration – note that point: reenactment, restoration – of an ancient culture: Egyptian, Sumerian, Minoan, Greek, Hebrew, whatever you please; but the aim is the total reenactment, the total restoration, the total reconstruction of a culture, a mode of thought, a mode of speech, that existed in the past.

Within this total reconstruction, both contributing to it and illuminated by it, lies the interpretation of each text in its concreteness, its particularity, all its strangeness and oddity, all its wealth of detail, all its fascination and profundity. This work of reconstruction – the general ideal of interpretation with respect to each particular text – is governed by its own internal norms and exigences. It cannot be dictated to by any ecclesiastical

19 Friedrich A. Wolf, *Prolegomena to Homer, 1795*, trans. Anthony Grafton et al. (Princeton: Princeton University Press, 1985).

dogmas, whether dogmas derived from the contents of scripture, or those about the nature of inspiration in the origin of the text. It accepts the data, all of them, and it demands the right to be free to discern in the data themselves their proper intelligibility, the process that explains their content and structure, their lacunae and repetitions, their oppositions and contradictions. It does not conceive history on the model of a law court in which you listen to the witnesses and pick out the ones that you think are reliable and believe what they say. It does not believe; rather, it regards history as science. Collingwood illustrated the point in his *Idea of History* by writing a little short story, a detective story, in which a crime is committed, and all the witnesses are lying, and all the clues are planted, but the detective finds out who the criminal is. It is not by believing – anybody. He studied all the concrete situations.[20]

On the other hand, romantic exegesis is apt to be powerless against the tone and current of the times. The art of empathy, *Einfühlung*, the scholarship that gradually acquires a commonsense understanding of the common sense of another people, language, culture, epoch is not easily combined with the grasp of fundamental philosophical and theological issues, their criteria, their possible solutions, their endless implications. And particularly, it is not easily combined under the circumstances that were especially dominant in the nineteenth century. Insofar as you have the original Lutheran view – nothing is clearer than scripture – then any complicated views on hermeneutics and exegesis are just out of the question; it is the plain meaning of the text for the plain man that counts. Further, in response to the application of Hegelian idealism – Hegel's laws for the development of history apply not only to history in general but also to scripture, and they were found not to work – there was a general revolt against any type of a priori dictation. In consequence, what happens is that one fashion is apt to follow another. For a full account of this with regard to the Old Testament, you can see Hans-Joachim Kraus on the history of higher criticism of the Old Testament: *Geschichte der historisch-kritischen Erforschung des Alten Testaments.*[21] But to take a very simple instance, the fruits of nineteenth-century scholarship ended up pretty much with a picture of Jesus of Nazareth in terms of the ethical ideals of the nineteenth-century bourgeois, and they were summed up in Harnack's *Wesen des Chris-*

20 R.G. Collingwood, *The Idea of History* (see above, chapter 3, note 3) 266–74.
21 Hans-Joachim Kraus, *Geschichte der historisch-kritischen Erforschung des Alten Testaments von der Reformation bis zur Gegenwart* (Neukirchen: K. Moers, 1956).

tentums.[22] And on the appearance of Harnack's book, Loisy wrote his very simple *L'Evangile et l'église,*[23] in which he emphasized – what is obvious in the New Testament – that Jesus of Nazareth was above all concerned with eschatology, with the imminent coming of the kingdom of God; the texts were just full of it. Then the whole nineteenth-century picture collapsed; that was the turning point.

At the present time in New Testament studies, there is Bultmann, who represents something analogous to the classical type of exegesis insofar as he demands a philosophy to state his ultimate concepts; his philosophy, however, is just the opposite of the classical philosophy, which is in objective categories. For Bultmann, objective categories are myth, and everything has to be transposed into subjectivity. With regard to this existentialism, von Rad in the Old Testament does not have the systematic element of Bultmann, but he is concerned with describing the faith.[24]

6 Points Regarding Exegesis

From the presentation that I have offered, neither classical nor romantic ideals are simply mistaken, nor is either complete by itself. And while we do not have time to do anything very significant with regard to what I think must be aimed at, still I had best offer a few indications of the way I believe the problem has to be approached. Fuller indications are in *Insight,* chapter 17, on the truth of interpretation.

The first of three main points I would make is that the classical ideal has to be divorced from classicism.[25] The classical ideal rests upon a differenti-

22 Adolf von Harnack, *Das Wesen des Christentums* (Leipzig: J.C. Hinrichs, 1900); in English, *What Is Christianity?* trans. Thomas Bailey Saunders (London and New York: Williams & Norgate, 1904).

23 Alfred F. Loisy, *L'Evangile et l'église* (Paris: A. Picard, 1902).

24 There follows a sentence or sentences that are obscure on the recording. Eichrodt is mentioned.

25 Lonergan became aware quite early in his career of the error of classicism. In an interview of 1973 ('*Insight* Revisited') he refers back to his reading in the early 1930s of Christopher Dawson's *The Age of the Gods,* which 'introduced me to the anthropological notion of culture and so began the correction of my hitherto normative or classicist notion' (*A Second Collection* [see above, chapter 1, note 26] 264). That this was not reading back into his youth his views of forty years later is proved by a lecture he gave at Regis College (then Christ the King Seminary), Toronto, in 1949, 'Towards a Definition of Education'; here he referred to 'the error of classicism that an ideal is valid for all places and all times' (p. 1 of the lecture notes, Archives).

ation of consciousness, an awareness, a real apprehension of the difference between Thales and the milkmaid, between the theoretic life and the practical life. They are two entirely different types of consciousness. And one and the same consciousness can so develop that it transposes from one to the other. This classical ideal, this distinction between the theoretic life and the practical life, is to be distinguished and separated from classicism.

By classicism I mean the fruit of an unsuccessful education in which, first of all, there is no real grasp of theory of any kind – mathematical, scientific, philosophic, or theological. Theory is proposed and studied, but in the subject there is no real serious differentiation of consciousness; all we get as a theory are the broader simplifications offered by a professor to introduce or round off a lecture or a course, or the products of *haute vulgarisation.* But he is never bitten by theory; he has no apprehension, no understanding, for example, of the fact that Newton spent weeks in his room in which he barely bothered looking at his food, while he was working out the theory of universal gravitation.

Not only is there no real grasp of what theory means, at the same time there is no apprehension of the concrete either. Everything is just an instance of the universal, the ideal, the exemplar, the norm, the law, the model. The classicist has no apparatus for apprehending what it is to go beyond the universal law, ideal, exemplar, into the concrete. He does not really apprehend the concrete, the particular, in its endless detail and variety and difference. Thirdly, while he admits that the instances are not perfect examples of these universal abstractions, still the differences do not really count; they are not important; they are *per accidens. Plus ça change, plus c'est la même chose.* If you know the universal, you know all that is of any importance. There is no use getting down to the concrete. Consequently, classicism is nonhistorical, it has no capacity to apprehend history, it has no historical sense – it does not know what is meant by historical sense, namely, the apprehension of a mind at work in an entirely different way from one's own.

Yet he remained attached to the classical ideal of the Greeks and even used the word 'classicism' to speak of it: of 'the emergence of the intellectual pattern of experience,' he says: 'This is what is meant by classicism in its best sense, the Greek achievement' (*Topics in Education* 75). Here, however, three years later in this lecture of 1962, he makes a clear distinction between the classical ideal of the Greek achievement and classicism, a word which he now uses in a definitely pejorative sense (see chapter 9 below, at note 33; also *A Second Collection* 1–9, 98–99, and passim).

Such is the first point. The classical ideal has to be separated from classicism and the effects of classicism; otherwise, the results of classical exegesis are transposed into a classicist mentality. Then you get the views propounded in *The American Ecclesiastical Review* by Father King:[26] if you honestly wish to accept what the writers said, you do not need the devices of the exegete; it is only when you want to get around what they said that you appeal to the *genera litteraria*; and we are having much too much of this trying to get around.

The second point is that classical ideals not only have to be disassociated from the classicist caricature, which very commonly exists, but they themselves have to be superseded. The Greek differentiation of consciousness was a momentous event in human history, but there is a further element, a further differentiation, in modern consciousness. The Greek differentiation was theory and practice, and that differentiation is not enough to deal with any serious modern problem. The differentiation that we need in order to deal with our problems is threefold: common sense, theory, and interiority. Now to make clear just what that differentiation means was one of the major tasks in my little book *Insight*, but now I will give a few illustrations of what it implies.

First of all, there are the foundations of method. In any empirical science, what counts, what is important, is not the results but the methods. Scientists are not sure of their results; they are sure of their methods. The foundations of methods of philosophy, of philosophic doctrines, of theological doctrines move from the realm of theory to the realm of interiority, the realm of *Existenz*, self-appropriation, conversion (intellectual, moral, religious conversion), the realm of wisdom – really, the earliest expression of self-appropriation is the wisdom literature.

Secondly, theory moves from the realm of the absolute, the immutable, the eternal, to the realm of development and decline, to the realm of history, of genesis and dialectic, of positions and counterpositions. All doctrines in their concrete unfolding and expression have a date ('in their concrete unfolding and expression' means just the opposite of all doc-

26 Fr John J. King was a frequent contributor to *The American Ecclesiastical Review*, stressing the role of the *magisterium* in theology. Lonergan may have been referring to 'The *Magisterium* and the Scholar,' 145 (1962) 145–66, in which King takes issue with John L. McKenzie's views, or to 'The Holy Spirit and the *Magisterium Ecclesiae*,' 148 (1963) 1–26. Classicist views are evident in both, though it seems to be Lonergan's intention not to quote King but to draw the consequences of his thinking.

trines taken substantially, prescinding from accidental differences). There are doctrines propounded in precisely this manner in this milieu, under the conditions of this milieu, with determinants from that milieu and time. If you want to talk appositely in a later time to the same people, or to a different people at the same time, you do not do it in the same way. Consequently, the historical dimension enters into the realm of theory, not in the sense that every doctrine is a doctrine about history but in the sense that every theoretical expression has a date. This is not relativism, because the foundations do not lie in the realm of theory; they lie in the realm of interiority, and the foundations are invariant. It is a shift, a rearrangement, of the functions that, on the Greek differentiation, lie entirely in the realm of theory, which I divided between theory and interiority. Consequently, the problem which is raised by exegesis and dogma is not some incidental problem; it belongs to the groundswell of the centuries; it is something that has been building up over the past four or five centuries. Because it is a first-class problem, it is not something that is going to be solved in any simple and brief fashion.

The third point brings us into something more concrete or more apparently relevant to the issues. First, I would say that it is necessary to acknowledge the relative autonomy of scriptural research and scholarship. By relative autonomy I mean that it has its own ends and its own methods, and the only way it can attain its ends is by its methods. More specifically, its end does not seem to be to establish the dogmas. I believe Karl Rahner had remarked on one issue – I didn't see this myself, but someone else told me – that the doctrine of the beatific vision of Christ during his mortal life belonged to the deposit of faith, and it was up to the scripture scholars to find it in the New Testament. Whether he said this or not, I do not think it is correct.[27] The equipment of the biblical scholar enables him to give an account of what is explicit in the thinking of the scriptural writers. What

27 Lonergan does not dispute the view that theology must show the continuity between the sources and the doctrines of the church, for just around this time he quoted and accepted the mandate of Pius XII: it is the noblest task of theology to show how doctrines defined by the church are contained in the sources (*De Deo trino*, vol. 1: *Pars dogmatica* [see above, chapter 2, note 18] 5 – in a new introduction written for the 1964 edition). His point here seems to be that it is not the task of exegesis to do this. And for a later statement, see *Method in Theology* (see above, chapter 1, note 51) 353: '... the shift from a predominantly logical to a basically methodological viewpoint may involve a revision of the view that doctrinal developments were "implicitly" revealed.'

was discovered centuries later to be 'implicit' involves a different type of development, a concrete study of a quite different historical movement; and I do not think that the proper methods of biblical scholarship and research are such as to be competent to deal with that question of the evolution of dogma. It is not that similar methods, applied to the history of dogma, will not give the answers, but that these methods applied to scripture will not give the answers. In other words, historical study is the main category, and if you want to know how the dogmas developed from scripture, you study the period; you do not study the New Testament, but the process from the New Testament to the councils; and the study of the scriptures is the study of the scriptures in themselves. So much with regard to the end.

Secondly, methods do not arrive at truth at the first crack. In the sciences, there is a succession of hypotheses, and it is through mistaken hypotheses, and only through mistaken hypotheses, that better theories evolve. Moreover, not only is there this arriving at better hypotheses through mistaken hypotheses but also there is arriving at better methods through mistaken methods. It is only by entering into this process that one can correct any errors that there are in the process. An extrinsic approach leaves the problem in its entirety. This summer I read the book by Kraus that I have already mentioned, and when I finished the chapter on Wellhausen I said, 'Well now, what are they going to do with this?'[28] It was a magnificent display; it summed up all the nineteenth-century work on the subject. And I started the new chapter on archeology and saw what happened. It just filled out the assumptions of Wellhausen with regard to the earlier period. There is an answer that will come out of the application of the methods in their proper sphere; you have to wait for it, you have to let the process take its own way, but that is the only answer that is going to meet the issue in its own terms.

Thirdly, while this autonomy of the scientific or scholarly process, letting hypothesis follow hypothesis and method follow method, is the only way

28 'Wellhausen, Julius (1844–1881) ... He elaborated the problem of the structure of Genesis ... while his thesis on the relative dating of the component documents of the Pentateuch ... completely transformed OT studies ... In his later years he devoted himself to a critical study of the NT on similar lines ... [Here] his conclusions ... met with less ready acceptance, though his [work] laid down many of the lines for the later development of form criticism.' *The Oxford Dictionary of the Christian Church,* ed. F.L. Cross (London: Oxford University Press, 1958) 1444.

that is going to get results, still I know that I said that it is a *relative* autonomy. In other words, the autonomy is not absolute. Besides this process that is dealing intimately and proximately with the texts and historical study of all kinds in all their interdependences, there is a necessary function of criticism from the realm of interiority. The weakness I have already mentioned with regard to romantic exegesis is precisely the fact that, while the interpreter can be very critical in his account of the history and in his interpretation of the text, there is a more profound criticism needed of himself. If he does not supply it, it has to be supplied by someone else. That criticism from the realm of interiority is the counterpart of deductions from self-evident, eternal truths in the classical mode, and it works through the exegete's methods, through his attitudes, and so on. It is a type of criticism that is relevant to his work and consequently that will attack, on the level of his methods, the source of whatever aberrations may arise. In other words, it is the question of positions and counterpositions, not on the philosophical level as outlined in *Insight*, but on a theological level.

8

The Mediation of Christ in Prayer[1]

The notion of mediation begins with Aristotle within the field of logic. He distinguished between first principles, which are immediate, and conclusions, which are mediated by a middle term between the subject and the

1 A lecture given at the Thomas More Institute, Montreal, 24 September 1963. From 15 to 26 July of that same year, Lonergan gave an institute, 'Knowledge and Learning,' in the Graduate School of Gonzaga University, Spokane, Washington. At least some of Lonergan's notes for his lectures at Gonzaga are available in a photocopy of the autograph in File 357, number 1, in the Lonergan Research Institute Library. One of the lectures of the institute was on 'Mediation,' and Lonergan's notes for this lecture (eight typewritten pages) contain an outline of the major portion of the Thomas More lecture. A similar situation obtains between the Gonzaga notes and Lonergan's Thomas More lecture on the analogy of meaning (chapter 9 below).

The autograph itself of Lonergan's Gonzaga lectures on mediation and on the analogy of meaning (and of at least several other lectures in the Gonzaga institute) can be found in a file in the Lonergan Research Institute Archives called 'Various Papers.' The papers in this file are of special importance as well for the Georgetown lectures (Method of Theology) that Lonergan gave in the summer of 1964. For several years our only documentation on the Georgetown lectures was a set of notes provided by Sister Rose Wilker. The notes were brief but gave precious hints on the importance of the lectures for Lonergan's thinking just before the 1965 breakthrough on method. In the summer of 1992 Ivo Coelho, while working on his doctoral dissertation, alerted the editors of the Collected Works to the links between some of these 'Various Papers' and Sister Wilker's notes on the Georgetown lectures.

We have no verbatim record of the Gonzaga institute, but copies of personal notes by Jean-Marc Laporte and Bernard Tyrrell (Lonergan Research Institute

predicate. In the *Posterior Analytics*, book 2, chapter 4, he states, '... syllogism proves an attribute of a subject through the middle term.'[2] A first principle admits no middle term because it cannot be proved. Things that are proved are proved insofar as a middle term is inserted between the subject and the attribute. All men are mortal. Why? Because what is composite, what is put together, can come apart. All men are composite; they consist of parts. Consequently they can come apart, and their coming apart in a bad way is dying. The middle term 'compositeness' explains why the predicate 'mortal' is found in the subject 'man.' Just to drive home this use of the words 'middle' and 'mediation': in the middle term, the attribute is nonmediated; it is immediate, *amesos*. Where there is a conclusion predicated of the subject, a concluded attribute predicated of the subject, the attribute is mediated in the subject.

Hegel, because he was presenting an idealist philosophy in the form of a logic, extended the notion of mediation to everything. If everything aspires to the conceptual, then, to take one example, the ideal of a common law in

---

Library, File 357, numbers 2 & 3), who participated in the institute, indicate that Lonergan included a small section at the end of the lecture on 'Mediation of God.' The autograph also contains a handwritten mention of this topic. The expansion of this section in the Thomas More lecture (reflected in the title) is undoubtedly traceable to another set of outline notes, 'The Mediation of Christ in Prayer' (Lonergan Research Institute Archives, Batch V, folder 3, item b, 5 pages, handwritten). The close correspondence between these notes and the last section of the Thomas More lecture dealing specifically with this application of mediation suggests that Lonergan prepared this second set of notes for the Thomas More lecture. As further evidence, the notes are written on the reverse side of a first-page outline for 'Theology 101' in the Theology Department, Loyola College – most likely the scrap paper at hand in the room of the Loyola Jesuit Community where Lonergan was staying before the lecture.

While a graduate student in Toronto in the 1970s, Mark D. Morelli made a transcription (Lonergan Research Institute Library, Toronto, File 373) of the tape recording (TC 373) of this Thomas More lecture. Later he integrated the eight pages of notes on 'Mediation' with the transcription and edited the lecture for publication under the Thomas More title in *Method: Journal of Lonergan Studies* 2:1 (March 1984) 1–20. For the present version we worked directly from the tape recording of the Thomas More lecture. We have retained most of the decisions that Morelli made in his editing, but we judged that for the sake of history our text should present the Thomas More lecture, with the additional material from Lonergan's Gonzaga notes (LGN) given in footnotes.

2 Aristotle, *Posterior Analytics*, II, 4, 91a 14–15, trans. G.R.G. Mure, in *The Basic Works of Aristotle* (see above, chapter 2, note 6) 162.

which things are not fully thought out – the judge uses a good deal of discretion in settling a case – is inferior, as Hegel judged, to such a code of law as is represented by the Napoleonic Code. Similarly for everything: everything aspires to the level of the *Begriff*, to the level of the concept. The relations between concepts, consequently, are found in an imperfect form on an inferior level in everything else. They are just processes towards the concept. Consequently, in Hegel the notion of mediation takes on a universal role. On Hegel's use of the notion of mediation in its fundamental character in his philosophy, there is the book by my friend Henri Niel, who teaches philosophy in the Institut Catholique de Lyon; the title is *De la Médiation dans la philosophie de Hegel.*[3]

We shall use the word 'mediation' in a broad sense, in a universal way, as did Hegel. But we shall not do so on Hegelian presuppositions of an idealism.

Our assumption, then, shall be that the usage of the words 'immediate' and 'mediate' or 'mediated' in Aristotle can be generalized. For example, in Aristotelian logic the first principles are necessary, evident, true – necessarily true, and of their nature evident. In them necessity, evidence, and truth are immediate. And while in the conclusions you have necessity and evidence and truth, still it is a mediated necessity, a mediated evidence, a mediated truth. If we generalize the Aristotelian notion of the immediate and the mediated, then we can say of any factor, quality, property, feature, aspect that has, on the one hand, a source, origin, ground, basis, and on the other hand, consequences, effects, derivatives, a field of influence, of radiation, of expansion, or that has an expression, manifestation, revelation, outcome – we can say that this factor, quality, property, feature, or aspect is immediate in the source, origin, ground, or basis, and on the other hand is mediated in the consequences, effects, derivatives, outcome, in the field of influence, radiation, expansion, in the expression, manifestation, revelation.

Consequently, the notion of mediation, under the influence of this generalization, becomes an extremely vague notion. It is even more general than the notion of causality, and its significance arises, not in that vague-

3 Henri Niel, *De la Médiation dans la philosophie de Hegel* (Paris: Aubier, 1945). Fr Henri Niel, SJ, was instrumental in having the *verbum* articles translated into French, tried to interest Lonergan in giving some lectures in France (Lonergan's letter to F.E. Crowe of 11 December 1962), and contributed to *Spirit as Inquiry*, the *Festschrift* published for Lonergan when he reached the age of sixty (see below, chapter 10, note 3). Further on Niel, see above, chapter 5, note 30.

ness, but in the patterning that the notion of mediation itself can accept. This vagueness remains something that is material, and what becomes significant lies in the distinctions that we shall draw between a general notion of mediation, of which I have given you a definition – I will offer illustrations immediately – and secondly, mutual mediation; thirdly, self-mediation (and that in three forms: by physical parts, by consciousness, and by self-consciousness); and finally, mutual self-mediation. So we have: mediation in general, mutual mediation, self-mediation under the three forms of displacement upwards, displacement inwards, and deliberate transposition of center, and finally, mutual self-mediation.

When we use the word 'mediation' we are not settling anything specific or even anything determinately generic. We are using a very general expression that distinguishes between a source, an origin, a ground, a basis, and whatever results from it. But the interest will arise insofar as we proceed to the further notions of mutual mediation, self-mediation, and mutual self-mediation.

1 Mediation in General

To illustrate mediation in general we will offer four types of examples: one mechanical, one organic, one psychic, and one logical.

1.1 A Mechanical Example

In a watch, movement is immediate in the mainspring. Provided the watch is wound, the mainspring keeps things moving. The movement of the other parts is mediate; it is mediated by the mainspring, and it brings to light the function of the mainspring, which is to move itself and the other parts. But besides movement, there is control. It is not enough for a watch to be going; it also has to keep time. For it to keep time there is need of a control; and the function of control is immediate in the balance wheel and is mediated in the subsequent series of wheels and levers that are controlled by the balance wheel. The balance wheel is the source of control for itself, with some approximation to a simple harmonic motion that has a constant period. That constancy is transmitted from the balance wheel through the gate and escapement to all the other parts of the watch. Again, control is immediate in the balance wheel and mediated in the other parts of the watch; movement is immediate in the mainspring and mediated in the other parts of the watch.

1.2 Organic Examples

The supply of fresh oxygen is immediate in the respiratory system but is mediated in the rest of the body. It comes from the fresh air breathed in by the lungs. The flow of blood is immediate in the heart – the central pump is the reason for the circulation of the blood – but that flow is mediated in the arteries and veins. The source is the heart; the mediation is elsewhere. Nutrition is immediate in the digestive system and mediated in the rest of the body. Locomotion is immediate in the muscles, mediated in the rest of the body. Control is immediate in the nervous system, mediated in the rest of the body.

1.3 A Psychic Example

Next, a psychic example.[4] Anger, one can say, is immediate in what moderns call aggressivity and the medieval writers called the *irascibile.* But anger is not only in aggressivity (considering aggressivity as an organic part with a psychic correspondent), but it is mediated in the eyes, the look, the voice, the jutting jaw, the up-raised hand, the forward step, the violent images, the one-track thinking, the vigor of the will, of the angry man. It spreads out through consciousness into all parts. It is immediate in aggressivity or the *irascibile,* but it is mediated in the rest of consciousness.

1.4 A Logical Example

Finally, to revert to Aristotle, we have a logical example. Truth, evidence, necessity are immediate in first principles. They are there not because of something else but because of the nature of first principles themselves. But truth, evidence, and necessity are mediated in all conclusions.

So much for the general notion of mediation. Now, as I said, the interest of the term is not in the generality of an origin and consequences that can be applied in almost a hundred ways to an endless numbers of things, but in its further complications. And so we move on to the notion of a mutual mediation, the notion of the functional whole.

4 LGN (see note 1 above): 'What is immediate in intelligence (or will or senses or imagination or memory or affectivity or aggressivity) is mediated throughout the rest of consciousness and in bodily manifestations.'

2 Mutual Mediation: The Functional Whole

A functional whole is constituted by mutually mediating parts. Again, we will illustrate on different levels.

2.1 A Mechanical Example

We have already taken an example of mediation on the mechanical level, from the watch. But it is also a case of mutual mediation. The balance wheel controls itself and all the other moving parts, including the mainspring; and the mainspring moves itself and all the other parts, including the balance wheel. This is a mutual mediation. The functional whole is so constructed that there are different centers of immediacy and the mediations of different immediate centers overlap, so that a watch does not merely move or merely keep time; it does both. It has a constant movement, and consequently that *is* keeping time. You have to combine a principle both of control and of movement to have a watch. If you do not have a principle of movement your watch is not going; if you do not have a principle of control it does not keep time. You have to have these two combining. You get them combining by a mutual mediation. The balance wheel controls itself and the mainspring; the mainspring moves itself and the balance wheel. When you have this mutual mediation, you have the functional whole; it closes in on itself. So a watch is not merely a material whole, a case and what is inside the case; it is also a functional whole. There are different centers of immediacy, and their mediation spreads through the other centers. The two immediate functions mediate each other.

2.2 Organic Examples

An organism is a material whole, the skin and what is inside it. It is also a functional whole, a case of mutual mediation. And it is alive; the mechanism of the watch is not alive. But insofar as we consider an organism, not qua alive but as a functional whole, we find it is a matter of mutual mediation. The respiratory system supplies fresh oxygen not merely to the lungs but to the whole body. The digestive system supplies nutrition not merely to the digestive tract but to the whole body. The nervous system supplies control not merely to the nervous system but to the whole body. And the muscles supply locomotion not merely to the muscles but to the whole body. The result is something that has fresh oxygen and is nourished, is under control and is moving, because you have a number of immediate centers, and from each center there flows over the whole the consequences of that center.[5]

2.3 A Psychic Example

We said that anger is immediate in one's aggressivity but mediated in one's voice, look, eyes, jaw, raised arm, step forward, rancorous memories, violent images, one-track thinking, and vigor of will. But there is a mutual mediation because one's posture, one's look, one's imagination, one's will, one's thinking are typical of the angry man. The anger grows, and one tends towards an explosion. There is a mutual mediation or a feedback from the results of the anger into the causes of the anger.

2.4 A Scientific Example

Finally, we will take an example on the level of mind. Aristotelian logic has one immediate, and everything else is mediated. Necessity, evidence, truth are immediate in first principles and mediated in conclusions. But in empirical science there are two immediates. Empirical science is empirical through its attention to data; and it is science through inquiry, insights, hypotheses, deductions from hypotheses, processes of verification, and so on. What is scientific is immediate in the intellectual effort and work, in the inquiries, the insights, the hypotheses, the deductions. Empirical science is science because of that intellectual element. It is empirical because of the data. It is not like Aristotelian logic, in which there is only one immediate and everything else is mediated. There are two principles of immediacy, and the result is a compound as in the watch, a compound of functions, a mutual mediation that is known as empirical science.[6]

I have illustrated the notion of mediation in general and mutual mediation. I move on to the notion of self-mediation.

5 LGN: 'The whole organism (the sum of its parts, organs) has fresh oxygen from the respiratory system, nutrition from the digestive and vascular systems, local motion from the muscles, control from the nervous system. Each function of the organism is immediate in some organ or set of organs and mediated in the rest of the organs. If the immediate functions are A, B, C, D, E, ... and the mediated functions are respectively a, b, c, d, e, ..., then mutual mediation implies that A is abcde ..., B is abcde ..., C is abcde ..., D is abcde ..., and E is abcde ...'

6 LGN: 'The empirical element is immediate in data, mediated in empirical science. The scientific, systematic element is immediate in the hypothesis, mediated in empirical science.'

3 Self-mediation

3.1 The Living Organism

We can think of self-mediation as a whole that has consequences that change the whole. The first example is the organism. Both machines and organisms are functional wholes, but machines are made while organisms grow. The growth of an organism is a self-mediation. It originates itself by giving rise to physical parts within itself. The process is a process of division. The organism starts from a single cell, and by a process of division it proceeds to a structure of 2^n cells. That process of division is governed by a finality, as is illustrated by Driesch's experiments on sea urchins.[7] He placed the single cells between two plates of glass such that the division could not occur in accord with the structure of the sea urchin; and he discovered that if the sea urchin was allowed to grow up to, say, the sixteen-cell stage or, perhaps, the thirty-two-cell stage, and then the plates of glass were removed, it would correct the previous distortion and become a normal sea urchin. However, if it was kept between the two plates of glass for longer than that, it would never recover. These experiments were designed to show that there is no geometric pattern governing the way cells divided, but that there is a certain finality within the organism itself.

Now at any stage of its growth, the organism is alive at that stage and preparing later stages. As alive at that stage, it is a set of functional parts in a functional whole. There are different centers of immediacy, and the centers make the whole, giving the whole all the properties of each of the centers of immediacy. But as moving from one stage to another, it will also exhibit transitional developments, useful for a time but later disappearing. It is extremely useful for the infant to be able to feed at the breast, but it is just a transitional development. On the other hand, there are anticipatory developments that have no great utility at any particular given stage but are extremely useful later on. For example, the size of the child's brain is out of proportion to the rest of its body, but the brain does not increase in bulk the way the rest of the body does. In other words, there is something more to the organism than mutual mediation. There is the structuring that regards both functioning at the moment *and* future functioning.

7 Hans Driesch, 'Die isolirten [sic] Blastomeren des Echinidenkeimes,' in *Archiv für Entwicklungsmechanik der Organismen* 10, ed. Wilhelm Roux (September 1900) 361–410.

When one compares successive stages, one finds not merely an increase in size but a process of specialization, of differentiation. What earlier is performed in rudimentary, global fashion by single parts, later is performed in a specialized, highly efficient fashion by different parts. This process of specialization, of differentiation, is not just a matter of greater complexity – as in a Rube Goldberg cartoon, if I'm not referring to something a little too ancient – that would involve mounting inefficiency (more and more roundabout procedures) and mounting fragility (more parts to go wrong).[8] The process of specialization also involves the creation and exploitation of entirely new possibilities. The displacement upwards is not merely the multiplication of cells from the single-cell stage to a later stage where there are 2^n cells. Not only the single cell but also the 2^n cells are a mere substratum; and the organism lives – it has a reality that is something superior to the whole business of cells and their differentiation and specialization. The living of the organism is something quite different in kind from the living of the single cell or the multitude of single cells. It is the living of a whole organism. You can change all the cells every seven years, but you have this higher set of functions that emerge on this basis and develop and sustain themselves, as it were, on a higher level. There is, in that self-mediation of the first kind (the development of the organism), a displacement upwards, a displacement from the one or 2^n cells to the life of the organism which is something different from the life of the cells.[9]

Similarly, one can apply the notion of mediation not only to the single organism but also to the species.[10] The species may be said to mediate itself by the individuals. What lives does not live alone, and what grows also dies. But the species mediates itself by reproduction. Within the genus, the lower species mediate the emergence and sustenance of higher species. Trees do not grow in desert sand but in soil; herbivorous animals presuppose vegetative life; and carnivorous animals presuppose herbivorous animals.

3.2 Consciousness

We have been applying the notion of mediation to self-mediation, the

8 The expressions in parentheses are added from LGN.

9 LGN: 'The end, the *telos*, is the self-developing and self-sustaining functional whole that develops through the development, and functions through the functioning of its parts.'

10 LGN: 'From the particular living thing one can shift to the larger whole of the concrete universal.'

whole that becomes something different through its consequences, its outcome, its results. That difference consists in a displacement upwards. But there is another type of self-mediation; it is a displacement inwards, the displacement from the living of the tree to the living of the animal. This displacement inwards is consciousness. The organism mediates itself by developing physical parts and functioning by the functioning of the parts. The animal mediates itself not only organically but also intentionally. What is meant by the intentional? We shall attempt to indicate it by considering first the intentional element, and then the intentional summation.

3.2.1 The Intentional Element

The intentional element consists in three parts or aspects: the act of intending, the intended object, and the intending subject. The act of intending is any act or simultaneous set of acts that occur within consciousness.[11] It is apprehensive in hearing, smelling, moving, seeing, touching, tasting. It is integrated over time by memory and anticipative imagination. It is dynamic by affectivity or aggressivity. The intended object is made present to the subject by the act of intending. The subject is constituted as present to itself by the same act of intending.

We have used the word 'presence' twice but in two different senses.[12] One can say that the table is present in the room. One can say that you are present to me. But for you to be present to me I have to be present to myself, and my being present to myself is a different sense of the word 'presence' from the sense employed when I say that you are present to me. This presence of the subject to himself is not the result of some act of introspection, some act of reflection. The subject has to be present to himself for there to be anything within consciousness on which one could reflect, into which one could introspect. Were being conscious simply a matter of being looked at, then one would not be conscious when one is not looking at oneself, and one would still be unconscious when one did, because what one would look at would be something unconscious. The looking does not change its object.

11 A few years later (*Method in Theology* 30) Lonergan will 'distinguish non-intentional states and trends from intentional responses,' illustrating states by fatigue and so on, and illustrating trends by hunger and so on. Fatigue and hunger are within consciousness, but are probably not 'acts' in Lonergan's sense, so the statement of the lecture can stand.

12 On 'presence,' see above, chapter 5, note 21.

Consciousness is a presence of the subject to himself that is distinct from, but concomitant with, the presence of objects to the subject.

That is what I call the intentional element.

3.2.2 The Intentional Summations

What we are familiar with are the summations of intentional elements. Intentional acts are summated into living: the accumulation of experience, the acquisition of skills, of habits, of ways of doing things. Objects are summated into situations, and the summation of situations is the environment, the world, the horizon. Subjects are summated into the intersubjectivity of community, into 'we,' into the family, the swarm, the flock, the herd, the group. 'We' apprehend together the common situation, act together in the common situation, communicate about the common situation, live a common life, and share a common destiny. The summation of intentional acts, then, is threefold: (1) the summation of the acts themselves, which is one's living; (2) the summation of objects into situations, into a world; and (3) the summation of subjects into a 'we' who live together and perform all the operations of life, not singly as so many isolated monads but as a 'we.'

Now there is intentional mediation of the whole. The animal is an organism but it is also conscious. It moves within the intentional order, and just as the self-mediation that constitutes the growth or development of the organism involves a displacement upwards, so the intentional order involves a displacement inwards to the subject of consciousness. It also involves an extension outwards. The tree can respond only to things that act upon it, but the animal can respond to anything it perceives, to anything it apprehends. Finally, the displacement inwards gives rise to the group, to the 'we.'

3.3 Self-consciousness

A third form of self-mediation is self-consciousness. The animal mediates itself by intentionality. Still, the intentionality of the animal is not autonomous. The animal lives by instinct, and the instincts translate into consciousness the needs and functions of the animal. The animal does not plan, think out new plans and jettison old plans of animal living. Its mode of living is something that is settled, as we say, by instinct, by its nature. But human development is the mediation of autonomy. The child wants to do things for himself. Up to the age of one or two or three, everything is done for him; but the boy will quickly be saying, 'Let me do it! Let me do it!' He wants to tie his shoes for himself, put on his own clothes, and so on. The boy wants to decide for himself. There is the emergence of willpower and 'won'tpower'; he wants to make the decisions. The adolescent wants to find out for himself. Bringing up the child, educating the boy, the adolescent, the young man, is a matter of gradually enlarging the field in which he does things for himself, decides things for himself, finds out for himself. This process reaches its climax, its critical and decisive phase, when one finds out for oneself what one can make of oneself, when one decides for oneself what one is to be, when one lives in fidelity to one's self-discovery and decision. It is the existential moment that the drifter never confronts. He thinks as everybody thinks, he says what everybody says, he does what everybody does, and so do they. The mass of unauthentic humanity lacks the courage to take the risk of thinking things out for themselves – they might very well be wrong if they did. It lacks the resoluteness that decides and the fidelity that stands by its decisions. But the development that reaches its goal in the existential decision and in fidelity to that decision is the emergence of the autonomous subject.

There are, from the very nature of the case, two periods in human life.[13] In the first period one is concerned with objects, with coming to do things for oneself, to decide for oneself, to find out for oneself. This is all about objects. But this process of dealing with objects makes one what one is. One develops habits, becomes a certain kind of man or woman by one's actions. But there is that reflective moment in which one discovers that one is not merely dealing with objects but also making oneself. There arises the question of finding out for oneself what one is to make of oneself, of deciding for oneself what one is to be, and of living in fidelity to one's decisions. Such existential commitment is a disposal of oneself. Within human life, such disposal is not absolute. The firmest resolutions I make today or on New Year's Eve do not predetermine my choices during the subsequent days, or weeks, or months, or even minutes. They all remain free choices afterwards, just as if I had not made the resolution.

13 Compare the point made in Lonergan's trinitarian theology, where he studied the temporal and eternal subjects, and wrote, 'Quibus perspectis, elucet subiecti temporalis duo esse tempora' (*Divinarum personarum* ... [see above, chapter 6, note 7] 179; repeated in the third edition of that work, *De Deo trino*, vol. 2: *Pars systematica* [see above, chapter 2, note 18] 199). It is of some interest that the 1957 volume preceded Lonergan's lectures on existentialism at Boston College, 1957.

One can dispose of oneself but it is not an absolute disposing of oneself; one has to be faithful to it.

Again, this disposing of oneself occurs within community, and particularly in the three fundamental communities:[14] in the mutual self-commitment of marriage, in the overarching commitment to the state, and in the eschatological commitment to the church, the body of Christ, the New Law which is the grace of the Holy Spirit.[15]

Human community, materially, is an aggregate of human beings. But formally, it is an intentional reality, and that intentional reality is not merely a matter of knowing but also of deciding, of commitment. The community is what people mean it to be. Democracy in England and democracy in the United States are both democracy, but they are not democracy in exactly the same sense, because the English tradition and the American tradition are not the same. What is meant within the tradition and by people who live by the tradition is not exactly the same. There are as many kinds of states, as many kinds of homes, as there are different ideas of the state, of the family – the effective ideas of the community, ideas that are lived. To change the received idea of a community is to change the reality itself; as people have a different idea of the state, the state becomes something else; as they have a different idea of marriage, married life becomes something else. If you change the normative meaning – not merely the effective meaning but what ought to be, what people think ought to be – you change the possible attainment of community.

Just as we extended the notion of mediation in the case of the organism to the perpetuation of the species, so we can say that the community mediates itself in its history. The community is constituted by its common sense, its common meaning, its common commitment, its common apprehension of what the community is and what being a member of the community implies. That idea may be full or vague and sketchy; it may be satisfactory or unsatisfactory. But living that idea gives rise to situations; and if the situations that arise are deplorable, unsatisfactory, either that common sense of

14 There is regular reference from now on to these three communities, generally in the context of the three fundamental loves: of family, of one's fellow human beings, and of God. But this may be the first occurrence of the idea in its present form; the three communities listed in 'The Role of a Catholic University in the Modern World' (*Collection* [see above, chapter 2, note 13] 108–13, at 109) are characterized not by the object loved but by levels of consciousness.

15 LGN: 'By existential commitment one disposes of oneself, and one does so in love, in loyalty, in faith.'

community is corrected or it is not, and then there arises the course of the history of that idea of the community. The community reveals itself to itself by its living, by the way it meets its problems, by its revisions of its common sense, its common meaning, its common commitment, by the way things work out in development and breakdown, by growth and disintegration. By their fruits you shall know them. The history that is written about is the mediation, the revelation, of the common sense of the community. The history that is written is the fully reflective product of that self-manifestation. The two are continuous. The community reveals what it is in its living, and reflection on the living itself, in its problems, its successes, and its failures, reveals the quality of the common sense that constitutes the community. A written history, then, that attempts to think things out is the full stage in the reflection, the manifestation, of what the community is.

As a community mediates itself by its history, so the individual mediates himself, manifests himself objectively to others and to himself, by his living. In one's living one brings to light one's possibilities, and one realizes them in one's self-commitment. One discovers the inadequacies of one's self-discovery and the reservations that cripple one's self-commitment. One is true to oneself or falls short of one's ideals. One recovers oneself in one's repentance and fresh beginnings. The person is autonomous; he is what he has made of himself. But because his present resolutions cannot predetermine his future decisions, he is always until death a piece of unfinished business. Consequently, his living is the manifestation, the mediation, of his existential decisions.

Such is the autonomy of the individual, but it is not the whole story. From the community he has his existence, his concrete possibilities, the constraints that hem him in, the opportunities he can seize and make the most of, the psychological, social, historical achievements and aberrations that constitute his situation. One can perhaps think of destiny as the working out of individual autonomy within the community.[16]

We have thought of history as the mediation of the community and of its common sense, as the manifestation of the constitutive common sense of the community. We have thought of ruling one's life as the mediation of the existential decision by which the individual constitutes himself as autonomous. And perhaps we can think of individual destiny as the work-

16 LGN: 'and so the summation of destinies in a community is the history of the community.'

ing out of autonomy within, under the conditions of, human community. That brings us to our final complication of the notion of mediation, namely, mutual self-mediation.

4 Mutual Self-mediation

We started off from an extremely general and tenuous notion of mediation: anything is immediate insofar as it is a source, basis, ground; anything is mediated insofar as it is a result, consequence, outcome, insofar as it arises in a field of radiation, expansion, influence, insofar as it manifests, expresses, reveals, the basis.[17] We used that general notion to form notions of mutual mediation and self-mediation.[18] We distinguished three levels of self-mediation: displacement upwards in the organism, displacement inwards in the animal by consciousness, and finally the deliberate transposition of center that occurs when one becomes a fully autonomous being. One constitutes oneself as an autonomous being by one's existential decision.

But we remarked of existential decision that it occurs in community, in love, in loyalty, in faith. Just as there is a self-mediation towards autonomy, and a mutual mediation illustrated by the organism or the functional whole that is not just a machine, so there is a mutual self-mediation.[19] One's self-discovery and self-commitment is one's own secret. It is not a natural property that you can predicate of all the individuals in a class. It is an idea conceived, gestated, born, within one. It is known by others if and when one chooses to reveal it, and revealing it is an act of confidence, of intimacy, of letting down one's defenses, of entrusting oneself to another. In the process from extroversion, from being poured out on objects, to existential self-commitment, to fidelity, to a destiny, we are not Leibnizian

17 In LGN at this point, this is called 'simple mediation.'

18 LGN: 'Mutual mediation constitutes the functional whole: there are at least two principles, and each mediates the other or others. Self mediation means that the whole has consequences that transform the whole itself.'

19 LGN: 'Its occasion is the encounter, the meeting, keeping company, living together.' Compare, in the 1943 essay 'Finality, Love, Marriage' (*Collection* 17–52, at 31–32): 'startled by a beauty that shifts the center of appetition out of self ... *erôs* leaping in through delighted eyes ... imperious demand for company ... friendship with its enduring basis in the excellence of a good person.' The rest of the present paragraph, too, owes much to that early article of 1943.

monads with neither doors nor windows. We are open to the influence of others, and others are open to influence from us.[20]

Mutual self-mediation occurs in a variety of contexts and to a greater or less extent. Meeting, falling in love, getting married is a mutual self-mediation in which (in the foreign words of Pius XI) the father becomes the head, the mother the heart, of the family.[21] There is a mutual self-mediation in the education of children, of the infant, the child, the boy or girl, the adolescent, the young man or woman. There is a mutual self-mediation in the relationships of mother and child, father and son, and brothers and sisters. And there is mutual self-mediation between equals, between brothers and sisters, between father and mother, husband and wife; and between superiors and subjects, parents and children, teachers and pupils, professors and students, professors and staff, fellow students. There are matrices of personal relations in the neighborhood, in industry and commerce, in the professions, in local, national, and international politics.

To explore this field of mutual self-mediation is perhaps the work of the novelist. In his study of the master and slave, Hegel has given us an instance of the reversal of roles. Because the master makes the slave the slave, the slave is forced to work. He changes from an indolent, shiftless being into someone who does regular hours and works hard, and he becomes a rather fine fellow. The master, because he has everything done for him, ceases to be an upstanding, effective person and becomes rather flabby, becomes more and more dependent on the slave. Hegel works it out rather well and at length in his *Phänomenologie des Geistes*.[22] Gaston Fessard has a similar dialectic of Jew and Greek: the Jew and the Greek both met Christ, but the Jew changed from a member of the chosen people to one of those who had rejected Christ; the Greek was a pagan following the idols, adoring the idols, and leading a very unsatisfactory moral life; his meeting with Christ resulted in the transformation of a member of the goyim into a member of the body of Christ.[23]

20 The final words of this sentence are not clear, due to a changeover to side B of the cassette; and the reel recording carries the same distortion. Nor is the wording clear on the photocopy of LGN with which we worked. The suggested wording retains the balanced expression of the sentence.

21 'Si enim vir est caput, mulier est cor ...' *Casti connubii, DB* 2223, *DS* 3709.

22 G.W.F. Hegel, *Phänomenologie des Geistes* (Frankfurt am Main: Suhrkamf, 1970) 145–55; in English, *Phenomenology of Spirit*, trans. A.V. Miller (Oxford: Oxford University Press, 1977) 111–19.

23 Gaston Fessard, *De l'Actualité historique* (Paris: Desclée de Brouwer, 1960) 40–52, where the dialectic is used as a paradigm for historical interpretation.

Mutual self-mediation provides the inexhaustible theme of dramatists and novelists. It is also the imponderable in education that does not show up in charts and statistics, that lies in the immediate interpersonal situation which vanishes when communication becomes indirect through books, through television programs, through teaching by mail.

We have considered a long series of applications of the notion of mediation in a way that has no dependence on Hegelian logic with its idealist presuppositions, that rests simply on generalizing the notion of mediation found in Aristotle. Aristotle conceived only necessity, evidence, truth as a field in which there is the immediate and the mediated. By considering any factor, property, aspect to be immediate in one location and mediated in other locations, I have attempted to show how the notion of mediation can develop into a pattern of structures of mutual mediation, self-mediation, and mutual self-mediation.[24] That will do, I think, for the part of our talk having to do with the notion of mediation. We will go on now to apply this notion of mediation to the mediation of Christ in prayer.

5 The Mediation of Christ in Prayer

To apply what we have said about mediation in general to prayer, we

24 LGN: 'Our consideration of mediation has yielded a number of terms and analogies. We generalized Aristotle's mediation of truth, evidence, and necessity to any kind of consequence, result, manifestation. We went on to consider mutual mediation on the levels of mechanics, the organism, consciousness, and mind. We conceived three levels of self-mediation, of the whole having consequences that transform the whole. We had occasion to speak of growth, consciousness, autonomy, of displacement upwards, displacement inwards, and the consequent deliberate shift of center. We made mention of evolution, encounter, community, history, and destiny, and we have considered mutual self-mediation.

'I have spoken of such different instances of mediation that I may have produced mere bewilderment. The bewilderment arises perhaps because mediation is an even less determinate notion than causality. Hence, to say that A mediates B may mean any of a vast variety of things, and to know any of them is entirely a matter of studying them. The word 'mediation' does not teach us anything whatever about mechanics, biology, sensitive consciousness, rational autonomy. Still, mediation is not without significance. From simple mediation one passes to mutual mediation, an understanding of automatic devices, of organic functions, of functions within consciousness, of the difference between Aristotelian syllogistic and the method of empirical science. From mutual mediation one passes to three types of self-mediation, of the self-transforming whole. Finally, mutual mediation and self-mediation combine in mutual self-mediation.'

have to pick out a particular aspect of mediation. Our question is not about all the ways in which mediation can be applied to Christ, but about one particular way in which it is relevant to prayer. Mediation is an open notion, an open pattern of concepts, and can be applied in an extremely large number of manners. I will indicate, first of all, the obvious ways in which we spontaneously think of its objective application, and then go on to what I think is significant in prayer, namely, its subjective application.

5.1 *Objective Application*

Spontaneously, we think of Christ objectively in terms of Galatians 4.4–6: 'In the fullness of time God sent his Son, made under the law, made of woman, that he may redeem those under the law. And because we were made sons of God, he sent his Holy Spirit into our hearts crying, "Abba, Father!"'[25] Christ appears to us in terms of the love of Christ: 'Greater love than this no man hath, that he should lay down his life for his friends;'[26] in terms of the precept of Christ: 'A new commandment I give unto you: Love one another as I have loved you.'[27] The precept of charity was given not only by Christ, but it was only Christ that could give the precept, 'Love one another as I have loved you.' The example of Christ in his life, in his suffering and death, is set before us through all our religious teaching; and the work of Christ – in his redemption, in his sacrifice, in his satisfaction, and in the church that carries on his work – is all before us. Christ mediates between us and the Father, and the Holy Spirit mediates between us and Christ. That Christ mediates between us and the Father we find in 1 Timothy 2.5: 'There is one God and there is one mediator between man and God, the man Jesus Christ';[28] and that the Spirit mediates between us and Christ we find in 1 Corinthians 12.3: 'No one can say that Jesus is Lord

25 NRSV: 'But when the fullness of time had come, God sent his Son, born of a woman, born under the law, in order to redeem those who were under the law, so that we might receive adoption as children. And because you are children, God has sent the Spirit of his Son into our hearts, crying, "Abba! Father!"'

26 NRSV: 'No one has greater love than this, to lay down one's life for one's friends' (John 15.13).

27 NRSV: 'I give you a new commandment, that you love one another. Just as I have loved you, you also should love one another' (John 13.34).

28 NRSV: 'There is one God; there is also one mediator between God and humankind, Christ Jesus.'

except in the Holy Spirit, and no one in the Holy Spirit says anathema to Jesus.'[29]

This is all an account of Christ as mediator in the objective field.

5.2 *Subjective Application*

There is also another approach. In this we can see Christ as immediate and as mediator. Each of us is to himself something immediate: oneself as one is, oneself as *Existenz*, as capable of a decision that disposes of oneself and yet incapable of an absolute disposition; all that is to be known about oneself by analysis, by insight – yet not as so known, but rather as lived, as the *vécu* not the *thématique*, as the *actus exercitus* not the *actus signatus*. It is oneself as a prior given to oneself, all the data on one's spontaneity, one's deliberate decisions, one's living, one's loving. It is not one's thinking about all that but each of us in his or her immediacy to himself or herself.

Now in that immediacy there are supernatural realities that do not pertain to our nature, that result from the communication to us of Christ's life. In the Gospel of St John, in the first part, 'life' is a recurrent theme that begins in the prologue – 'In him was life and the life was the light of the world'[30] – and culminates, perhaps, in chapter 10: 'I have come that they may have life and have it more abundantly.'[31] 'Life' is a dominant theme in that first part; 'loving' becomes a dominant theme in the second part of John's Gospel. We are temples of the Holy Spirit; we are not our own. St Paul expresses this reality in an extremely vivid, vigorous, almost vulgar passage in 1 Corinthians 6.15–19: 'Shall I take the members of Christ and make them the members of a harlot? You are not your own – *non estis vestri* – you are temples of the Holy Spirit, you do not belong to yourselves.'[32] Temples of the Holy Spirit, we are members of Christ: 'Saul, Saul, why persecuteth thou me?'[33] Paul did not persecute Jesus; he perse-

29 NRSV: 'Therefore I want you to understand that no one speaking by the Spirit of God ever says "Let Jesus be cursed!" and no one can say "Jesus is Lord" except by the Holy Spirit.'

30 NRSV: 'What has come into being in him was life, and the life was the light of all people' (John 1.3–4).

31 NRSV: 'I came that they may have life, and have it abundantly' (John 10.10).

32 NRSV: 'Do you not know that your bodies are members of Christ? Should I therefore take the members of Christ and make them members of a prostitute? ... Or do you not know that your body is a temple of the Holy Spirit within you, which you have from God, and that you are not your own?'

33 NRSV: 'Saul, Saul, why do you persecute me?' (Acts 9.4)

cuted the Christians; but there was an identification between them and Christ. We are adoptive children of God the Father.

That is our reality, the higher part of our reality. It is something in us that is immediate and becomes mediated by the life of prayer. It is not immediate in the sense in which our bodies and our souls are immediate to us. They are ours by nature. Being a temple of the Holy Spirit, a member of Christ, an adoptive child of God the Father, is something that is ours essentially by a gift. Still, in the concrete, it is part of our concrete reality, and in that sense it proceeds through the mediation of prayer from being a sort of vegetative living to a conscious living. It can be merely a vegetative living, if one is in the state of grace, if one keeps out of sin, if one does good deeds. One does all this only by the grace of God. But its occurring only by the grace of God is not something with a label on it. It just occurs, and we do not stop to think. It is a life within us that goes on, that is promised to us by Christ, that fructifies in us. Our ideas about it can be as vague and inconsequential as the ideas of Topsy: when she was asked how she came into the world she said, 'Ah 'spect ah just grow'd.' But this life of grace within us can become a habitual conscious living. When I say 'habitual' I mean that one is not thinking of it all the time but that one easily reverts to it, that one can be, as it were, distracted from worldliness in as easy and as spontaneous a manner as when one in love is distracted from everything except the beloved. It is not a matter of study of oneself or analysis of oneself. It is a living, a developing, a growing, in which one element is gradually added to another and a new whole emerges. That transformation is the mediation of what is immediate in us. What is immediate in us is that de facto we are temples of the Spirit, members of Christ, and adoptive children of the Father, but in a vegetative sort of way. That can move into our conscious living, into our spontaneous living, into our deliberate living; and that is growth in prayer.[34]

Just as we are immediate to ourselves by consciousness without any self-knowledge, and through our consciousness by philosophic study and self-appropriation we can come to a fuller knowledge of ourselves, so also what we are by the grace of God, by the gift of God, can have an objectification within us. What is immediate can be mediated by our acts, and gradually reveal to us in an ever fuller fashion, in a more conscious and more

34 This is an implicit application of the turn from substance to subject (see note 27 to chapter 3 above), made explicit in the 1964 lecture '*Existenz* and *Aggiornamento*.'

pressing fashion, the fundamental fact about us: the great gift and grace that Jesus Christ brought to us.

This mediation is potentially universal. The precept is 'Pray without ceasing' (1 Thessalonians 5.17). In loving our neighbor we are loving Christ. In making ourselves good Christians and better Christians we are loving Christ. In this process, which is universal, which can regard every act, thought, word, deed, and omission, there is a complete universality, a possibility of the complete growth of every aspect of the person. And in that growth, not only is there the mediation of the subject by his acts, but the acts have as always an object, and in that object the center, the focal point, is Christ. It is Christ, not as apprehended by the apostles, by Paul and John, by the church, by Christ himself, by the Spirit; it is our *own* apprehension of him. It is, as it were, putting on, acquiring, our own view of him. We put on Christ in our own way, in accord with our own capacities and individuality, in response to our own needs and failings. It has its foundation in tradition and revelation, but it arises from what is immediate in the subject. It develops in response to the capacities, the needs, and the growth of the subject.

It is, then, a self-mediation. There is the mediation by our acts of what is immediate in us through the grace of God. Though the object of those acts is not exclusively Christ – it is everything – still, everything turns back to Christ in one way or another. That is, it is not merely a self-mediation in which we develop, but it is a self-mediation through another. One is becoming oneself, not just by experiences, insights, judgments, by choices, decisions, conversion, not just freely and deliberately, not just deeply and strongly, but as one who is carried along. One is doing so not in isolation, but in reference to Christ. The Father predestined us to be conformed to the image of his Son, through the merits of Christ, through the grace of Christ, through the example of Christ. Consequently, there is an element not merely of personal development, but of personal development in relation to another person.

This development of the person in relation to another person is not only a self-mediation through another; it is a mutual self-mediation. It is not a mutual self-mediation like that between equals, between husband and wife, between brothers and sisters; it is not a matter of simultaneous mutual influence. But it is nonetheless a very real mutual self-mediation because Christ himself, as man, developed; he acquired human perfection. The human perfection that he acquired could have been quite different from the perfection that de facto he did acquire. If he sought the perfection that was suitable to him as a divine person, we would not expect it to have been the perfection of a person who lives a life of poverty and suffering, who dies in abandonment, unjustly and cruelly. Christ chose and decided to perfect himself in the manner in which he did because of us. We think of the way of the cross primarily as the cross of Christ. But primarily the way of the cross is the way in which fallen nature acquires its perfection. We attain resurrection through death because death is the wages of sin, and death entered into the world through sin. It was because he was redeeming a fallen humanity that Christ chose to perfect himself, to become the perfect man; by his own autonomous choices, he was thinking of us and thinking of what we needed to be able to attain our own self-mediation. Just as it is by relying on, adverting to, the precepts, the example, the love of Christ that we attain our own self-mediation with reference to him in this life of prayer, so also the life of Christ himself was a self-mediation with reference to others, and the others are we and all men.

The life of prayer, the mediation of Christ in the life of prayer, is then, I should say, a mutual self-mediation. One can think of attaining perfection through suffering, which is the human lot, in terms of abstract principles, of overcoming evil by good, of transforming evil into good, of the general theme of death and resurrection. But instead of an abstract principle we have a mutual self-mediation. We choose that way because, as I said, we choose the cross of Christ: 'If any man would come after me, let him take up his cross daily and follow me.'[35] We think of the cross as the cross of Christ; but primarily the cross is something that belongs to all humanity. Christ chose it because of us, and we choose it because of him.

To carry the point further is, in a sense, a matter only of private meditation, of private living. The life of prayer is something on the level of what is lived, of the *vécu*, and any talk about it is thematizing it. But we have developed some notions, some categories: self-mediation and mutual self-mediation, applied to our own subjectivity, to what is immediate within us; and initially and fundamentally in a very obscure fashion in terms of objects: temples of the Holy Spirit, members of Christ, adoptive children of God the Father, which nevertheless have their subjective manifestation, their revelation in us that they are within us. These objects are the immediate in an ontological immediacy. And that ontological immediacy is pro-

35 NRSV: 'If any want to become my followers, let them deny themselves and take up their cross daily and follow me' (Luke 9.23).

moted to a psychological, an intentional, immediacy through the life of prayer.

The life of prayer, then: Christ is mediator in the life of prayer insofar as the life of prayer itself is a transition from the immediacy of spontaneity through the objectification of ourselves in acts. The acts of living and the acts within praying are referred to Christ. By that process we perfect ourselves, we become ourselves, we become autonomous individuals, we have a self-mediation that is related to another person. There is a similar process in the becoming of Christ as man; and in that case he was becoming himself with reference to us. In both cases the fundamental theorem, as it were, is transforming evil into good, absorbing the evil of the world by putting up with it, not perpetuating it as rigid justice would demand. And that putting up with it acts as a blotter, transforms the situation, and creates the situation in which good flourishes.

9

The Analogy of Meaning[1]

We will attempt to indicate the reality of meaning. We are apt to think that 'sticks and stones may break my bones but names will never hurt me,' that meaning is a minor matter in human life. We wonder what the point of the study of language is, which after all has nothing to do with meaning;[2] or the study of logic, or the study of mathematics, which has more meaning of a different kind. The purpose of my talk tonight is to put together some notions on this subject.[3]

1 A lecture given at the Thomas More Institute, Montreal, 25 September 1963 (and so on the evening after the lecture that appears in the previous chapter was given). A transcription of the tape recording of the lecture and of Lonergan's answer to the first question that followed was made by Philip McShane in April 1973 (File 375, Lonergan Research Institute Library, Toronto). Our editing worked from the original tape recording (TC 375 and 376, Lonergan Research Institute Library) but benefits from McShane's transcription. We also completed transcribing and editing the question session from the tapes.

Lonergan's lecture notes from the Gonzaga University institute 'Knowledge and Learning' earlier in the same summer (see above, chapter 8, note 1, including information given there on the autograph) contain notes for a lecture on the analogy of meaning. We will follow the same policy as in the previous chapter, indicating in footnotes important material from these notes that did not find its way into Lonergan's lecture at the Thomas More Institute. Again, we will use the symbol LGN to refer to these notes.

2 The relative clause is ironic, as is clear from Lonergan's tone of voice.

3 Lonergan added, 'I did it originally from the viewpoint of a book on the method of theology.' Before this talk, Lonergan had given a course 'De methodo theologiae' in the second semester, 1961–62, at the Gregorian University, Rome, and had conducted an institute 'The Method of Theology' at Regis College, Willowdale, Ontario, 9–20 July 1962. In addition, he had given a

The answer to the question, What is the analogy of meaning? would be somewhat technical, but our approach will be rather descriptive. One could start logically by asking, 'What is meaning?' and pointing out that any answer to the question either would have a meaning or it would not. If it had no meaning, it would be useless and senseless; but if it did have a meaning, you would be presupposing what you are talking about; you would be in some sort of a circle. But a second thought on the same topic brings to mind that meaning is in a sense self-explanatory. The meaning of meaning is a meaning. The question answers itself. The present lecture could proceed either analytically or descriptively to state that a little more concretely.

An analytic approach would be through the notion of being, the inquiring mind which intends everything and which unfolds itself on the level of experience (the level of data of sense and/or consciousness), secondly on the level of understanding and conception, and thirdly on the level of reflection and judgment. This gives us a meaning on the level of experience, a meaning on the level of understanding, a meaning of a different type on the level of judgment. The analogy of meaning is simply the comparison of those three levels of operation.

But our procedure, as I said, will be rather descriptive. It will be an enumeration of the realities that result from meaning, that are constituted by meaning. When we speak of meaning as constitutive, we do not mean that meaning is the sole constituent, but that it is *a* constituent. It is something without which that reality does not exist. The theme will be that, while there are many very interesting and very true things that can be said about man without mentioning meaning – because man is subject to the laws of physics, the laws of chemistry, the laws of biology; he is studied in a metaphysical psychology that speaks about potencies and habits and acts; he is a man when he is sound asleep or knocked unconscious or in his infancy or in his doddering senility, and meaning has pretty well nothing to do with that – while all that is true, still, all of man's waking life, all his imaginings, all his feeling, knowing, speaking, doing would undergo an essential

---

previous lecture on 'Time and Meaning' at Regis College, Willowdale, 16 September 1962, as well as at two other locations that same fall (see above, chapter 5). Further, he was soon to add a third lecture on meaning, 'Dimensions of Meaning' (see above, chapter 5, note 1). All of these are sources for understanding the development of his thinking on many fronts, not the least of which is the topic of meaning.

change if meaning were omitted. Meaning is a formal and constitutive element of human living, and to remove meaning is to remove art and symbol, literature and history, natural and human science, families, states, religions, philosophies, and theologies.

1 Meaning as Constitutive of Human Communication

The most obvious field or domain in which meaning is constitutive is human communication. We will consider seven instances or types of human communication. Our purpose will not be to explore any one of the seven but rather to give a rapid survey that will illustrate the different things meant by meaning, and thereby to introduce us to the concrete analogical reality that meaning is.

1.1 Everyday Language

We will consider first of all everyday language. Everyday language is the language of the home, of conversation, of speaking with acquaintances, relatives, friends. It is the language of the schoolroom and playground, of commerce and industry, of newspapers, radio, television, of politics, and of prayer.

In the use of language, and particularly in the use of everyday language, one can distinguish three components, three vectors, three dimensions. First, even though the first person may not be expressed, language usually has a component of the first person; it is expressive of the person; it is somehow in an optative mood, manifesting his desires or his fears or his tendencies. Again, language is in the indicative mood; it sets forth, proposes; it expresses not merely the subject, but also something, it proposes something; as this dimension tends to a pure form, it moves to the third person, the *im*personal. Finally, language *im*presses; as it expresses the speaker, so it impresses on the hearer; it is addressed *to* a second person; it has the imperative mood.

These three components can be separated out, as it were, in special cases. Technical language aims at being strictly impersonal. It speaks in the third person, or impersonally. It aims at being purely indicative. It omits all feeling, all free play of imagination, all verbal flourishes and magic; it is dry as dust. Literary language is a work, a *poiêma*; it is not just said to someone but rhymed and rhythmed, and it may be simply spoken or also written out. When it is written out, it is a permanent but mediate communication;

the person to whom one is speaking is not there; the language is simply written down, and seen later. This written language, this literary language, tries to convey through words what in ordinary speech is communicated by presence, voice, countenance, gesture. Like a musical composition or a play, it has to be reenacted, interpreted. Unless the reader is, as it were, reenacting in himself what is intended to be communicated by the literary language, nothing happens; the books remain on the shelves. C.S. Lewis in a recent book, *An Experiment in Criticism*,[4] made the criterion of the good book the good reader: a good book is a book that is read by a good reader; and he proceeds to define what a good reader is.

Everyday language, on the other hand, is not mediated but immediate; it is to the person there. And it is not permanent but transient; the words are uttered, and they pass on. The language can be purely expressive, as in exclamations (Ah! Ouch!), or purely imperative (Stop!), but commonly it is at once expressive, indicative, and impressive. It is modeled on the human situation. Grammars speak of persons, number, tense, mood, and they reflect the human situation, in which one person speaks to another about a third, at a certain time, in a certain mood. Everyday language develops from an oppressive concreteness. Those of you who have read the first volume of Ernst Cassirer's *Philosophy of Symbolic Forms*[5] will have noticed the way he insists on the concreteness of a primitive language. They do not have a very general term like 'two' but they talk about a pair of this and a couple of that – all the different words we have for 'two' – and so on for everything else.

The significance of everyday language for human existence is illustrated by the well-known description of Helen Keller's discovery of the *word* – the terrific moment in her life when she first discovered the utility of words, the possibility of signifying things through words. That passage in her autobiography provides a very real clue to the profound veneration for the name that we find in ancient cultures.[6] It would seem that the human psyche floats with the weightlessness of images and the caprices of affectivity and aggressivity until it pins things down in words, with names. The image is formed and changes into something else, but if you have a word

4 C.S. Lewis, *An Experiment in Criticism* (Cambridge: Cambridge University Press, 1961).

5 Ernst Cassirer, *The Philosophy of Symbolic Forms*, 3 vols., trans. Ralph Manheim (New Haven: Yale University Press, 1955); vol. 1 is entitled *Language*.

6 Helen A. Keller, *The Story of My Life* (see above, chapter 5, note 15).

you pin down what you are meaning. Our first illustration, then, of the reality of meaning is in the reality of communication by everyday language. The language would be meaningless, would not be language at all, without the meaning. The meaning is constitutive of the communication. Remove the meaning, and the language as such disappears.

1.2 Intersubjective Meaning

A second form of communication I call intersubjective meaning. To form a general idea of it from a concrete instance, think of acting.[7] Or again, think that the transition from spoken to written language involves an enormous abstraction.[8] Contemporary linguistic study is study not of the written but of the spoken word, because spoken language is not merely the use of words but also the use of the presence, the co-presence of persons, and the acting; there is much more that goes on besides the mere utterance of the words. To analyze that further element in communication that I call intersubjective meaning is an occupation of the phenomenologists. Max Scheler wrote a celebrated book on the forms of sympathy, in which he is simply describing the manifestation of a type of meaning that is spontaneous, that is not contained in words but that is a great part of human living.[9]

My own illustration of that is from an experience I had. In my daily walk in Rome there is a ramp up which I go to enter the Borghese Gardens. One day there was a child running in front of its mother, and it stumbled on the concrete. I was at least thirty feet away but spontaneously I leaned forward to prevent the child from falling, although it was a quite useless gesture. There is a community that is prior to the distinction between 'I' and 'thou.' A scream not only startles us but frightens us. The distinction

7 *Understanding and Being* (see above, chapter 2, note 13) throws some light on this cryptic reference to acting; see 'The Dramatic Pattern of Experience,' pp. 328–29: 'To be in the dramatic pattern of experience is to be *not* thinking about it. If I spoke as though I were an actor, I'd be consciously in the dramatic pattern of experience. And being consciously within it is already acting it, or not being in it, in a sense. Insofar as the actor *acts* as though he weren't acting, he is a good actor.'

8 In Lonergan's posthumously published 'Philosophy and the Religious Phenomenon' (*Method: Journal of Lonergan Studies* 12:2 [1994] 125–46) the transition from spoken to written language marks something of a stage of meaning. See editorial note *j* to that article, p. 146.

9 Max Scheler, *The Nature of Sympathy* (see above, chapter 5, note 3).

between me and you, the speaker and the hearer, is something that somehow is subsequent. St Thomas illustrates the mystical body (the church) or the body politic by the fact that, as the arm automatically rises to protect the head against a blow, so there is a similar sympathy between human beings. That part of meaning is already at work before we speak. There is already a meaning in the fact that someone knocks at my door and comes to see me, in his or her coming to me and my going to him or her. The fact of the encounter recalls, releases, sets in motion, the dynamism evoked, developed, modified, by past encounters. There is a mutual recognition, a tacit acknowledgment of the past, an implicit agreement to continue it or to change it, perhaps a struggle for the upper hand as in one-upmanship.

On this level of intersubjective meaning, there is all that is revealed by tone of voice, by cast of features, by the fleeting play of smile, by seriousness, by vivacity, by silence. Human communication is not a matter of a soul hidden in some unlocated recess of the body and employing some Morse code of signals to communicate with others. Rather, there is no separation between soul and body; the bodily presence is the presence of the other to me. Through every shift of eyes, countenance, lips, or color, of voice, tone, volume, or of fingers, hands, arms, the meaning comes through. The soul expresses itself through the body, and the body is not an instrument that is separated from it. It is part of one and the same thing.

1.3 Incarnate Meaning

From intersubjective meaning one can move on very easily to what might be called incarnate meaning. A person, either in his totality or in his characteristic moment, his most significant deed, his outstanding achievement or sacrifice, *is* a meaning. That meaning may be cherished, revered, adored, re-created, lived, or it may be loathed, abominated, contemned. The persons in the drama of the passion and death of Christ all have that embodied and incarnate meaning. Such is the meaning of the crucifix, the meaning of our Lady standing at the foot of the cross, the meaning of Judas, of Peter's denial, and so on. They all contain profound meanings: there is a meaning contained simply in the person, in the person's actions, in the person's deeds. I have given you a religious example, but the same can be verified in national heroes. That type of incarnate meaning is perhaps the fundamental theme in Georges Morel's three volumes on *Le Sens de l'existence chez s. Jean de la Croix.*[10] Heidegger had given us an apostate's view of the meaning of existence, and Fr Morel went to John of the Cross to give us a Christian, a saint's, incarnate meaning of human existence.

1.4 Symbols

A fourth type of meaning, one that again escapes the level of words, of clear concepts, of flat affirmations and negations, is the meaning of the symbol. By a symbol is meant an affect-laden image. There is the image, and either it evokes the affect or the affect evokes it. They correspond to one another. The affect finds expression in the image, resonates in the image, finds form and concreteness in the image; on the other hand, the image is dynamic, alive, moving, insofar as it is connected with the affect. Images or symbols have been studied in many different ways. In the Freudian account, symbols are expressions of family relationships, especially family relationships gone sour, and very sour, as illustrated by the Greek tragedies built about the story of the Seven against Thebes.[11] Carl Jung is concerned with symbols of transformation, of conversion, of death and resurrection, with the preformation, on the level of the unconscious and of the sensitive soul, of man's higher spiritual activities.[12]

Besides these somewhat clinical interests in symbols, there has been a rather detached study of symbols by Gilbert Durand, *Les Structures anthropologiques de l'imaginaire: Introduction à l'archétypologie générale.*[13] He takes as his basis the dominant reflexes. One is going to slip and fall; the spontaneous reflex effort to regain one's equilibrium cuts off any other activity. Similarly, swallowing is a dominant reflex. Durand starts from these dominant reflexes. Knowing about one's equilibrium, maintaining one's equilibrium, is something that we have to learn. Children have to learn to be able to stand up and keep their balance and walk, and they spend a great deal of time in learning all this. Not only do they learn to stand and not tumble, walk and not crawl, but there is a great deal of affective shifting going on at

10 Georges Morel, *Le Sens de l'existence selon s. Jean de la Croix* (see above, chapter 5, note 9). Lonergan's next sentence in the present lecture might clarify a similar reference to Morel and Heidegger at this point in chapter 5.

11 Aeschylus, *Seven against Thebes* (see above, chapter 5, note 5).

12 LGN (see note 1 above): 'The psyche as the born cooperator with the spirit, as anticipating and pre-forming man's spiritual destiny.'

13 Gilbert Durand, *Les Structures anthropologiques de l'imaginaire: Introduction à l'archétypologie générale* (see above, chapter 5, note 6).

the same time. As a result, we think of what is good in connection with what is upright, what ascends, what is moving towards the light; one is assuming a position in which one can freely use one's arms and hands, in which one can hold the sword and the scepter, in which one can manipulate things. All that is good. On the other hand, to fall is to go down to what is dark, into the slime, the mud, into all the symbols of what is disgusting, something that you loathe, that you hate, that terrifies you, that you are afraid of. And so there are built about the dominant reflex of maintaining one's equilibrium symbols of ascension, which are connected with the good, and symbols of the fall, which are connected with everything that you loathe or instinctively hate, that terrifies you, that are horrible, and so on. All these symbols are put together in the image of St George on horseback slaying the dragon. St George has gone up on the horse; he is master of his animals; he is in the position in which he is able to use his arms freely; he is manipulating the spear which he is driving down the dragon's throat. And the dragon is a synthesis of everything you find horrible, disgusting: it is scaly; smoke is issuing from it; it has claws, horrible teeth, and an enormous tail that threatens imminent death. You have all the symbols of ascension and at the same time of the fall combined in that set of symbols, on which Durand spends some 200 pages.

But there is also the transformation of the meaning of the symbols. One can think of falling, but to go down, to descend, is not the same thing. Food descends down your throat in a style that is quite pleasant. It is dark down below; and it is not so terrible. Falling may be terrible, but going down, re-lax-ing, taking things easy, is not so terrible after all. Drop all the effort and tension involved in ascending and mastering. Destroying the enemy – forget about all that! Take things easy. All the symbols of horror and loathing are mitigated into something that is not too bad after all. One gets a synthesis of all these symbols in Jonah and the whale. Like the dragon, the whale is a synthesis of everything that is terrible and horrible and threatening. But Jonah goes down into the whale's belly, and he comes out three days later not the least bit worse off for it.

Finally, there are the symbols of synthesis, the combination of the two attitudes, the possibilities of shifting from one to the other. The tree rises erect from the plain in the sunlight and spreads out its branches and its leaves to obtain energy from the sun through the chlorophyll; but at the same time it sends its roots deep down into the dark soil. The serpent has been described as the animal that is subject to the verb 'to tie': it is what joins together, what links, brings together. The *Tao* of Chinese symbolism has the same sort of meaning. All these meanings exist, and they exist upon a level which is not conceptualized, on the level of the psyche as intersubjective meaning, incarnate meaning, symbolic meaning, particularly the intersubjective and the symbolic – meanings that, in their type, are fully constituted on their own level. It is not that we first have meaning when we inquire and ask, 'What is it?' There is already a meaning for human living on this previous level.

1.5 *Artistic Meaning*

Another form of this type of meaning, though it goes quite beyond it, is artistic meaning. I shall not attempt to offer any analysis of the different forms of art. What satisfies me most of all from the little I have read on the subject is Susanne Langer's *Feeling and Form*,[14] in which there is a general theory of art and its application to the various types of art – painting, sculpture and architecture, dance and drama, various types of poetry, and so on. There is also a book published about two or three years ago by René Huyghe on art and the soul, *L'Art et l'âme.*[15] It is profusely illustrated, and it studies the meaning in pictorial art.

But in general, what is artistic meaning? It is a break from routine meaning. In routine meaning we are the ready-made man in the ready-made world. The meanings are all settled beforehand, and we take them on and fit into them. The light is red and we stop; it is green and we go ahead; that is, as it were, a brief synthesis of the meanings that can dominate the greater part of our lives. The meanings are ready-made, and we put them on like a ready-made suit; they constitute our living. The artistic intention is to break that routine, and by the fact that it is broken there emerges a new subject in a new world, with fresh meaning. And that meaning is again, fundamentally, primarily, the type of meaning of the symbol, of the incarnate meaning; but the artist has to take it and sharpen it, bring it to the point, unfold it, develop it, present it, express it effectively.

We have been talking about meaning as constitutive of communication. We considered everyday language, intersubjective meaning, incarnate meaning in example, affective meaning in the symbol, nonlinguistic expression in art; and we turn, finally, to literary and technical meaning.

14 Susanne K. Langer, *Feeling and Form* (see above, chapter 5, note 13).
15 René Huyghe, *L'Art et l'âme* (Paris: Flammarion, 1960).

1.6 Literary Meaning

The Greeks discovered and formulated logic, and when they had finished they discovered that logic was not the way people de facto think and speak. So they went to work and studied poetics and rhetoric, and worked out the figures of speech. De facto the poet or the orator does not first of all think out what he is going to say and then add on the figures of speech to make it concrete and vivid. His thinking already occurs in this other, not strictly logical form. Besides logic and the logical unfolding of an idea in a treatise, there are also the laws of imagination and of affect, and they are quite distinct from the laws of logic, the laws of the treatise.[16]

Literary meaning floats somewhere in between the two.[17] Besides using the defined concepts and the implications of propositions, literary meaning also exploits intersubjective, incarnate, symbolic, and artistic meaning, and in the measure that this occurs there emerge the modes of thinking, of operating, that were first analyzed, I believe, by Freud in his account of dream work. There is a movement[18] from the class concepts of logic towards the representative figure: think of the first and second Adam. Again, from the univocal concept one moves to simultaneous multiple meanings. A word as well defined, as employed logically, has just one meaning, and one proceeds consistently, always using the word in precisely that sense or giving notice to the contrary; but in the measure that the laws of imagination and affect take over, the same word occurs with several meanings at once, and all are intended.[19] Again, instead of the logical law of excluded middle (either *A* or not-*A*), insofar as the laws of imagination and affect take over, there is overdetermination, ambivalence; there is love, but not merely love, also hate, and with respect to the same object. Again, where the logician will prove, the literary thinker will reinforce, he will repeat, he will enumerate, he will give you variations on the same theme,[20] he will build up accumulations that head to a climax. According to the

16 LGN: 'Properly, logic and the treatise express not facts but ideals. But besides the ideal of clarity and exactitude, embodied in the treatise, there is also the exigence for self-expression and the aim of communication.'
17 LGN: '... between the laws of discursive thought and, on the other hand, the laws of image and affect.'
18 LGN: 'displacement.'
19 LGN gives as examples 'death, life.'
20 LGN adds 'contrast.'

famous phrase of the character (I forget which) in *Alice in Wonderland*, 'When I say something three times, it's true.'[21]

Again, the logical approach is satisfied with the simple negation, It is not so; but the poet posits the object to overcome it, piles up other things against it till it is annihilated. That is the only way imagination and affect can negate. Again, from the single theme, the single level of representation, there is a movement towards condensation, the combination of a whole series of different themes within the same phrase or sentence. This is so conspicuous in Shakespeare, in, for example, the early part of *Macbeth*, when Macbeth states:

> And Pity, like a naked newborn babe,
> Striding the blast, or Heaven's Cherubin, hors'd
> Upon the sightless couriers of the air,
> Shall blow the horrid deed in every eye
> That tears shall drown the wind.

He starts off with pity, a naked newborn babe, which somehow is striding the blast; moves on to heaven's cherubin, horsed on the sightless couriers of the air; and then the horrid deed of murdering the king is blown in every eye, and the eyes start weeping and the wind is drowned. We see here a condensation of a variety of different themes that, from the viewpoint of logical analysis, is very paradoxical but, from the viewpoint of poetic expression, is extremely effective; it fits in with the spontaneous condensations that follow the laws of imagination and affect.

1.7 Technical Meaning

Finally, there is technical meaning. Only primitives get along without any technical meanings at all. The great objection, the standard answer from publishers is, 'The book is too technical for us to publish.' Well, once you get away from the primitives, the technical meanings start. The build-up of technical meanings has been described by Ernst Cassirer in his *Philosophy of Symbolic Forms*,[22] by Karl Jaspers in his book on *The Origin and Goal of His-*

21 Lonergan's memory was somewhat faulty here; the remark he quotes was made by the Bellman at the very beginning of Lewis Carroll, *The Hunting of the Snark: An Agony in Eight Fits* (New York: Mayflower Books, 1980) 3: '"I have said it thrice: What I tell you three times is true."'

22 LGN adds *Essay on Man*.

tory,[23] by Henri Frankfort and others in *Before Philosophy*.[24] Frankfort's work in that book, and also in *Kingship and the Gods*,[25] was exploited by Eric Voegelin in the first volume of his *Order and History*.[26]

Briefly, the ancient high civilizations – Egypt, Babylon, Crete, the valleys of the Indus and the Hwang Ho, the Mayas in Central America, and the Incas in Peru – developed the mechanical arts of irrigation, architecture, tools, and the organizational arts of bookkeeping, the state, armies, navies. But at the summit, they were locked in myth.[27] They would be completely intelligent with regard to anything that was practical. So too, Malinowski speaks of a very primitive tribe in the Trobriand Islands; as far as planting the seed and harvesting the grain was concerned, they were just as intelligent, just as rational, as anybody else; but all the rest of their lives was penetrated through and through by myth and magic.[28] The first high civilizations drove myth and magic right out to the perimeter. They organized the state, they organized any type of material achievement, but their religion, their cosmology, and their politics were penetrated with myth, and the concepts fundamentally were mythological.

The breakdown of these ancient high civilizations resulted in a breakdown of the myth. By revelation in Israel and by the *logos* in Greece, there developed something that met the questions that the myth had met in its own way. Plato's early dialogues depict Socrates asking the Athenians, What is temperance? What is fortitude? What is virtue? What is justice? What is knowledge? While the Athenians knew perfectly well what all these things were, they could not answer Socrates because he had a new gimmick. He wanted universal definitions, definitions that applied *omni et soli*, to every case and to no other. He was introducing a technique of thought, and to introduce that technique was a breakthrough from the hold of imagination and affect upon human thinking. Aristotelian ethics worked out the answers to Socrates' questions, the universal answers, the universal definitions, but these answers were technical. The technical word, technical thinking, was developed particularly in that Greek milieu.

23 Karl Jaspers, *The Origin and Goal of History* (see above, chapter 3, note 38).
24 Henri Frankfort, Henriette Antonia Frankfort, et al., *Before Philosophy: The Intellectual Adventure of Ancient Man* (Harmondsworth, Middlesex: Penguin, 1949, 1963).
25 Henri Frankfort, *Kingship and the Gods* (see above, chapter 7, note 11).
26 Eric Voegelin, *Israel and Revelation* (see above, chapter 3, note 19).
27 LGN: 'King was Son of God, ruler of the cosmos, ruler of the state.'
28 Bronislaw Malinowski, *Magic, Science and Religion* (New York: The Free Press, 1948; reprinted Westport, CT: Greenwood Press, 1984) 17–36.

The transition to technical meaning involves a differentiation of consciousness, a new type of subject that differs from the old as Thales differed from the milkmaid. Thales was gazing at the stars and did not see the well at his feet, and the milkmaid laughed: how on earth can he expect to know anything about the stars when he cannot see a well right at his own feet? But still, Thales had become a different type of psychological subject from the milkmaid. There was a prior period when every subject was just like the milkmaid. This development involves a differentiation of worlds. Eddington speaks of the two tables in his office. One was brown and hard and solid, made of wood, containing drawers, useful; and the other was mostly a vacuum – here and there there were electrons and protons floating about, but you could not *imagine* what they were.[29]

This development involves also a different language. When the chemist or botanist or depth psychologist starts talking to you, he is talking another language, a technical language, a language invented to describe a different world for a different subject.

This development also creates a different society. The man who spends his day doing modern physics and then goes home to his wife and children is migrating from one world to the other. There is a different type of development of understanding, a different type of inquiry and investigation, from that of common sense, one with its own rules, its own criteria, its own laws. There is a movement from 'We both understand what is meant, so why waste our time trying to define it?' to definition; from proverbs, which fulfil the same sort of function as rules of grammar – rules with lots of exceptions, but it is worth while paying attention to them – from proverbs to principles and laws that must hold in absolutely every case or else they are completely worthless; from seeing the point to logical deduction and detailed verification.

I have been speaking of meaning as constitutive of human communication, and I considered some seven ways in which that meaning takes form. There is meaning in everyday language, and if you write out the language you are omitting an awful lot, you are omitting the intersubjective element where there is meaning that is not conceptual, not verbal, but still very real, very vital, and very effective. There is incarnate meaning, which is the intersubjective meaning raised to a pitch of intensity – the meaning of the crucifix or the meaning of the hero. There is the affective meaning of the

29 Sir Arthur Eddington, *The Nature of the Physical World* (see above, chapter 5, note 26) xi–xv.

symbol, whether you think of the Freudian or Jungian symbols or the nonclinical symbols studied by Durand. There is the meaning of the work of art, which is a breakaway from the ready-made meanings of a ready-made life. There is literary meaning and technical meaning. All are forms of human communication.[30] In all of them there is the constitution of the communication as such by meaning. Remove the meaning and the thing ceases to be what it is.

2 Meaning as Constitutive of Human Potentiality

Meaning is constitutive not only of communication but also of the human being, of the man. For those who are not infants, morons, knocked unconscious, insane, meaning is constitutive of living. Not only does meaning constitute communication, it constitutes *us* insofar as we are specifically men and women, specifically human beings. It is not the sole constituent. A man in a coma is still a man. A man in an insane asylum is still a man. All that is missing is the meaning. But when you say that all that is missing is the meaning, you realize that meaning constitutes the significant or important part of human living.

In the first place, meaning is constitutive of human potentiality. Unless we are able to mean, we are not able to be men or women, except in the sense in which the insane are men or women. Meaning is constitutive of the symbols that express our affectivity and aggressivity, that express our existential psyche,[31] our deep drive for transformation and integration. It is constitutive of our projects, of our imagination bodying forth longing and dread, hope and fear, love and hate, joy and sorrow, delight and pain. It is constitutive of our tactics and strategy, our plans and counterplans, our aims, our goals, our ideals, our intentions. It is constitutive of our yet-to-be-realized ambitions and achievements. It is constitutive of our endless questions, our acts and growing habits of understanding, our explorations of possibility – mere possibility – in mathematics, in logic, and in fiction, in the novel and in the movies too. It is constitutive of our doubts, our affirmations and negations, our beliefs and opinions, our convictions and our certitudes. It is constitutive of our loving, our loyalties, our allegiance, our faith, our resolutions and fidelity, our deliberations and decisions. Not

30 See above, chapter 5, note 2.

31 LGN adds 'equilibrium, swallowing, mating,' a reference to Durand's dominant reflexes.

only is it constitutive of what we could say, could do, could make, either on our own or with the help of others, but also, *Deo volente*, it is the ground of all that is distinctively human, the potentiality for the region or realm or field in which arise good and evil, right and wrong, truth and error, grace and sin, saving one's soul and being damned.[32]

We have spoken of the differentiation of consciousness, of two subjects, worlds, languages, societies, modes of understanding, methods of inquiry and investigation. Meaning is constitutive of the potentiality for that differentiation. It is constitutive also of the potentiality for one-sidedness. If one distinguishes between classicism and classical culture and uses classicism in a pejorative sense, one has a fairly common form of one-sidedness.[33] Classical culture has a grasp of theory. It knows what it is to be like Thales, to be absorbed totally in a theoretical problem, as was Newton when he was working out his general theory of gravitation and for a number of weeks could barely attend to eating his meals or to sleeping; he stayed in his room and worked away; he had the idea, and it possessed him. Classical culture is not at all unaware of theory. But classicism has no grasp of theory. It never got beyond popularizations, the simplifications of professors that were out to hold the attention of the tail of the class. On the other hand, classicism also never apprehends the concrete in its concreteness, its particularity, its individuality. It can think only of the universal, the normative, the ideal, the exemplar, the law. The concrete differs in some accidental way from that, but that does not matter – *plus ça change, plus c'est la même chose.* You think of everything in universal terms, and you do not get the point in the universal, in the theory. Another type of one-sidedness is scientism. It is highly developed on the theoretic side but it remains rather primitive in common sense, in human affairs, in philosophy, in religion.

Meaning is constitutive, then, first of all of human communication and secondly of human potentiality. As meaning is constitutive of human

32 The last four sentences of this paragraph are meant, it seems, to follow Lonergan's standard three higher levels of consciousness: questions and understanding, doubts and affirmations, love and loyalty. The fourth sentence ends with religious consciousness, but the insertion of the community factor ('either on our own, or with the help of others') obscures the sequence. Still, if that is the case, the obscure last sentence opens up a valuable field of investigation: the community factor intervening between the level of decision and the level of religion. See also §§5 and 7 below in this chapter. LGN has 'always by God's help' instead of '*Deo volente*' (God willing).

33 See above, chapter 7, note 25.

potentiality, so also it is constitutive of human knowing, human living, and human society.[34] Let us take up these three topics one by one.[35]

3 Meaning as Constitutive of Human Knowing

Meaning is constitutive of human knowing, not in the sense of knowing where any single cognitive act of man may be called knowing – seeing or hearing, smelling or tasting, feeling or touching, inquiring or understanding, each a separate instance of knowing – but in the specifically human sense in which a man knows; not insofar as he merely experiences without understanding anything at all – he is just eating; nor in the sense that he experiences and understands – that may be just a bright idea that is all wrong; but insofar as he experiences, understands, and affirms or denies truly. In other words, human knowing in the specifically human sense of knowing is a compound of three different types of elements. Just as in Thomist metaphysics prime matter is not a thing but just a part of a thing, and material substantial form is not a thing but just a part of a thing, and *esse*, existence in that sense, is not a thing but just a part of a thing, and the thing is the compound of all three, similarly human knowing, in the specifically human sense of knowing – the knowing that animals do not possess and that angels do not possess – is a compound of three components: an experiential, an intellectual, and a judicial component. In that sense, meaning is constitutive of human knowing. It is a compound of the meaning on the level of sense – the intersubjective, symbolic, incarnate meaning that is already visible on that level – and the meaning on the level of understanding and the meaning on the level of judgment.

Aristotle, in the *Posterior Analytics*, the first chapter of book 2, reduced all questions to four types: Is it? Is it so? What is it? Why is it so? And in the second chapter of the same book he remarked, 'These, then, are the four kinds of question we ask, and it is in the answers to these questions that our knowledge consists.'[36] Knowing consists in answering questions. Meaning-

34 LGN: 'It also is constitutive in the integration of the world of community and the world of theory: historical consciousness, existentialism.'

35 The editors have added the last sentence. Lonergan said, 'I think I had better leave those topics till the next hour and have a break.'

36 'The kinds of question we ask are as many as the kinds of things which we know. They are in fact four: – (1) whether the connexion of an attribute with a thing is a fact, (2) what is the reason of the connexion, (3) whether a thing exists, (4) what is the nature of the thing ... These, then, are the four kinds of question we ask, and it is in the answers to these questions that our knowledge consists.' Aristotle, *Posterior Analytics* (see above, chapter 8, note 2), II, 1, 89b 21–25; II, 2, 89b 36.

less questions and meaningless answers are neither questions nor answers. If our knowledge is constituted by answering questions, our knowledge is constituted by meaning. It follows that for Aristotle meaning is constitutive of human knowing. If we look at what St Thomas did we find that he spent most of his time asking and answering questions. And since he was a follower of Aristotle there is a fair presumption that he too considered questioning and answering to be human knowing.

Now this view of human knowing is extremely paradoxical for the perceptionist, for a man like Kant – to whom our knowing is in immediate relation to the known only through *Anschauung*, taking a look (for Kant, what you take a look at are phenomena) – or for Gilson, for whom our knowledge is not merely idealist and logical, but is of things that really exist outside the mind insofar as, beyond taking a look with our eyes, we also take a look with our intellects. According to the formulation, or the caricature, we look with the eyes of the body and we see particulars; we look with the eyes of the mind and we see universals. We look again, and we see the nexus between universals, and so reach principles. We look still once more to see the connection between propositions, and so we arrive at syllogisms. Knowing consists in looking, on that view.[37] I believe that it is a Scotist view, and that our knowing consists rather in meaning.

To discuss this question at any length would take you through the whole argument of *Insight*. I have just pointed out that there is a different realist view represented by Gilson and an idealist view represented by Kant, in both of which knowing essentially is looking.[38] But there is another view, and on that view we know that knowing in the strictly human sense is achieved when we break from the world of the infant, from the world that is reached, seen, heard, into the world as mediated by meaning, the world of 'is' and 'is not.' The world that is mediated by meaning is the world of the believer, the world of the theologian, the world of a realist philosophy, the world of natural and human science, and the world of common sense.[39]

37 LGN: '... questions and answers are a mere epiphenomenon, a manifestation, expression, of the looking that constitutes knowing.'

38 LGN: 'An idealist holds that, if we did perceive, we would know; but in fact we do not perceive reality; and so we do not really know; all we can achieve are the immanent activities of meaning, and all we reach by meaning is the meant.

'We are boxed within a world of meaning, and as we cannot get beyond it, we can never know anything more than what we mean.'

39 LGN on this paragraph (and the very end of the preceding): 'It happens to be my opinion that human knowing (as distinct from animal knowing, which also occurs in man) is true meaning.

The world as mediated by meaning is the world that is communicated by teaching and learning. Teachers and professors at least have to carry on *as if* true meaning were knowledge. By wonder, by the problem, by the question, the data are promoted to a world of intellectual meaning. By insight, understanding, the data are enriched with possible meaning. By expression, definition, deduction, verification, one prepares the way for judgment, for the pronouncement that the possible meaning is true or false. I think that if the teacher tells his pupil to take a look at universals or at being, to see the nexus between universals with the eye of the soul or the eye of the mind, he is wasting his own and his pupil's time, because those looks do not exist. However, that is just an opinion.

4 Meaning as Constitutive of Human Living

Finally, meaning is constitutive of human living. It is not the only constituent. As I have already remarked, an infant is alive and a human being, a person in a coma is alive and a human being, a person in an insane asylum is alive and a human being. But besides the operations of the respiratory, vascular, digestive, lymphatic, endocrine, and nervous systems, and local movement, there is another far more important, far more significant component of human living in its concreteness, the component that consists in meaning. It is by that that we differ from the infant, the person in the coma, the person in the asylum; and by that difference the importance of meaning in human life can be estimated.[40] The potentiality of human living is the potentiality for meaning. Knowing is meaning as true, and when we add to meaning the act of will – what we mean is what we choose – we effect the transition to deliberate human living: the actuality of living by

---

'I disagree with the perceptionist's fictions.

'I disagree with both perceptionists and idealists in their claim that true meaning is not knowing.

'I grant, of course, that to accept what I call the realist view, what is also the dogmatic view (in the R.C. sense of dogma), presupposes a conversion.

'One has to break from the world of the infant ... and enter a different world, the world as mediated by meaning, by "is" and "is not."

'The world as mediated by meaning is the world of the believer, the world of the theologian, the world of realist philosophy, the world of human and natural science, and the world of common sense.'

40 LGN: 'The closer one's living resembles that of an infant, of a moron, of a man in a coma, the less the importance of meaning.'

one's choices, one's decisions, or alternatively by one's drifting, one's failure to confront issues and decide.[41]

5 Common Meaning and Community

I have spoken of meaning as constitutive of the potentiality and the act of human living, and as constitutive of human knowing and of human communication. Now the communication is the transference, the transmission, of the form of human knowing and living from one person to another. There is such a thing as common meaning, a meaning shared by many individuals. And as meaning is constitutive of human potentiality, so common meaning is constitutive of the potential community.[42] People are potentially a community insofar as they can understand one another, understand what each means. Learning a language is not learning word-for-word equivalents with the language one already knows. It is learning to think of everything in a quite different fashion, and if one has not learned that, one is the helpless victim of one's own language. Strangers are strange to us because their meanings are not the same as ours, because their ways of seeing and doing things are not the same as ours, because their values are not the same as ours. A European is odd in America, and an American is odd in Europe. The differences are far more radical when one moves to Africa or Asia. Where the Greeks differentiated consciousness by distinguishing the practical and the theoretic life, there is a differentiation of consciousness at the base of Indian culture, but it seems to be the differentiation effected by distinguishing common sense, practical living, on the one hand, and mystical contemplation, on the other. There is a radical difference in the whole structure of Eastern and Western cultures.

Just as common meanings constitute the potentiality for community, so diverse meanings constitute the potentiality for different communities and for conflict between them. A common sense, a common religion, a com-

41 LGN: 'Basically meaning is constitutive of distinctively human potentiality.
'But the potentiality becomes actual in two ways: it reaches the actuality of knowing by judgment; it reaches the actuality of one's living by one's choices, one's decisions, or alternatively by one's drifting, one's failure to confront issues and decide.'

42 More clearly in LGN, especially in reference to what is to follow: 'As meaning is constitutive of human potentiality, human knowing, and human living, so common meaning is constitutive of community on the respective levels of the potential community, the community of knowledge, and the communities of commitment.'

mon philosophy, a common specialty create a community in knowledge. A common capacity to understand things in the same way creates a common culture. But there are many cultures, and the multiplicity of cultures creates division, difference, and the possibility of incomprehension, misunderstanding, suspicion, fear, distrust, misinterpretation, misconstruction, and the beginnings of the development of defensive and offensive mechanisms.[43]

Besides the potential community and the community of knowledge, there are communities of commitment. The commitment may be absolute or relative, conditioned, qualified. Absolute commitment is represented by the family, the state, the church. It is an absolute commitment that is entered upon when two people marry to live together. There is the overarching commitment of members of the state to one another and to the state. The first is a commitment in love, the second a commitment in loyalty. Finally, there is the commitment in faith to the eschatological community of the church. These commitments give meaning an objectivity that realizes the meaning, realizes the institution, in each family, in each state, in the church and all the variations of the church.[44]

That constitutive meaning of the institution is something that is specifically human, and because those meanings change and develop, because they reveal their inadequacies and need to be perfected, they constitute the history of ideas, of doctrines, of concepts, of meanings. The United States is a democracy, and England is a democracy, but they are not democracies in exactly the same sense. The Englishman, by his parliament and his institutions, does not mean something that corresponds point to point with what the American means by his democracy. They are two different democracies, and the differences are constituted by the common meanings to which two peoples are committed. Similarly in the family, there is the meaning of the family, and it is the meaning that the members of the family apprehend and are committed to that is realized in the family. One can set up a normative idea of the family, a normative idea of the

43 LGN: 'The stratification of community

'The Revolt of the Masses against the complexity of meaning, the abstruseness of meaning, in modern technology, economics, politics

'The breakdown of the intermediate groups that mediated the meaning from the summit to the rank and file.'

Lonergan adds by hand, 'Nisbet, *Quest for Community*, OUP [Oxford University Press].'

44 LGN: 'Conditional, limited commitment, in subordinate communities: partnership, corporation, legal firm, medical profession, teacher or professor.'

state, a normative idea of the church, but they are abstractions. They are not the concrete reality that is constituted by the meanings known and willed by the persons involved. Consequently, for institutions to be known in their concreteness, in their individual reality, they have to be studied in their histories. To change those meanings is to change the reality. The reality of the family becomes a different thing when divorce becomes a common possibility. You have changed the meaning, and changing the meaning changes the reality because the meaning is constitutive of the reality.[45]

6 Meaning in Human Science

We have been considering meaning as constitutive of the individual in his potentialities, his knowing, and his living; prior to that we considered meaning as communicated in seven different ways, running through the whole gamut of possible meaning; and we just moved on to a consideration of common meaning, illustrated by the absolute commitments of love, of loyalty, of faith, and by the limited commitments of having a job and doing one's job, of entering into a partnership, of having acquaintances, of forming an association, and so on. But because human reality is constituted by meaning to so great an extent, it follows that human science, scientific knowledge of man, if it is to be knowledge of human reality, will be knowledge of meanings. To know human potentiality is to know potential meaning. To know human knowledge is to know meanings that are true. To know human living is to know meanings that inform, that are constitutive of, modes of human living. To know human communities in their potentiality, insofar as they are communities of knowledge, academic communities, or insofar as they are communities of commitment, again is to study meanings as they are effective in groups of human beings. Precisely in the measure that meaning is constitutive of human living and of human commitment, human science is a study of meaning.

That is the point that was made by Wilhelm Dilthey. His first notable

45 LGN: 'Meaning as constitutive of living and of communities of commitment is meaning as dependent on will.

'There is a normative component but there is also an actual component: the family ought to be what one ought to mean by the family, but the family at best is what one actually means by the family.

'States are not just instances of what ought to be; they are concrete embodiments of what peoples have de facto chosen them to be.'

work, about 1881, was an introduction to the study of the human sciences; and one of his fundamental problems was drawing the distinction between what Germans call the *Naturwissenschaften* and the *Geisteswissenschaften*.[46] That distinction does not exist in our milieu. We distinguish the natural sciences such as physics, chemistry, and biology and (with the Ford Foundation) the behavioral sciences. But Dilthey's distinction conceived *Naturwissenschaften* as sciences in which the data are simply what is given: the color, the sound of such an intensity or volume, such a pitch, such a timbre or tone, the variety of smells and tastes and shapes, and so on. The data of physics are simply what is given to the senses, whether through instruments or not; and similarly for chemistry and biology. But the human sciences are not simply a matter of the bare data, as in the natural sciences, but of the data as already carrying a human meaning.[47] If you were to study 'Lectures at the Thomas More' and came down to D'Arcy McGee[48] and studied the color on the walls and the seats, and the colors and the shapes of the people that are here, and so on, you would not find out in a thousand years what was going on. To know what the lectures are about, you would have to know that there is such a thing as meaning and the communication of meaning. That is something you start from. It is not a scientific hypothesis that possibly may be relevant to the thing – 'We'll have to think about that, it's one form of hypothesis'; it is something you start from, it pertains to the data as data of a human science. Again, if you want to do a study of law courts and go in with a machine that will measure the decibels of the sounds made by the different speakers or the arrangement of people in the room on different sides and places, and so on, you will not understand anything about the law court. To get a start you have to have a common apprehension of what a law court is and what its function is. Any scientific knowledge of the law will be a further understanding that will presuppose that meaning that pertains to the constitution of data for a human science as such.

Again, because so great a part of human reality is meaning, human science is historical. You arrive at human science insofar as you arrive at an understanding of common meanings: of one common meaning, of several

46 Wilhelm Dilthey, *Einleitung in die Geisteswissenschaften* (Leipzig: B.G. Teubner, 1922 – original 1883); in English, *Introduction to the Human Sciences*, ed. and trans. Ramon J. Betanzos (Detroit: Wayne State University Press, 1988).

47 LGN: 'the given as possessing a constitutive meaning.'

48 Courses and lectures of the Thomas More Institute were generally offered during this time at D'Arcy McGee High School, 220 Pine Avenue West, Montreal.

common meanings in their interrelations, their conflicts, their amalgamations, their origins, their unfolding, their development, their shifts, their breakdowns. Because human reality is constituted by meaning and that meaning changes over time, takes on different nuances in different milieus, history is an integral part of any human science.

Further, hermeneutics, the science of interpretation, the fundamental rules for exegesis, for saying what is meant by a text or a statement or a document, is a fundamental branch of any human science, because hermeneutics is concerned with saying just what is meant, and human reality is constituted by meaning. Consequently, a science of human reality will be a science that is dependent on hermeneutics.

To turn to a more practical field, education is basically the communication of meaning and the techniques of meaning.[49] It is concerned with that part of human life by which the normal human being differs, by meaning, from the infant, the insane, the person sound asleep or knocked unconscious.

7 Meaning in Theology

Those are very brief reflections: applications, or indications of the wider significance of a study of the analogy of meaning. To take a final point, theology goes a step further; it adds something on to human science. Human science arrives at its goal when it knows correctly what men mean. But what men may mean may be true or false, right or wrong. When I am interpreting Kant or St Thomas, whether both are correct or not I can interpret both correctly. If the rules of hermeneutics are observed, I can interpret perfectly in both cases. But the word of God differs from the word of man. It is a datum, and it has a meaning, as have the data of human science. But it adds something on to that. The meaning of the word of God, because it is God's, has a fundamental, basic, unquestioned validity, a truth; it is something not to be refused, not to be rejected.

If you have followed me and have happened to agree with me on what I have been saying of meaning as constitutive of human potentiality, of human living, of human communication, of human communities, whether potential communities or communities of commitment, you will see the full

49 LGN, on a handwritten page, lists among the 'techniques of meaning' art, symbol, language, literature, and logic. Another is listed, but Lonergan's handwriting at this point is illegible.

impact and the full import of divine revelation. Revelation is God's entering into the world of human meaning.[50] As meaning is a principal component and constituent of human reality, so God's entering into the world of human meaning by a divine revelation is God's entering into human reality at its most significant and its most important level. The data for the theologian differ just as much from the data of human science as the data of human science differ from the data of natural science. The data of natural science, I said, were simply what is given. Data become data specifically for a human science – for a sociology, an economics, a psychology – insofar as there is a prior prescientific meaning included with the data. But that prior prescientific meaning may be true or false. It may be antiquated or up to date. It may be good or bad. It may be right or wrong. It may be magnificent or ludicrous. The data for theology add a third component: the speech of God to man. The word of God, whether taken as the word of the Bible, or the word of tradition, or the incarnate Word that is the incarnate meaning of the Son of God – that meaning is not only given, not only has a meaning, but also has a value, a truth, that has a divine origin.

8 Conclusion

So much, then, for a descriptive account of the analogy of meaning. The word 'meaning,' particularly in English, has a vast variety of meanings. One pair of authors, I believe, arrived at 900 meanings for the English word 'meaning' – I forget their names.[51] But to put some order into that multiplicity, we have attempted tonight first of all to consider different types of meaning that are constitutive of the reality that is human communication. Then we considered meaning as constitutive of human potentiality, of the field of our choices, the field of what we can become, the field of what each of us can make of himself. Thirdly, we considered meaning as constitutive of human community; there are various potential communities insofar as

50 LGN: 'Word of God is God's entry into human reality as constituted by meaning.'

51 The reference is possibly to C.K. Ogden and I.A. Richards, *The Meaning of Meaning: A Study of the Influence of Language upon Thought and of the Science of Symbolism*, 4th ed. (London: Kegan and Paul, Trench, Trubner & Co., 1936), but their formal list of the meanings of meaning gives only sixteen uses (twenty-three if you count subdivisions); in any case their interest is far more on the philosophy of language, thought, and symbolism than it is on counting varieties of meaning.

there is a common meaning, a common apprehension of the common meaning that we call common sense; there is actual community insofar as many are committed absolutely or relatively to the same meaning. Meaning, constitutive of the individual's living and the living of the group, and of the communication between the individuals within the group, is a principal part of human reality and consequently a principal part in the object of human science. That principal part is what makes the essential difference between science that is specifically human and, on the other hand, natural science. And finally, since there is a word of God, there is a further case of meaning that differs just as much from the object of human science as the object of human science differs from the object of natural science.

I thank you very much for your very kind attention. I believe there are to be questions.

Question: In your last point there, the theological view: would that involve an explanatory account of meaning?

Response: Well, it would be concerned with the meanings of the Bible, with the meanings of the Fathers, with the meanings of the theologians and the heretics and the councils. That would be positive theology, theology in *oratio obliqua*, theology as giving an account of what other people have known or thought they knew about God. And the different parts would pertain to what are called different *loca theologica*, different fields. The authority of what is found in the Bible is something greater than what is found in a single Father, and what is found in a series of Fathers is something more clearly relevant to an account of the word of God than what is found in only one who is singing outside the chorus, and so on; there are differences. That is the field of positive theology.

Now there is also, just as in ordinary affairs, what Georg Simmel referred to as *die Wendung zur Idee*, what we may call in English 'displacement towards system.'[52] Take the field of economics as an illustration of it. For a while, starting from the sixteenth century, there was the law that one must export more than one imports, so that one will have more gold in the country – mercantilism. It was an idea, and it worked. And people went beyond that – the physiocrats in France and Adam Smith in England – and held the contrary doctrine, the doctrine of free trade, no government

52 Georg Simmel, *Lebensanschauung, Vier metaphysische Kapitel* (Munich and Leipzig: Duncker and Humbolt, 1918) 29–98.

interference; the governments were helping the practice of mercantilism. This is another economic theory. There was not merely the theory but the practice. It went beyond free trade to the gold standard, and then managed money, and creeping socialist thought – we used to call it free enterprise – and there arose the socialisms. In all cases you can distinguish between a beautiful, perfectly logical theory and, on the other hand, what de facto occurs in the concrete, which is something simpler.

Similarly in, for example, the movement from the doctrine in the New Testament to the later doctrine about Christ, there has been a displacement towards system. There are many things said about Christ in the New Testament, and to give you just the barest list of them would take at least an hour. But there is not the unequivocal statement that you have in the Council of Nicea that the Son is consubstantial with the Father. What is taking place is a movement from a more direct form of communication to definition, a movement from the way the Athenians thought to the way Socrates thought. There are no problems of exegesis on Euclid's *Elements.* You have to study to know what he means. But once you have studied him and seen the point, you know what he means, and everybody has exactly the same ideas about what Euclid means. There are no commentaries written on Euclid to explain what he means. You can understand it just as well from Euclid. But if you examine what has been written on the Gospel of St John in the last twenty-five years alone, you have an almost endless bibliography, and you have a dozen full-scale commentaries; they are all explaining the same text, but they are not all explaining it in the same way. There is a problem of exegesis that arises with this immediate type of communication. 'You know what I mean, and I know what I mean,' and we are getting along fine, so long as someone doesn't start butting in and saying, 'Well, what precisely does this word mean?' and so on. To settle what was meant, to state clearly what was meant, you have to move to this other plane. At least that's my concept of it.

When you do that, you discover you have mysteries. There is not so clearly a mystery when you remain with the statements of the New Testament, but when you say, 'A man is God,' you have something that seems very, very queer. So there arises speculative theology that attempts to attain some imperfect, analogical understanding of the mysteries. And we have a third theology now, the dogmatic, that says exactly what was meant by the scriptures but in a different way. Systematic theology describes the understanding of the mysteries in a systematic manner. You can have a fundamental basis of method, the grounds of method – fundamental in that sense – in which one moves from the objects of theology to the theologian. There is an awful lot of disagreement going on, and the trouble is not merely with the object. It is also with the subject, with the theologian – with the kind of men they are. The study of the theologian as a subject in his operations gives you a fundamental theology. And this fundamental theology, if it understands the theologian as a subject, is off to understanding all the theologians, all the Fathers – they're all human beings too. It is fundamental not merely to the dogmatic and the systematic but also to the positive theology. In that way, you more or less complete a circle.[53]

Now there are several ways in which this set of different things – positive and systematic and dogmatic and fundamental theology – can be considered. When we are expounding things to people who are already converted, we do it one way. But we can be thinking of people who are not converted, and all their blocks, and then we go about it another way. Or we can be considering the relations between theology and other fields – the relation of theology to philosophy, the relation of theology to science, the relation of theology to literature, the relation of theology to the practical aspects of religion, to catechetics, preaching, liturgy, and so on. And such expansion goes under the general rubric of theology as wisdom, as ordering all things.

Question: The next question had to do with how one can discuss the meaning of art when one is unable to find common denominators, when there are differing people looking at objects.

Response: At the beginning I drew a distinction between an analytic and a descriptive account of meaning. And the account I gave tonight was descriptive, telling, stating, enumerating the different fields in which meaning is found. You are raising the question of possibilities. The conditions of the possibility of anything are the same questions: What is its

53 This paragraph shows Lonergan on the verge of a major development in his concept of theology and its method. For several years he had remained in the context of the twofold order of thought: the analytic and the synthetic. In this lecture (as in the contemporary volume *De Deo trino*, vol. 1: *Pars dogmatica* [see above, chapter 2, note 18] 5–14 and in the likewise contemporary lectures at Georgetown University, 'Method of Theology,' July 1964 [see the notes on these lectures in the Lonergan Archives, Toronto]), the synthetic remains constant, but the analytic has subdivided into positive and dogmatic approaches, and a quite new concept of fundamental theology is emerging. The process will reach a landmark development in 1965 with the concept of the eight functional specialties of theology.

essence? What is the one thing that makes it what it is? And to answer those questions one has to use an analytic approach.

Now what is the analytic approach? Well that, I would say, is in terms first of all of the notion of being, what is intended in any question. There are all sorts of questions, and they are unlimited. You are an obscurantist if you draw the line here and say, 'Any questions beyond this point are ruled out of court,' without any consideration, without any reason. And any answers – no matter how many answers you give to the questions that are raised – just provide a springboard for further questions. Questions are unlimited. Questions arise from wonder, from inquiry, from reflection. According to Aristotle, wonder is the beginning of all science and philosophy. Wonder is the ground that promotes us from the data of sense to the operations of intelligence, and from the operations of intelligence to the operations of reflection; there is that fundamental drive that can be given all sorts of names; that drive is one, it correlates knowing and being,[54] and it has a single source. Now that source lies in inquiry as its correlate in the subject, in the psyche, in the sensitive soul. One of the more prominent conclusions (I say this subject to correction) of contemporary dynamic or depth psychology is the preformation of intellectual activities on the psychic level. It is something that is very conspicuous in Jung's approach. There is in the human psyche a preparation for the intellectual operations. The finality of intelligence towards speaking is prepared by the finality of sense itself, and it is there that you will find a radical unity of meaning – on the side of the meaner, of the one that means, the side of the subject. The objects are related to one another through this common root.

Question: The question asked about the meaning of the 'analogy of meaning' in the title of the lecture: 'analogy' seems to imply an analytic account. **Response:** Perhaps the title is not altogether relevant to a descriptive account. But what I was describing was different senses of the word 'meaning.' I was emphasizing the types of meaning that are on the psychic level: the intersubjective, incarnate, symbolic, artistic, and their influence on literary meaning, and taking more or less for granted the scientific, the philosophic, and the theological types of meaning, of which I spoke very briefly in terms of technical meaning.

There is meaning that is already constituted on the level of sensitivity.

54 We are interpreting here. There was a gap in the tape at this point: 'correlates [gap] being.'

It's a real meaning: you don't go about the streets smiling at everyone; people would misunderstand you. The meaning of the smile is a meaning that takes on all sorts of different significances; there is the smile of welcome, the smile of recognition, the smile of friendliness, the smile of the person who is pretty tired of this, the smile of resignation, the enigmatic smile, the ironic smile, and so on indefinitely. Smiles have a meaning, they all have a meaning. These meanings are multiple, and to sort them out you have to go on to an entirely different type of meaning – the meanings of understanding and conception, the clear and distinct ideas of Descartes. And there is meaning in a still further sense that is quite different when you say, 'It is' or 'It is not'; that is full meaning. But there is meaning that is constitutive of human reality, for example, in the community of commitment, in the family, the state, the church; the meaning is something realized objectively in the group; it functions in the group; it develops in the group. It is the reality of the country – of Canada, of the United States, of England, and so on. It differs from country to country, and it develops historically.

There are four different types of meaning: on the level of the psyche, as in the smile; on the level of intelligence, as in the definition; on the level of judgment – 'That's what it really is'; and the meaning that is constitutive of the human community. Then the analogy is between those four, and the movement is the combinations of them. Now a particular application of that comes up in the distinction between natural science, in which the meaning *is*, arises simply from, the human intelligence of the scientist, and human science, where there already is a meaning. The scientist may arrive at a fuller level of meaning in his theory about society (the sociologist in his theory about economics or his theory about psychology), but there already is a meaning constitutive of the object, and that meaning may be true or false, right or wrong. And there is a meaning of the word of God – and that's yet a third level – insofar as it is just meant or realized in the community: the difference between the gospel as preached and the gospel as practiced.

Question: The question was indistinct, but concerned the 'field of being' and meaning. The questioner had a difficulty with the proposition that the field of meaning is more inclusive than that of being.

Response: A false statement has a meaning. That's why we find the root of meaning in the meaner, because the meaner can go astray. Meaning can be a larger field than being; it can be occupied with everything that isn't and not just with what is!

Question: With the finality of meaning, can we inquire after a prime analogate?
Response: Well, yes. Being, the real world, the qualified universes, mathematical realities, the square root of minus 1, the merely logical, the merely hypothetical, fiction, the world of art; and then the world of error, the world of myth, the world of aberration, the world of the insane – there's meaning there, too. The analogy would be in the spheres, and the fundamental one would be what is, what is realized, particularly the meaning that is realized. But it is the sort of thing, you know, that operates on the flying trapeze to some extent – this meaning. There is the being that is constituted by the meaning.

Question: I still can't see why meaning is broader than being.
Response: Do *you* mean anything? Do *I* mean anything when I say, 'Don't read it, it can't be fun?' Supposing I'm wrong.
Questioner: Well then, it's meaningless.
Response: No! – because you wouldn't know I was wrong, if it was meaningless.
Questioner: There you're meaning something other than what I mean by what you're meaning.
Response: Newton's hypothesis of universal gravitation: is that true?
Questioner: I don't know.
Response: Well, according to modern physics, it isn't true; it's a good approximation for earlier centuries but it is no longer accepted. I believe Newtonian mechanics is corrected by relativity mechanics that has been largely successful in the last fifty years. There is meaning that is not a statement of fact, of what actually is so. For example, there are different types of geometry, Euclidean and non-Euclidean, and non-Euclidean is subdivided. They're not all statements about what actually is, but they all have a meaning. And because our mind is transcendent, because it proceeds by divisions within the transcendent and can go astray, you have the phenomenon of meaning being broader than the field of what actually is.
Questioner: I would be inclined to disagree with you. How can you have a meaning about something that is not? When one goes astray, how can you go astray about what is not, unless you are going astray from what is?
Response: But is the 'going astray' meaning? or is it not meaning?
Questioner: I would be inclined to say it is meaning, definitely some kind of significant meaning. But I fail to see how divorce lacks some kind of family life.

Response: Well, the false ...
Questioner: What is the meaning of falsity?
Response: What is the meaning of falsity? The noncorrespondence between what you say and what is. But what you say, though it doesn't correspond with what is, still it is not meaningless, not necessarily meaningless.
Questioner: I agree.
Response: That is the whole point I was making.

Question: In your description of communications, what type of meaning have you employed?
Response: Oh, everyday language mainly; occasional excursions into technical language.
Questioner: You mean the description of the reality of meanings in communication has been operating out of one base or from several?
Response: No, everyday language was the first type I described, wasn't it?
Questioner: Yes, but what did you describe it in?
Response: Everyday language! (Laughter)
Questioner: You wouldn't call it technical language?
Response: Well, perhaps there were a few technical terms like imperative mood and indicative mood, number and tense: they are technical terms that arise in grammar; grammar is of historical origin.

I thank you very much!

10

Philosophical Positions with Regard to Knowing[1]

The course we are beginning has to do with knowing. I propose tonight to point out a series of ambiguities and confusions that can arise with regard to knowing. These are not purely theoretical: if they are not avoided, people very easily get discouraged and give up their efforts to know.

I will speak on four topics: first of all, knowing; secondly, knowing knowing;[2] thirdly, the objectivity of knowing; and fourthly, knowing and intersubjectivity.[3]

1 A lecture given on 29 September 1964, at the Thomas More Institute, Montreal, as the opening lecture in a course entitled 'Philosophic Positions with Regard to Knowing.' In March 1973, Howard Logan, SJ, transferred the reel recording to cassettes (TC 421 & 422, Lonergan Research Institute Library, Toronto). Mark D. Morelli made a transcription of the lecture from the cassette recording, completing it by 10 June 1973 (File 421, Lonergan Research Institute Library). In our editing we worked from the cassette recording itself, but received important assistance from Morelli's transcription.

Lonergan began the lecture by thanking Fr Eric O'Connor, who had introduced him, and adding, 'It's a great pleasure to be coming back here even after twenty years; it shows I've led a good life and I'm still alive.' Lonergan first lectured at the Thomas More Institute in 1945–46, the first year of the Institute's existence, giving a series of lectures, 'Thought and Reality.'

2 Since cognitional theory was so central to Lonergan's thought, it was inevitable that he should from time to time speak of 'knowing knowing' and of 'understanding understanding.' It was likewise inevitable that typists should drop the second member, writing simply 'knowing' and 'understanding,' and that proofreaders should fail to spot their error. This happened both in *Insight* (above, chapter 2, note 9; see, for example, p. 801, note *d* to chapter 16, and p. 806, note *a* to the 'Epilogue') and in the first publication of 'Cognitional Structure' (see *Spirit as Inquiry* [see below, note 3] 532, and compare *Collection* [see above, chapter 2, note 13] 208, the second sentence of § 3).

1 Knowing

The word 'knowing' may be used generically: animals know, men know, angels know, God knows. Again, it can be used generically with regard to particular human activities: seeing, hearing, tasting, smelling, touching, feeling; inquiring, understanding, thinking; reflecting, weighing the evidence, judging. They are all different activities, and each one of them can be called knowing. You have a generic use of the word, used with regard to totally different kinds of knowledge: human knowledge and animal knowledge, and then again different human activities each one of which may be called knowing.

A first and fundamental point is that human knowledge that is *specifically* human is not any single activity but a *set* of activities. When I see, generically I can be said to know. But my seeing may be perfect as ocular vision yet I may be without a glimmer of understanding. Then my seeing is just gaping, and no one would call mere gaping human knowing. While seeing, by itself, is knowing in the generic sense of the term, still it is not what we mean specifically by human knowing. Again, one can understand what one merely imagines, come up with a brilliant idea, be enthralled with one's cleverness in thinking something out. But this is not knowing, because it is not understanding data. It is understanding merely what one imagines, and what one imagines has no corresponding data of sense or data of consciousness. Mythic consciousness – what is called 'mythic thought' – involves a great deal of understanding but it is not understanding experience; it is understanding what one imagines. Understanding alone, without experience, is not human knowing, just as experiencing – seeing, hearing, tasting, touching – without understanding falls short of human knowing. Again, one can pass judgment on something that one does not understand, but then one is exercising not human knowing but human arrogance. Or again, one can pass judgment without any regard to the data

3 The marked similarity of this lecture to the essay 'Cognitional Structure' that Lonergan contributed to the *Festschrift* for his sixtieth birthday (*Spirit as Inquiry: Studies in Honor of Bernard Lonergan, S.J.* [Chicago: St Xavier College, 1964]) is explained by the fact that they are practically contemporaneous. The *Festschrift* article went to the general editor on 26 September 1964 (letter of F. Crowe to Justus George Lawler, 26 September 1984), so Lonergan would have written the article in the late summer, a month or two before this lecture. 'Cognitional Structure' now appears as chapter 14 in *Collection.*

of experience; and in that case one is setting fact aside. A judgment that has no relation to any data of experience, no connection with it, is just 'in the air'; it is apart from matters of fact.

The point that I have been attempting to make is that, while there are several different kinds of activities that pertain to human knowing, still single activities by themselves are not properly human knowing. Seeing alone is not human knowing. Understanding alone is not human knowing. Judging alone is not human knowing. Human knowing is a *set*, a *structure*, of different activities.

What do I mean by a structure? We can start with the notion of a whole. A whole may be simply a conventional or an arbitrary unit, such as a gallon of milk. Its parts are equally conventional or arbitrary parts. You can have any size. You can take the conventional parts – the quarts, the pints, and the cups – or you can take arbitrary parts, any fraction you happen to think of. You can draw up a large number of interesting arithmetical and geometrical relations between the parts. But that type of whole is not a structure.

In contrast, there are highly organized products of nature and art, in which every part is related to the others. Every part is just what it is because of its functional relations to the other parts. To drop out any one part is like having an automobile with three wheels, and to add one is like having an automobile with five wheels. The parts determine what the whole has to be. Such a structure may be *static*: the parts are made of material things. Or it may be *dynamic*: the parts are operations. Human knowing is a dynamic structure *materially* because its parts are operations, but it is dynamic not merely materially but also *formally*: it assembles itself.

An organism grows; it starts from the one-cell stage and divides into two (usually by karyokinesis, I believe), and then into four. Gradually, the organism builds itself up; it assembles itself. Similarly, human knowing assembles itself. In this dynamic structure that is human knowing, there is a level of experience – any sense activity: seeing, hearing, tasting, touching, smelling, feeling. But there is a second level. People ask questions – Why this? Why is it there? It wasn't there yesterday! Who moved it? What is it? all the questions one can ask. And there are not only the formulated questions but also the prior intellectual curiosity. In answer to the questions there are insights and thoughts, concepts, formulations, hypotheses, theories. The thoughts provoke a different kind of question, on a third level: Is that so? Are you sure? Might it not be otherwise? And so there is reflective understanding and judgment.

This is a structure of knowing. I illustrated the existence of the structure by saying that experience alone is not enough for human knowing. Seeing can be merely stupid gaping, and that is not human knowing. Understanding, insights, alone are not human knowing – your insight may be into something that you merely imagine, or into something part of which you experience and part of which you imagine. And judgments alone are not human knowing – if you judge what you do not understand, you are being arrogant, and if you judge without reference to data of experience, your judgments are all 'in the air.'

Now human knowing is a structure of activities. It is materially dynamic because what is put together are activities. It is formally dynamic because (1) you cannot avoid the experiences, you cannot be sound asleep, sleeping like a log, *all* the time; (2) experiences lead to wonder, to inquiries, and from these you get insights and thoughts; and (3) thoughts may be merely thoughts, they are not yet knowing, and so you have to reflect, weigh the evidence, and judge.

Human knowing, then, is not a single operation but a dynamic structure of different operations. The operations are not similar. You cannot start off from seeing and say, 'An insight! Ah, you have the word "sight" in there after the "in"; it must be something like seeing.' It is not something like seeing; it is something quite different from seeing. A person ordinarily sees just the color that is there to be seen, unless he is colorblind. He sees the shape that is there to be seen. He does not have to see it, and see it, and see it, and accumulate acts of seeing before he sees something. He sees right at the first crack. But with insights it is an entirely different story. Insights are a dime a dozen, and most of them are wrong. A second one complements the first, qualifies it, and corrects it. And the third complements, corrects, and qualifies the first two. It is only after you have had a hundred that you begin to get a grip on some subject and to gain some light on the matter. Insights are not like seeing. They differ from it very much, and if someone tries to think of them on the analogy of seeing he will come up with a notion of something that is not like understanding or insight at all. He may talk a great deal about 'intellect,' but what he tells you about intellect bears no relation to intelligence.[4] Insight is precisely the exercise of intelligence in the ordinary meaning of the word.

The relations, then, between the different parts are not relations of simi-

4 On intellect and intelligence, see above, chapter 4, note 7.

larity. (We will come to a point later on when we bring up the question of objectivity, and then you will find that people will feel that unless these other activities *are* like seeing they cannot be knowing at all. And then it is not just a bad guess, but there is a big principle preventing them from paying attention to anything that is not like seeing.) The parts are parts in a functional whole. Each part performs its role within the whole. There is no similarity between the tires on a motor car and the differential; each performs its function within the whole, and each performs it not because all the parts are similar to one another but because they fulfil complementary functions. One is not, then, to construct the whole from the parts by analogy or similarity.

But if one is not to do so by analogy or by similarity, what on earth is one to do? One has to appeal to immediate experience. That is quite easy with regard to seeing. Anyone can have an immediate experience of seeing and connect that experience with the word and the concept 'seeing.' To have the experience as often as he pleases, to turn it off and on, all he has to do is blink. By opening and closing his eyes he will turn on and off the experience of seeing. What do you mean by 'seeing'? Exactly that experience. A blind person cannot experience seeing; it is just the same for him whether he opens or closes his eyes. But for a person who is not blind, it is a quite simple matter to experience seeing as often as he pleases and to connect the name with the experience. The same is true with hearing, provided you have a soundproof room into which you can enter and out of which you can exit. In general, sensitive activities are fairly easy to experience immediately and identify. But exactly the same procedure has to be employed with regard to insights and thoughts, reflective understanding and judgment, and then it is not so simple.

You cannot have an act of understanding and insight just when you please, by blinking your eyes. To have the experience of an act of understanding, of an insight, you have to be learning something you did not know before. Or you have to be reenacting in yourself a previous process of learning. While we use our understanding all the time, insights are, as I said, a dime a dozen, most of them are habitual, we do not notice them, and so they are not useful for identifying in oneself the experience of an act of understanding, because the thing is so obvious to you that you cannot quite make out what a person who asks you to identify an insight is talking about. The best instances of insight, too, are not commonsense understanding, because it is very, very difficult to define accurately what the insight in question is. The best examples are from the sciences, from mathematics, and particularly from geometry, where you have a very clear-cut diagram. Shall I give an example?

I imagine you have heard me give this one before. There is a limited number of good examples, but Euclid s first proposition in his first book is one of them. The problem is to draw on the base of a straight line *AB* an equilateral triangle within the plane of the blackboard. Take center *A* and radius *AB* and draw a circle; take center *B* and radius *BA* and draw another circle. The point of intersection is *C*. Join *CA* and *CB*. Radii of the same circle are equal, so *CA* and *AB* are equal. The radii of the other circle are equal, so *AB* and *CB* are equal. And things equal to the same thing are equal to one another, and so *CA* and *CB* are equal. Therefore we have an equilateral triangle, as desired.

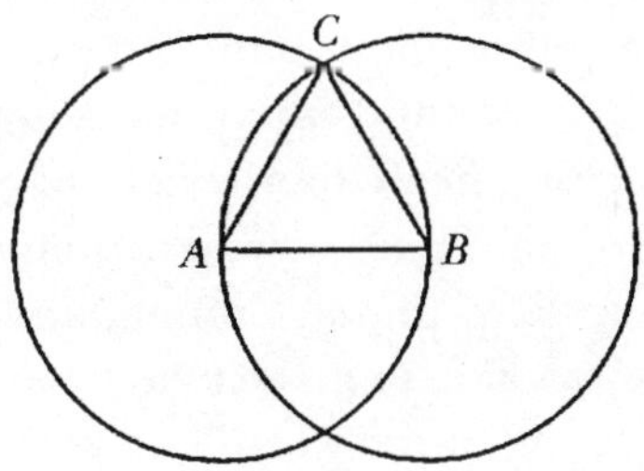

Now to pin down the insight you all have had, we ask, Where is the fallacy? Euclid does not prove that the two circles will intersect. They need not intersect. You can have two circles in the same plane that do not intersect one outside the other or one inside the other, and so on. Not only does Euclid not prove this, but he *cannot* prove it with his definitions, postulates, and axioms. Consequently, modern Euclidean geometers introduce different axioms that Euclid did not think of. But he s right! How does he know? Not from his concepts or definitions or axioms or postulates. How do you all know that these two circles will be like that and that they must intersect? You see it; you see a must in the sensible data. Seeing that is having the insight. (You don t see a must with your eyes, of course!)

There are other examples, but I am not talking on insight tonight. I have written a little book on the subject, where you will find more examples.[5] But what I *am* talking about is that, to know this cognitional structure, you

5 Bernard Lonergan, *Insight* (see above, chapter 2, note 9). Further examples of insight may be found in the first two chapers.

must identify the activities. Just as you can easily identify an act of seeing, so you must more laboriously search for acts of understanding, of reflective understanding, and of judgment. To know what knowing is, you have to have immediate experience of each one of the activities that occur in the structure.

There is just one further point to be made about knowing, namely, that this structure is not a chronological order.[6] Over time, over the years from infancy, a person accumulates experiences in memory. Over the years one accumulates insights, builds up habits of understanding. Over the years one's judgment matures. One starts experiencing from infancy. Understanding starts developing a little later. One is supposed to be able to make certain elementary judgments by the age of seven years. In several books, Piaget has given a detailed plan of the development of the intelligence of children.[7] You will hear more about him, I'm sure. Judgment starts developing about the age of seven, and when our knowledge increases it does not mean that we are getting new experiences *and* new insights *and* making new judgments. Rather, something new has come in either on the level of experience or on the level of understanding, and we are able to make a judgment that we were not able to make before.

So much for the meaning of the word 'knowing.' The word can be used generically to denote any one of these activities, or to denote animal knowing, or to denote angelic knowing, or to denote God's knowing. But specifically human knowing is not some one activity. It is a set, a structure, a dynamic structure of different activities, and to know what knowing is you have to know each one of the activities, and not by analogy, not by saying that one activity is partly like seeing and partly different. (Of course, if you ask, 'What do the "partlys" mean?' people will say, 'Well, that's being a little too exigent!') It is on the basis of immediate experience of each activity that one knows what knowing is.

6 The stress, it seems, is on 'structure': the structure, 'immanent and recurrently operative in ... cognitional activities' (*Insight* 11), is given in human equipment, but it unfolds and is appropriated in its parts only with time. This is especially clear in the compact way the whole structure is contained in the affectivity of children, till gradually 'distinctions develop between the different levels' (*Dialogues in Celebration*, ed. Cathleen M. Going [Montreal: Thomas More Institute, 1980] 310–11, in an interview with Lonergan, 'Questions with Regard to Method: History and Economics' 286–314).

7 See above, chapter 3, note 25.

2 Knowing Knowing

Now, if knowing were looking, knowing knowing would be looking at looking. It would all be very simple. But because specifically human knowing is a structure, knowing knowing is a reduplication of the structure. One performs the set of operations with respect to the set of operations. The major difference is at the level of experience: when we spoke earlier of experience, we meant seeing, hearing, tasting, touching, feeling; now we mean consciousness and introspection. Any of the operations in the structure that one performs occurs consciously. Insofar as the operations occur consciously, one knows that one knows. When you ask the questions, What is it? and Why? you do not do so unconsciously. When you get the point, when you catch on, you catch on not unconsciously but consciously; you 'know' something has happened, you 'know' that you are knowing, in the generic sense of the word 'know.' Similarly, when you are asking, 'Is that so?' you are aware you are asking it. And when you are weighing the evidence and you see that this has to be the answer and you make the judgment, you are aware of what is going on, and you are aware that this particular set of activities has reached a term. You know something, and you know that something has been settled, insofar as you use consciousness.

Consciousness, then, is a mirroring of knowing in the sense in which we all know: experiencing, understanding, and judging. We all know in that sense. And we all know that we know, not in the sense that we all have analyzed the structure of human knowing, the set of activities constitutive of human knowing, but in the sense that when we perform these activities we do so consciously. We are aware of what is going on.

What is that awareness, and what has to be added to it to advance from consciousness to this 'knowing knowing' which is the reduplication of the structure, namely, the whole set of activities with respect to the whole set of activities?

First of all, then, with regard to consciousness, distinguish three senses of the word 'presence.'[8] The clock is present in the room. The presence is merely physical, material. The clock does not know the room, and the room does not know the clock. Secondly, there is the presence of an object. You are present to me, and I am present to you. This is the presence of something to someone, the presence of an object to a subject. But there

8 On 'presence,' see above, chapter 5, note 21.

is a third type of presence, and it is the type of presence in which we are interested, namely, the presence of the subject to himself. That is not the presence of an object. You do not have before you me as an object *and* yourselves as another object, so that you are distracted by one of them and shifting from one to the other. The object is totally present to you, and you are present to yourself; but your presence to yourself is in another dimension. It is not on the side of the object. There is the spectacle and the spectator. As the object is present to the spectator, simultaneously and concomitantly the subject is present to himself. If he were not present to himself, if he were not all there, if he were dead to the world, nothing would be present to him. For him to be present to himself he does not have to get out into the parade of objects and take a look at himself. He is present to himself all along, as long as he is awake – and even if he is asleep, provided he is dreaming: the subject is present to himself in his dreams with a fragmentary presence. The third presence, again, is the presence of the subject to himself, not as an object, but by the mere fact that he is exercising any of these cognitional activities, or again by the fact that he is exercising any affective or voluntary activities. In this presence, the subject is present to himself at the receiving end, not at the objective end.

Now the presence that one has to oneself is not homogeneous. It is not the same sort of thing through and through. There are different levels of consciousness. I have already said that the dreamer is conscious up to a point, with a minimal type of consciousness. When he wakes up and begins to experience, he is *empirically conscious*. That is something better than dreaming. One is awake, lying on the beach, with not a thought in his head, not a question; he has empirical consciousness. But you can have a further level of consciousness. When he starts to wonder about something, to ask some questions, he is moving up to *intellectual consciousness*, to inquiry. He is the intelligent author of his acts of inquiry, of his insights, and of his thoughts. And there is a third level of consciousness, *rational consciousness*, in which he asks whether his thoughts are true. Beyond that there is *rational self-consciousness*, when he is concerned with the good, deliberating, deciding. So consciousness is not all of one piece. It rises together with cognitional activities and goes beyond the level of cognitional activities to the level of self-consciousness, in which one is deciding about things and other people, and ipso facto making oneself the kind of man or woman one is.

We have been speaking of consciousness as the subject's presence to himself. But we also mentioned introspection. Introspection is adverting to consciousness, adverting to the data of consciousness. I spoke of blinking one's eyes and of the way one can turn off and on the experience of seeing. Whenever you are seeing, you are seeing consciously – you cannot be unconscious and see – but when you are seeing, you need not be adverting to seeing. Normally what you advert to is the seen, not the seeing. Introspection is a shift of attention from the object to the subject, from the colors and shapes that are seen to the seeing. In blinking your eyes, you direct the question to the experience of seeing, and so your attention is drawn to the subject. Similarly, whenever you understand anything, you do so consciously, but you do not do so introspectively. You do so introspectively when you provoke insights by puzzles, experiments, and so forth, and watch for the experience of the insight under the conditions you have set yourself.

So we have the structure (knowing) and the reduplication of the structure (knowing knowing). Knowing knowing is not just consciousness. You always have that when you know anything: you are aware of what is going on, you are knowing. But merely to have that does not mean that you have worked out the structure by introspection with regard to each one of the activities. With introspection, for example, you not only use the word 'judgment' and have some vague idea of what judgment is or some definition of it, but you identify your own judgments in your own experience and the process of judging; and similarly with regard to the rest of the operations.

The next step in knowing knowing is to move toward an understanding. The mere fact that we drew up this scheme shows that we had some understanding of human knowing. Our understanding can be increased by multiplying all the instances of human knowing, by studying the way knowing develops, and so on. But we will try to indicate briefly some insight into the experience of knowing, and then move on to judgment about the insight into consciousness.

First of all, in order to convey a general insight into the subject as a knower, we will speak about the *inevitability* of experiencing, understanding, and judging. I have already mentioned one inevitability, namely, you cannot sleep all the time, you cannot be one of the Seven Holy Sleepers. You wake up at least to have something to eat, and then experiencing starts. Once you are awake, you cannot avoid it. You cannot go around with your eyes closed. And you cannot avoid sound, particularly if you live in the city; sounds are banging in from all directions all day long. You cannot rest your feet on the ground without feeling that, and so on. The part of knowledge that we call experiencing cannot be avoided; it is inevitable.

Nor can one be content merely with experiencing. One can claim that one is not an intellectual. One can argue that it is a 'bad thing' to be an intellectual. One can say that people that are smart do not get very far; they may be bright in school but what happens to them later on is very sad, and so on. But when one is saying all this, one does not mean that one is stupid. One may be willing to play the buffoon, but one wants to do it intelligently. One cannot renounce one's intelligence, and the greater the effort one makes to do so, the more one betrays that one is by nature intelligent. One cannot get around the fact that one has intelligence and that these questions keep popping up all the time. One gets insights, and one has one's thoughts; they are inevitable.

Similarly, one very quickly encounters the inevitability of reflection and judgment. I was talking recently in Los Angeles on the topic of objectivity.[9] People wanted to know how you can know, how you can be certain; if you could not account for that, they thought, you were not going to know at all. They were rationally conscious, and very intensely so. The 'elevator'[10] was working very strongly. What they were interested in, of course, were the objects. They were not adverting to themselves as rationally conscious, and so it was not for that reason that they were *asking* the questions, How can you be sure? Are you really sure? But if your knowing is just on the first two levels, the levels of experience and understanding, then there is no difference between fact and fiction, reality and appearance, philosophy and myth, astrology and astronomy, alchemy and chemistry, history and legend. Those differences are all a matter of judgment. It is by judgment that you reject what is merely insight into imagination and accept understanding of experience. To distinguish between the two, you have the process of reflective understanding and judgment. You do not give that up. No one wants to be a nut! That 'not wanting to be a nut' is just a rude way of expressing the exigence of rational consciousness, the demand to know whether or not it really is so. 'You have given us a beautiful theory. Is it

9 Lonergan is here referring to the third of three lectures he gave at Loyola University of Los Angeles earlier in September of the same year (1964) as part of a lecture series celebrating the golden jubilee of the University. The three lectures were titled 'Insight' (21 September); 'Self-appropriation' (22 September); and 'Being and Objectivity' (23 September). This additional information has been kindly provided by Mark D. Morelli.

10 Lonergan refers to a blackboard diagram that he has been using for this part of the lecture. The 'elevator' (what Lonergan elsewhere refers to as the 'operator') here is the questions for reflection that move one from the level of understanding to that of reflection and judgment.

true? Is this what human knowing is?' You will certainly ask that question sooner or later, and it will be the decisive question. Is my knowing really this structure of experiencing, understanding, and judging? Well, if I ask that question, that is what is meant by being rationally conscious, being on this third level: asking for sufficient evidence before one will make a judgment, and once one finds sufficient evidence, not being able to be reasonable, to be oneself, and *not* judge.

So let's put that question: Is our knowing really that? May this be just a hypothesis, a theory, that covers some of the facts that are easily presented in a half-hour's time? Will there not be many more elements and aspects to knowing that, if they are not known now, may be found out next year or after ten years or after a hundred years? Is not this just like any other hypothesis, subject to revision? New data will come up. People will understand the thing better. The better understanding will be something different, and they will see that it covers all the old data and more data besides, and does a better job of it. They will prefer the new theory, and they will say, 'This one is to be accepted, and that one thrown out.' We are raising the question for reflective understanding and judgment, Is this what the structure of my knowing is? Might it not it be revised? It is a plausible tale, but can I be certain here and now? You are all asking the question, and so you are all on the level of reflective understanding. At least that part of the theory is verified.

Now to answer the question you have to consider the possibility of a revision. What does one mean when one says a theory will be revised? To have a revision of a theory, first of all you need new data that the old theory does not account for. And to have new data you need the element of experience, either internal experience or external experience. Without new data, there is no revision.[11] Not only do the new data have to be significantly new, but also you have to have a new insight that you did not have before. Otherwise you would not have a new theory. In the third place, the new theory has to cover all the old data *and* the new data as well, or you cannot have the judgment, This is a better theory. So any possible revision involves experiencing, understanding, and judging. In other words, any possible revision will presuppose the same old story. One may make this structure more complete,

11 This may apply only to revisions that involve a new positive and creative understanding, for, as we shall soon see, there can be revision in the sense of refutation of a faulty position 'not because someone experienced or did not experience something, but because it is against normative objectivity' (below, §3.1).

but to revise it one has to keep to the structure. That is the possibility of making a judgment now, namely, that while this account of knowing does not tell anyone all there is to be known about knowing, still no matter how much he revises it, he will be coming back to the same structure.

We have set up knowing as a structure, not as a single operation but as a set of operations, and we have spoken about the way one identifies the operations in one's experience. Secondly, we spoke about knowing knowing, and distinguished between being conscious of one's knowing and being conscious of one's knowing on the different levels of empirical, intellectual, and rational consciousness. Being conscious of one's knowing on the different levels is not only consciousness that something is going on inside; it is consciousness that one really is knowing, because when one satisfies intellectual consciousness one is aware that one has understood, and when one satisfies rational consciousness one makes the judgment, That is so, and one knows one has settled the matter to one's own satisfaction.

So we have knowing, and then knowing knowing simply as consciousness. But knowing knowing in the full sense is repeating the structure with respect to the structure. We went through the three elements that are involved in repeating the structure. First, there is consciousness of the elements. Secondly, there is introspection into the several different activities. Thirdly, there is insight into the existence of the structure from the inevitabilities of the subject, who cannot avoid experiencing, cannot renounce his intelligence – even though he is anti-intellectual, he thinks that this is the intelligent thing to be – and cannot avoid the question of reflective understanding, the question whether or not this structure is just a nice theory, something that can be revised, or whether it is something that has to be presupposed as a possibility of revision.[12]

3 The Objectivity of Knowing

We have discussed knowing and knowing knowing, and now we will raise the question of objectivity and see how it relates to the praise of subjectivity[13] that is still current in some circles.

12 Lonergan suggested taking a break at this point before going on to the question of objectivity.

13 Though this line seems to put subjectivity in a pejorative light, the reference is to one-sided praise of subjectivity; this is shown, not only by positive remarks later in the same lecture, but also by the concern with subjectivity in other writings of Lonergan, earlier or contemporary (see *Collection* 302, editorial note *m* to chapter 14, and compare the index in the 1992 edition of *Insight* with the index in earlier editions).

3.1 The Position on Objectivity

Because knowing is a structure, not a single activity, objectivity is not a single property but a *set* of properties. If knowing were a single activity, then some one property of that activity would be its objectivity. Because knowing is a structure of different activities, objectivity is similarly a pattern, a set, of properties. From the list of philosophers that are to be found in the brochure for this course, it is clear that you will be encountering empiricists, rationalists, idealists.[14] For the empiricist, objectivity resides in the element of experience of the data. If you have the data, your knowing is objective; if you do not have the data, your knowing cannot be objective – period. For the rationalist, the objectivity of knowing resides in necessity. If the judgment is necessary, if it can be demonstrated, if it is self-evident, then you know. The rationalist idea and the empiricist idea of objectivity are totally different. It seems they are not talking about the same thing. For the idealist, as for the relativist, objectivity has to do with coherence. Experiencing all by itself is just stupidity. Intelligence has to come in; and when it comes in, intelligence is not more experience; it is putting order into the data of experience. What counts is always this element of intelligence. Insofar as your insights build up into a coherent view that accounts for all the data – if you think you have all the data, the whole world by the tail – you can be an idealist; if you think you are never going to get there, you will be a relativist.

Why is it that human knowing leads to such different theories of objectivity? It is because human knowing is not some one activity with a single property; it is a compound of different activities, and its objectivity is a compound of different elements in objectivity.

There is an *experiential*, a *normative*, and an *absolute* component of objectivity. The experiential component of objectivity is the givenness of data. To make clear and precise just what is meant by the givenness of data I will ask you, 'Is my hand white?' I hope you will all say, 'Yes,' and then check.[15] The experiential component in objectivity is not saying anything; saying it

14 The course description (a copy of which was kindly provided us by Dr Heather Stephens of the Thomas More Institute) lists the following: Plato, Aristotle, Aquinas, Descartes, Newton, Vico, Kant, Hegel, Kierkegaard, Darwin, Freud, Dewey, Heidegger, Cassirer, Lonergan.

15 The checking is missed entirely in a mere written record of Lonergan's words. It is clear from § 3.1 below that here, as in other lectures where he used the same example, the checking consisted in holding up his hand, asking 'Is it white?', and then inserting a sheet of white paper behind the hand, where the marked contrast showed that it was not white at all.

presupposes a certain amount of insight, probably a certain amount of judgment. But just taking a look or listening or touching – this is rough or smooth, and so on – is the givenness of the data, and nothing more. All data are equally valid as data. I don't know if any of you ever saw the movie *The Lost Weekend.* In one scene the fellow is lying in the hospital bed, and the plaster cracks and out comes an enormous spider, a tarantula. That is a perfectly good datum for abnormal psychology, not for natural history. Whatever is given to whatever subject is a datum. Putting the data into different categories is a further activity of intelligence and judgment. Experiential objectivity is simply the givenness of the data.

A second component in objectivity is normative objectivity. The enemies or adversaries of Lord Russell say that his postulate that regards the hierarchy of classes can be expressed as follows: there is no valid proposition that regards all classes. They say Lord Russell's postulate is a proposition, and it regards all classes. According to the postulate all such propositions are invalid. Therefore, Lord Russell postulates the invalidity of his postulate. It is incoherent, self-refuting. That is an exclusion of objectivity, not because someone experienced or did not experience something, but because it is against normative objectivity. One of the elements in normative objectivity is that you do not contradict yourself; and the absence of contradiction is a criterion of objectivity, a quite different criterion from the criterion of experiential objectivity. In the one objectivity of one human knowing there are quite different properties because human knowing is not some single operation but a set of different operations. I have given you a negative example of normative objectivity, namely, a contradictory proposition attributed to Lord Russell. Whether Lord Russell would accept that as an expression of his postulate regarding the hierarchy of classes is another question which we fortunately need not go into; but it illustrates the point, negatively, of normative objectivity.

What is the positive meaning of normative objectivity? We spoke about the 'elevators' from experience to the level of inquiry and understanding, and from understanding and thinking to reflective understanding and judging. This represents the intelligence and reasonableness of the subject. Because he is intelligent he asks What? and Why? and How? and so on. Because he is reasonable he asks whether that really is so. Is it what you *think* or is it something that is really true? There are exigences in the intelligent and rational subject that require that he try to understand and, when he understands, that he think coherently and express exactly what he has understood, and with respect to exactly what data that act of understanding holds. Similarly, reflective understanding, the rationality of the subject, has its exigences. And the sum of the exigences of the intelligent and rational subject constitutes the requirement of normative objectivity.

Now you will notice that in experiential objectivity the data are given. Normative objectivity – the exigences, the rules, that are not formulated but that are constitutive of man's intelligence and reasonableness – is like an 'if ... then': *if* these data, *then* this judgment. Normative objectivity gives you a hypothetical proposition. If you start out from these data you will formulate this judgment, so that the combination of experiential and normative objectivity will result in what I have called the 'virtually unconditioned.' I have to be very brief on that; you will find more in *Insight*, chapter 10.

Briefly, an unconditioned may be formally unconditioned, and then it has no conditions of any kind whatever. There is only one instance of that: God. Or it may have conditions and the conditions are fulfilled, and then it may be called a virtually unconditioned. What does reflective understanding do? A general formulation is that it combines the 'if ... then' of normative objectivity with the experiential data satisfying the 'if,' and so grasps a virtually unconditioned. If we say, 'If *A*, then *B*,' normative objectivity gives you what may be expressed as a hypothetical proposition; and in the hypothetical proposition, *B* is conditioned. There is a *B if A*. Experiential objectivity gives you the *A*. The two combined give a virtually unconditioned, and that is what reflective understanding grasps. When you grasp the virtually unconditioned, you judge; you say, 'It is so.'

The point to grasp is the difference between a judgment simply placed, and all the qualifications that can be made. One can say, 'It appears to be so,' 'It seems to me,' 'I'm inclined to think,' 'Perhaps one would say,' 'Possibly it's so,' 'Probably it's so'; and whenever one puts in a qualification like that, what one says is qualified, conditioned, by the subject. When one asks, 'Is this a piece of chalk?' and replies, 'It is' – that's all there is about it! You can chatter about it if you want, but no one has any doubt – this is a piece of chalk; that's what it is. You are saying something that is independent of the subject. The subject has grasped a virtually unconditioned. What is unconditioned has no conditions. What has no conditions at all has no conditions in the subject; what has no conditions in the subject is independent of the subject. It is not a matter of 'seeming to him,' 'appearing to him,' what he is 'inclined to think,' what he 'might say,' what he thinks 'would probably be true,' and so on. It is what is so, and you can say, 'It is so,' insofar as you have reached the unconditioned.

Briefly, then, the notion of objectivity that ties in with human knowing as a structure is a compound notion in which there are three components: experiential, normative, and absolute. And the third, the absolute, results from a combination of the other two. The normative gives you the equivalent of a hypothetical proposition. The experience itself, the data, the color of the hand – not the proposition that it is not white, but what you see when you compare the white paper with the not-so-white hand – is the experiential component. That experiential objectivity combines with the normative to give you the absolute objectivity; and when you reach absolute objectivity you say that something is so.

So much for three well-known philosophies: empiricist, rationalist, idealist. Each of them takes some element of the objectivity of human knowing and runs it for what it is worth.[16] On the other hand, what I believe is the true view of the objectivity of human knowing is a combination of three properties. And you have the combination of three properties because human knowing itself is a structure.

3.2 Naive Realism and Objectivity

Now we will do a little more complicated song and dance on the topic of objectivity and work our way to subjectivity. When you arrive at absolute objectivity and you say that something *is*, for whom does that mean anything? It is independent of the subject, but that is not what any man of common sense means by 'objective.' When I say it is objective that this lectern is out here, I mean that there is something hard here that I can put my hands on and everyone can see. What is objective is out there. You can perform a simple experiment on the subject of objectivity. You can ask Jack or Jill to raise a hand and look at it. The hand is out there, and the eye is here. The eye sees the hand. The hand is the object, the eye is the subject. And being objective is seeing what is there to be seen and not projecting

16 Since Lonergan mentions three philosophies and goes on to relate them to elements or properties of objectivity, which in his philosophy are three, it would be easy to suppose that the three philosophies pair off with the three properties of objectivity. But that would be incorrect. Empiricism does pair off with experiential objectivity, and idealism pairs off with normative objectivity. But rationalism cannot be paired with Lonergan's absolute objectivity; at best it can be said to head that way: 'there is something to the rationalist insistence on necessity, for a conditioned whose conditions are fulfilled is virtually an unconditioned' (*Collection* 214, and see 212–13).

something into the hand that is not there to be seen. It is an absence of projections from the subject. It is the subject seeing what is there to be seen. In that instance you grasp the essence of objectivity, and for knowing to be objective you have to have the essence of objectivity in it. Consequently, it is like 'Either you see something that is there to be seen, or not.' If you are seeing something that is there to be seen, then understanding is like ocular vision, at least essentially. It has to have the essence of objectivity in it; what is not objective is not knowing; knowing means knowing objectively. And in the judgment, It is so, what are you seeing? Well, you are seeing that your knowing corresponds to the thing. Truth is the correspondence between the cognitional act and the object known. You know the truth, you know the correspondence. And if you know the correspondence objectively, you see the one that is there to be seen; that is what it has to be.

That is what I would call the naive-realist notion of objectivity. You grasp the objectivity of knowing, the essence of it, by considering a simple example that everyone acknowledges to be objective knowing, and you generalize: the essence of objectivity must be found in every instance of objective knowing. Therefore, that is to be found in thoughts, in insights, in reflective understanding, and in judgment. Otherwise, these activities do not pertain properly to immediate knowledge. They may be useful for inferences and long trains of reasoning and all forms of indirect knowing, but they are not constitutive of the really basic instances in which you are knowing what is there to be known and exactly that, nothing more and nothing less.

3.3 The Kantian View

After the naive-realist notion, there comes what is approximately the Kantian view. I will give you just the basic elements. I look out my window, and I can give two reports. I can see a field or a street, and I can say, 'The field is green,' or 'The street is grey.' I can also say, 'The field seems to be green, it looks green,' or 'The street looks grey.' Both are possible reports on my experience when I look out my window. But when I say, 'The field is green,' 'The street is grey,' I am using language that purports to tell me the real properties of real things. When I say, 'The field is green,' 'The street is grey,' I seem to be talking about a real field, a real street, with a real property. When I say, 'It looks green,' or 'It looks grey,' I'm talking just about the appearances. Now when I say 'is,' I am not talking only about seeing.

You do not see 'is.' 'Is so' involves a judgment. When I say that the field 'looks' green, the street 'looks' grey, *that* is when I am talking about what I really see, the way things look. Seeing is just a matter of the way things appear, not the way they are. To know the way they are, you have to be on the level of judgment. What is true of seeing is also true of hearing. What you hear is the way things sound; and similarly for all other sensitive experiences. They report not reality but appearance. Consequently, when you inquire, you inquire about appearances; when you understand, you understand appearances; when you think, you think about appearances; and when you reflect, you reflect about your understanding of appearances. When you have grasped the unconditioned, it is with regard to what is unconditioned about appearances, and so your judgments are only about appearances, and you never know reality. That is a brief account of the Kantian position.

3.4 Objectivity and the Universe of Being

We note something common to both of these positions, namely, that fundamentally knowing is a matter of taking a look. It was apparent from the way I presented the naive-realist viewpoint: you see what is out there; objectivity is a matter of seeing what is there to be seen, not projecting upon it your interpretation or your bright ideas in connection with it. Seeing is not just a matter of data. Seeing the tarantula in *The Lost Weekend* and my seeing my hand are all on the same level; there is no big difference there. For the naive realist, objectivity resides in, the model for it is in, looking.

The Kantian formulates his position a little more carefully. At the beginning of his Transcendental Aesthetic, Kant says that whatever may be the mediate relations of our cognitional activities to objects, the one case in which there is an immediate relation to objects is in what he calls *Anschauung*, which is usually translated 'intuition' and may also be translated 'looking.'[17] If you live in a picture world, then the one possibility of knowing it is by taking a look. The only way you can know a picture is by looking at it. And in a picture world the condition of objectivity is looking. If you live in a universe of being, of what is, you do not have the difficulties I started out from by saying, 'Well, I would rather get at something independent of the subject, at what is. That has nothing to do with real life.' So the trick is: sub-

17 Immanuel Kant, *Kritik der reinen Vernunft*, A 19, B 33; in Smith's translation (see above, chapter 6, note 19) 65, where *Anschauung* is translated 'intuition.'

stitute a picture world, which is fairly easy, a very plausible tale, because we are mostly involved in the picture world a lot of the time.

The universe of being (of what is: that it is; and what is not: that it is not) is something different, and it is arrived at gradually. There is the world in which we live from the age of zero months until we reach the age of reason. We work out our distinctions between reality and appearance sufficiently for that age. We change them later on after reaching the age of reason and passing through adolescence and becoming adult, and so on. But when one starts to think about knowing, there is a great temptation to revert to childhood, and to revert to the criteria one first thought out at that time.

The existence of that problem was forced upon me many years ago. I was visiting my brother in my hometown of Buckingham, and there were two boys about four and five (perhaps three and four, I'm not sure) and another boy about eight with them. It was night, and the other boy about eight was saying, 'There's a bear in the side hall!' and these two fellows were terrified; they would run to their mother with their news that there was a bear in the side hall, and she would tell them not to be crazy, and so on, and they would become reassured. Then he would take them aside again and say, 'There's a lion in the side hall!' and they would be equally terrified. They had not yet reached the age where they distinguished between a story and what is really so. Before you reach the age of reason, you work out some sort of distinction between what you dream and your waking life, the stories you hear and what is really so. But if you work it out along the lines of seeing with your eyes what is objectively there, and then try to apply that to your cognitional theory, you will end up, on the one hand, as a naive realist or, on the other hand, equally well and much more consistently as a Kantian.

Kant says that what our senses give us are appearances. But in fact, our senses give us neither appearance nor reality. It is a judgment to say that something is not apparent but real, and it is just as much a judgment to say that something is not real but apparent. Both are matters of judgment. On the level of experience what have we? Data. We have just experiential objectivity. If you try to place more at that level, you evoke another philosophy, which does not give that level credit even for what it is.

So much for an indication of the puzzles connected with objectivity. We started off by considering three types of philosophers, each with quite different criteria of objectivity. We said that each was saying something true and none was saying the whole truth, because there is to the objectivity of human knowing a set of three different properties, and you need all three to have one objectivity. Just as knowing is a structure, so the objectivity of human knowing is a set of properties. But that set of properties does not bring us to the ordinary everyday assurance, to the ideas one simply forms about what the real world really is. When people start talking about being, about what is, normally their reaction is mystification. 'He's talking philosophy, and everyone knows that that must be nonsense. It is not natural science. It is not human science. It is not common sense. What is this "being" that the philosophers talk about when they talk about what is, and so on? God knows.'

That difficult, complex notion of objectivity is not easily accepted. You take an easy notion – looking at your hand, grasping the essence of objectivity there. What results from that? You eliminate rational psychology from the field; cognitional psychology is simply eliminated. You will find whole manuals on rational psychology with no mention of human intelligence. Why? Because human intelligence has the objectivity not of ocular vision but of intelligence, a normative type of objectivity, something that sense does not have. Sense has its own component of objectivity; and intelligence and reasonableness have their requirements of objectivity, and they are quite different. Just as you cannot conceive understanding on the analogy of seeing or hearing, so you cannot conceive the objectivity of intelligence and reasonableness on the analogy of sense. If you try to conceive it on the analogy of sense, you start importing or creating a purely fictitious account of what knowing is.

4 Knowing and Intersubjectivity

I have given six theories of objectivity: empiricist, rationalist, idealist, naive-realist, Kantian, and my own theory of objectivity as a compound. As you can imagine, there are many people who study all six theories and many more, and what do they do in the end? They throw up their hands: 'Objectivity is for the birds.'

To lead a human life you have to have meanings. To have a human community you have to have common meanings. A community involves a common field of experience. It involves, for a second level of community, common understanding, not mutual incomprehension. When mutual incomprehension is met, the other fellow is not only wrong, mistaken, he is simply incredible, out of this world: 'You wouldn't believe it, but this is actually what he said and did!' And so on. You need common judgments. There is a split in community when some start saying that this is true and others start saying that it is false and just the opposite is what is true. In the last place, finally, there are the communities of commitment in which will enters in. There is a common will, whether founded on love as in the family, or loyalty as in the state, or faith as in religion. There are, then, communities on the level of experience, on the level of understanding, on the level of judgment, and above all on the level of rational self-consciousness when one deliberates and decides and chooses. Human living is strictly human when you move to that fourth level where people are acting, relating with one another. That human community is impossible without meanings, common meanings. If we are going to live, we have to have common meanings. Philosophy cannot help us. There are endless theories of knowledge and endless theories of objectivity. You can listen to them all, and all it does is make you dizzy.

But we have to exist. The conscious subject has to assert himself, has to make his claims. And there is a tendency so to insist on intersubjectivity, on the subject, and on interpersonal relations that the subject takes over, will takes over, and objectivity is given short shrift. Instead of Jack or Jill looking at a hand and saying, 'This is what seems to me,' or 'My hand appears white,' or 'My hand is white,' 'There are four fingers on it and a thumb,' or whatever you please, Jack and Jill become interested in one another. The problem of the 'out there' is transcended. The intersubjective situation, the vital interchange of mutual presence – all the aspects of intersubjectivity studied by psychologists – and the importance of decision in leading a human life are given full emphasis. A mistaken notion of objectivity is brushed aside. The empiricist, positivist, naive-realist, Kantian notion of objectivity is transcended because one deals not with subject and objects; you have two subjects, and the two subjects are not totally separate. Besides 'I' and 'thou,' there is 'we,' 'us,' 'ourselves,' 'ours' – a viewpoint for living. Implicitly, objectivity is recognized. Jack and Jill are not thought of as characters out of a social worker's casebook. They are not unperceptive; the experiential element in knowing is there. They are not stupid; the intellectual element in knowing is there. They are not silly; the rational element in knowing is there. They have objective knowing, but they do not know it because they cannot get hold of any theory of objectivity that satisfies them. You get an insistence on subjectivity, a rejection of a mistaken notion of objectivity, but no recognition of what objectivity really is. And what is the penalty? The penalty is being lost in a very small group. Intersubjectivity goes so far – 'our circle.'

To deal with anything on a larger scale, with the city, with the state, with the church, to deal with the problems of industrialization and commerce and all the rest of it, you need a theoretical, technical type of knowledge. You cannot do it without some valid, carefully thought-out notion of objectivity. The scientific work can be done up to a point on a positivist or an empiricist basis. But the subject tends to be neglected, and the exigences of the person tend to be neglected, and that, it seems to me, is a fundamental problem of our time. In other words, everything that is said in praise of subjectivity and intersubjectivity and *Existenz*, of the subject determining what his own living is to be, making himself at the present time, is all excellent. But it contains such an affirmation of subjectivity as to appear at least to exclude, to rule out, the objective. And that tends to give the small circle or the solipsistic point of view that gets separated from the larger concerns of man's life on earth.

I wish to thank you for your kind attention. We'll answer, insofar as possible, any questions that anyone cares to ask.

Question: Is it possible that your presentation is largely in the picture world, and therefore you have to do things on the board?

Response: No. Understanding occurs with respect to images. I could describe a schematic image on three levels and say: imagine on the first level the experiences, on the second level the acts of understanding, on the third level the acts of judging. You have to have an image to understand; the quote from Aristotle on the front page of *Insight* says that intelligence grasps forms in images; St Thomas, in the first part of the *Summa theologiae*, question 84, article 7, says that without images one cannot actually understand anything whatever in this life, no matter what the habitual accumulation one may have acquired of what he calls *species intelligibiles*, no matter what intellectual habits one may have already acquired. If one knows the whole of mathematics, without any image of some kind, at least of symbols, one is not going to understand anything because the object of human understanding, of insight, is provided by the image. To avoid long and complicated explanations on how to form the image, it is much simpler to draw a diagram on the blackboard.

But living in the picture world is a matter of imagining knowing. People do not really live in picture worlds, but they imagine knowing and they take their image of knowing too seriously. They imagine the subject and they imagine the object, and the problem of objectivity is the bridge, how to get 'out there.' When the problem of objectivity is put that way, you are going to have an imaginative solution because your problem is in the image. It is a spatial problem of exteriority: 'How do you get out there? By seeing.' Insofar as your problem is put in terms of the unconditioned, when one knows what is, one is stating that something is so, independently of me. One must have reached an unconditioned. It has no conditions in me – what is, is so whether I know it or not. When you put the issue of objectivity discursively, you are forced to the notion of the unconditioned, and you can find that only in judgment. The fundamental thinker on that unconditioned is Newman in his *Grammar of Assent*, the section 'Assent Considered as Unconditional.'[18] In Plato and Aristotle, largely in the medieval writers, in the whole of German philosophy, that idea of assent as unconditional, as absolute positing, is lacking. The judgment is conceived as a composition of concepts, a synthesis of concepts, as in Plato's *symplokê tôn eidôn*,[19] and that is not judgment. In any hypothesis there are endless concepts linked together, but you are not saying whether it is so or not so – you're not judging.

Question: I gather that your theory of objectivity is a compound. Could you elucidate exactly what you mean by a compound theory of objectivity?
Response: There are different elements in it; it's not one property. Experiential objectivity is something totally different from normative objectivity. I gave the example of the color of my hand as a datum, as one component in objectivity, the datum as given – simply as given without any commentary. Another illustration of objectivity is coherence. If a proposition or a postulate is self-refuting, it can't be a part of objective knowledge. And this normative component plus the experiential combine to give you a third, the objectivity of what you call a fact. A fact is not the same as a datum. A datum qua datum is never defined. Data are fuzzy until you get concepts applied to them that mark them off.

I was speaking with a group of philosophers and scientists, and the question came up of the indefinite progress of science. A chemist remarked that the discoveries in chemistry in the last five years have immeasurably

18 John Henry Cardinal Newman, *An Essay in Aid of a Grammar of Assent* (first published, London, 1870), chapter 6.

19 The reference is probably to *The Sophist* 259e: *dia gar tên allêlôn tôn eidôn symplokên ho logos gegonen hêmin* ('For our power of discourse is derived from the interweaving of the classes or ideas with one another' – trans. H.N. Fowler [Cambridge: Harvard University Press, 1942]).

increased the field of data.[20] What did he mean? Not that we have new senses, but that advance in theory increases our capacities to apprehend, to attend precisely. You need concepts to tie onto data to make them precise. A fact is something that's sharply defined. It's something known by a judgment. It's something contingent, not what must be so. When you get an absolute positing that's particular – this piece of chalk is in my hand – we're stating a fact, which isn't simply a datum of experience or a pure product of intelligence and reasonableness. It is a third component.

Question: Why do you use the word 'normative' objectivity for intelligence?
Response: Because we said that knowing is not merely materially a dynamic structure – its components are activities – but also formally dynamic; it constructs itself. It doesn't construct itself just any way at all. It's intelligence that puts the questions that move one beyond experience to insight and thought. It's one's reasonableness that puts the different types of questions that move one to reflective understanding and judgment. And they not merely move, not merely are 'elevators' moving from one level to the next, but they also control the activities that occur, set their standards. You can't judge without sufficient evidence, and if you have sufficient evidence you have to judge. The 'can't' and 'have to' are not in terms of physical necessity, physical force, but in terms of the necessity imposed on one by one's own rationality.

Question: Would this be the totally subjective position if I said, 'What's out there doesn't exist except insofar as I define its existence'? Is that the subjective position?
Response: The subjectivist position, as it starts in Kierkegaard and is developed in the existentialists, is an insistence on the rationally self-conscious subject, which is a still further level of consciousness. Its concern is with not drifting. The drifter does what everyone else is doing, he says what everyone else is saying, he thinks what everyone else is thinking, and everyone else is doing the same thing. They're all drifting. They're waiting for Il Duce or the Führer or the Caudillo to come along and carry them off their feet.

20 In 1973, Lonergan identified this chemist as 'chairman of the department of chemistry' at Loyola University (now Loyola Marymount University) in Los Angeles. See *Philosophy of God, and Theology* (see above, chapter 3, note 24) 61–62.

The opposite of that is the one who develops authentically.[21] Take the child; you underestimate the development of a child and try to put on its shoes: 'Let me do it!' The child wants to do things itself, and boys want to decide for themselves, and adolescents want to find out for themselves. And teachers, parents, and others have to take account of that development, have to let their charges do more and more for themselves, decide more and more for themselves, find out more and more for themselves. There comes a critical point where one finds out for oneself that one has to decide for oneself what one is going to do with oneself. That's the moment of *Existenz.* You find out for yourself that it's up to you to decide for yourself; and when you decide for yourself you make the existential decision, you decide what kind of man you are going to be. That existing is on the further level, not of judgment but of decision and choice and rational *self*-consciousness, when one is dealing with oneself. It presupposes a meaning for a life.

But philosophy has been given up as bankrupt or as irrelevant to living. 'At least I have to exist' – as illustrated by Kierkegaard's religious faith in the teeth of Hegelian philosophy. He couldn't refute Hegel. When he said, 'I exist, and I have to live, and I have to be a man, and I have to be a Christian,' and so on, that affirmation of the subject in Kierkegaard is blind, it ties in with faith as confidence, the Lutheran tradition of faith, not faith as believing truths. But it came alive again this century in various types of philosophy which at least apparently are anti-rational and anti-intellectual. They're extremely intelligent at the same time, like Heidegger and all those philosophers; they do philosophy extraordinarily well. But the question of objectivity is brushed aside. What is particularly being brushed aside is positivism; we need to get beyond positivism if we are to lead human lives. That's a very common form of it. By positivism we mean what the scientists can tell us; and what they can tell us doesn't connect with the problems of living, and deciding, and being oneself. Now is that clarifying the matter for you any? All I can hope to do this evening is to give a general location.

Question: When you were talking about the virtually unconditioned, 'If *A*, then *B*,' *A* would have to be experienced. Is *B* on the normative or on the

21 On the language of 'authenticity,' becoming recurrent in Lonergan's work around the time of this lecture, see editorial note *r* to '*Existenz* and *Aggiornamento*,' *Collection* 306. Such language appears also in 'Cognitional Structure,' a paper, as we have said, practically contemporaneous with the present one.

then *B*,' *A* would have to be experienced. Is *B* on the normative or on the reflective level?

Response: It's the prospective judgment. Before you make a judgment, it's prospective. It isn't something you haven't thought of before; it's something you don't know yet. You have thought of it: Is that so? You have your prospective judgment in your question for reflection. If there is a link between that and experience, then you have that element, the contribution from normative objectivity. The experience gives you the fulfilment of the conditions. The experience as experience is not fulfilment of conditions, but under reflection you ask whether these experiences fulfil conditions. The notion of conditions comes from elsewhere.

Question (continued): And the prospective judgment comes ...

Response: It comes on the level of thought, and it's put as conditioned: Is that so? It's so if I have the evidence for it.

Question: The first three levels are inevitable. It's inevitable that I see, it's inevitable that I understand something of what I see, like a pattern, like the pattern on the wall?

Response: It's inevitable that you *try* to understand and normative ...

Question (continued): At what point is it inevitable?

Response: Well, it comes in human living. You have to act, you can't get around acting. It starts off on the spontaneous level. There's a process of maturation in the human being. This inevitability is the sort of thing that's bound to happen, but it doesn't exclude the possibility of low IQ's and so on, in which it happens very rarely or thinly. What's strictly inevitable is that you can't be intelligent and not want to understand. You're saying the same thing. It is illustrated by saying that if you're playing the fool, you want to do it intelligently.

Question (continued): Then can someone decide to drift, or does he just drift?

Response: Usually they just drift. They may say it's too bad to be this way and make resolutions, but resolutions do not predetermine the next day's choices. So even if a person decides not to drift he may still be a drifter. It is always precarious, as the existentialists say. Making oneself is never finished in this life. One never knows how one's going to end up.

Question: Can you still be intelligent and drift?

Response: Oh, yes.

Question (continued): But without exercising the will rationally you'll keep on drifting?

Response: Yes, usually with God's grace, as the relation comes in on the fourth level too.
Question (continued): Then rational self-consciousness ...
Response: ... is a fourth level.
Question (continued): Does it equate with rational consciousness?
Response: It's beyond it.
Question (continued): Cooperating with grace?
Response: Well, grace can come in anywhere, but particularly on the level of decision and choice.
Question (continued): Even in rational consciousness?
Response: It *can* come in there. Prophecy is supposed to be a matter of particular help on the level of judgment, of what is so.
Question (continued): There are many interpretations ...
Response: Yes, that is also true. I said, 'is supposed to be.'

Question: How can one hope to have a common subjectivity if the basis of his experience, the experiencing of experiences, is an individual thing?
Response: There is such a thing as intersubjectivity. A shriek not only startles but frightens us.
Question (continued): Not everybody.
Response: Perhaps not everybody, but there is all the same such a thing as intersubjectivity. Fundamental work has been done by Max Scheler on the forms of sympathy.[22] A simple example. The course of my daily walk in Rome is up a ramp. One day a child was running ahead of its mother, and the concrete there was shattered in a spot, and I was twenty feet away. I saw that child beginning to fall, and spontaneously I leaned forward – as if it were two feet away – to prevent it from falling. Spontaneously, without thinking. Just as, if you're going to be struck, you raise your hand without thinking. If you're going to lose your balance, there are spontaneous reactions. There are also spontaneous intersubjective reactions. They are prior to the level of the distinction between the 'I' and 'thou.'
Question (continued): Yes, but there are people who go through life with grey glasses, pink glasses, or green glasses ...
Response: Yes.
Question (continued): ... which means that there shall be entirely different experiences.
Response: Yes. Without any experiences of intersubjectivity, you say?

22 Max Scheler, *The Nature of Sympathy* (see above, chapter 5, note 3).

Question (continued): With very few.
Response: I don't think so; but it's a question for the empirical psychologist. It's commonly recognized. There's a total adaptation when you meet someone. If I'm in my room working and a student knocks at the door and comes in, well, it requires a certain amount of time to readapt. I usually get favorable reactions when I talk about instances of intersubjectivity. People seem to know what I mean.

Question: On these last questions – the subjective aspect: you went on to showing simply how the difficulty in formulating objectivity had led to these other problems, or that they are sort of ignoring the problem of objectivity. Have I got it correctly?
Response: Yes, yes. In other words, for a lot of students in Rome, the European section, there's no use insisting on objectivity; but if you talk subjectivity, well, you start talking sense.[23] In Germany, France, Belgium, Holland, Northern Italy, objectivity is finished. 'Well, that's all right for natural scientists, and so on. When you're talking on a subject like religion, you just have to blot that out. You'll putter around with diagrams and never get anywhere.' They're conceiving objectivity in a positivistic fashion usually. But the complexity of the philosophies, going through them all and so on, finding your way through, is such that they're blocked on that. They're convinced that there's no way out, no use trying. Especially the 'no use trying' – that's always a perfect block. It saves a lot of work.

Question: Is this a result of the Kantian ...
Response: Kant is fundamental. Kant has not generally been thought through; he is not out of date yet. Jaspers, for example, proves an extremely rich writer and penetrating, and all the rest. Kantian limitations run straight through all his thinking. Now there are other people who try to get around these somehow or other; Heidegger contains potentialities of getting beyond Kant, but he can't push through. He's never written the second part of his *Sein und Zeit.* Kant is still a problem.

23 This quite negative opinion of his European students is to be balanced by what Lonergan says on their positive influence on his own development in Rome: 'I was learning all the time myself; I was moving into the European atmosphere in which phenomenology was dominant. There were highly trained students from Germany and France, Belgium and Northern Italy' (*Caring about Meaning* [see above, chapter 3, note 27] 105).

Question (continued): This is a case of subjectivity – a lack of objectivity?
Response: No, no, no. Subjectivity need not imply any negation of objectivity. I said that the people insisting on subjectivity will also insist on being perceptive and not being stupid, not being silly; and that's what being objective is. If you're not unperceptive, you have the experiential component. If you're neither stupid nor silly, you'll have the normative component; and the normative component will drive you to the unconditioned before you make any judgments. And so you'll have what is objectivity. What's missing is a *theory* of objectivity; and then there are the blocks on that from the picture world, and all this sort of thing.

Question: I'm sorry I may appear a little dense on this, but would you redefine the shift to external reality in terms of 'The grass is green'?
Response: Well, they leap beyond that. 'I'm not worried about your appearances. You're a person talking to me, seriously putting me a question. I realize that, and there's no use my wasting my time discussing whether the grass is green, or looks green, and all that sort of thing. All these philosophers during the nineteenth century – they were bothered with that, but let's forget it. Get down to personal relations and human living, living in community. What is it to be a man?' – or whatever happens to interest one, and so on. It's a shift of the question into a new field.
Question (continued): The whole question of objectivity/subjectivity is outdated, it seems.
Response: Well, they want to outdate objectivity and insist on the subject, the becoming of the subject, and so on. They're serious people, in a human way, uninterested in a certain type of technical philosophy that has had the stage, such as Hegelianism – although Hegelianism is coming in strongly again in certain forms. You'll get more of this in other lectures coming in this course.

Thank you ever so much for your kind attention.

11

Theology as Christian Phenomenon[1]

Believers are one thing, theologians another. Often enough, it is difficult not to think of the theologians as a group of parasites that, if not utterly odious, at least do more harm than good. However, it is difficult to offer a course on faith and say nothing whatever about theology;[2] and the purpose of the present lecture is to offer you an outline, an indication, a set of suggestions, not indeed on the theory of the nature and method of theology, but upon the way it works in the concrete.

My first point will be that theologians, like believers, are human beings – men, and today also women. I prefer to spend some time on this rather platitudinous point, because the way in which men and women in general experience and inquire, understand and think, reflect and judge in other affairs is not without its parallels and analogies in matters of faith and theology. So my first point will be neither upon faith nor upon theology, but upon the way the human mind develops.

On this point, I will use a book written about four years ago in German

1 A lecture given at the Thomas More Institute, Montreal, 1 October 1964. The reel-tape recording of the lecture was transferred to cassettes by Howard Logan, SJ, in March 1973 (TC 423, 424, Lonergan Research Institute Library, Toronto). The late Michael O'Callaghan made a transcription of the cassette recording in February 1976 (Lonergan Research Institute Library, File 423). This editing works from the cassette recording and benefits from O'Callaghan's reliable transcription.

2 The lecture introduced a course entitled 'Faith: An Exploration of the Christian Commitment.' We are grateful to Dr Heather Stephens of the Thomas More Institute for this additional information.

and recently translated into English, *The Discovery of the Mind* by Bruno Snell.[3] The principal chapters in this book give a very beautiful illustration of man's discovery that he has a mind. The book recounts the manner in which the Greek poets and philosophers gradually came to objectify and state the fact that they had minds and wills, bodies and souls. Because it is obvious to us, we may be inclined to take it for granted that the same facts must always have been obvious to everyone. My point in spending what may seem a disproportionate amount of time on this mere illustration is that it introduces very effectively the notion of historical development and historical perspective.

The first section, then, of the lecture will be devoted to the development of the notion of mind in the Greek poets and philosophers; the second part will be the development in the Christian apprehension of Christ. They have a similarity, insofar as both are cases of development; they differ because in one case what is developing is natural human knowledge, and in the other case what is developing is Christian dogma.

1 The Greek Discovery of Mind

We will begin, then, from the illustration. According to Bruno Snell, the word *sôma,* which in later Greek means body, in Homer means corpse. Moreover, there is not any Homeric word that corresponds to what the later Greeks, and we ourselves, mean by body. In Homer there are several words to denote the various parts of the body. There are other words that denote various aspects of the body taken as a whole. But there is no one word that corresponds to the whole under all its aspects, as does our word 'body' and the later usage of the Greek word *sôma.*

Moreover, as Homer had no word for body, so also he had no word for what we mean by soul. He speaks of the *psychê,* the life breath; when a man dies, ordinarily the life breath, the *psychê,* goes out through his mouth, but if the man has a large gaping wound it goes out through that. He speaks of the *thymos,* which is the seat, perhaps the organ, of motions and emotions. He speaks of *nous* (or usually of *noos* in Homer), which means intelligent imagination. But there is no one general word to denote soul.

3 Bruno Snell, *The Discovery of the Mind: The Greek Origins of European Thought,* trans. T.G. Rosenmeyer (New York: Harper Torchbooks, 1960); an unabridged republication appears as *The Discovery of the Mind in Greek Philosophy and Literature* (New York: Dover Publications, 1982).

Further, as he lacks the notions of body and soul, so there do not occur in Homeric descriptions interior processes of the soul. Homer's heroes change their minds, but the change is not depicted as an autonomous interior process, which is the way we all think of it. On the contrary, a god or goddess intervenes, and the hero, so to speak, has his mind changed *for* him. So, in the first book of the *Iliad,* Achilles is enraged when Agamemnon deprives him of the slave girl Briseis; he is ready to draw the sword and lay about him, but he is tapped on the shoulder and turns around and marvels to see Athena behind him. She tells him that he has good reason to be angry but all in all, in the long run, he will be better off if he lets go his sword and refrains from slaughtering fellow Greeks. Achilles obeyed the goddess, Homer tells us. For internal process there is substituted a divine intervention.

I have been speaking of the limitations of Homeric vocabulary and Homeric thought with regard to man and internal human process. In the older lyric poets – in Sappho, Alcaeus, Stesichorus, Simonides, Bacchylides, and in the greatest of them all, Pindar – there occurs one marked development. They have the same general outlook on man as Homer, with one development. They describe singular and intense personal experiences: Archilocus those of the warrior, Sappho those of the lover, and so on. The point is that, where Homer's descriptions are limited to outward actions or to the intervention of a god, the older lyric poets describe not ordinary living as it is internally experienced, but only singular, remarkably intense events in internal living.

What began with the older lyric poets was advanced by the tragedians. Aeschylus, in the play *The Suppliants,* depicts just one thing: a decision. The daughters of Danaus are fleeing from the Egyptian youths; they seek refuge and asylum on an island where Pelasgus is king. The whole play is the decision of the king to risk war with the Egyptians by giving asylum to the maidens. In other words, the play consists in objectifying, in setting before one's eyes as a spectacle, the inner process of deciding, of making a choice. Free will is a property of man, but it is one thing to have a free will, and it is another to be able to think about one's own free will as one does about any other object. To take that step was an achievement of Greek tragedy. To take a series of similar, ever more complex steps that set forth men's inner lives as objects was the work of Sophocles and Euripides.

Upon the work of the Greek epic, lyric, and dramatic poets, there supervened the more technical and more thorough work of the Sophists and philosophers. The poets in their verses or in their dramas symbolically disclosed man's inner self. They effected a first objectification of the inner life of man. The philosophers exploited the disclosure in their analyzing, distinguishing, relating, establishing, deducing. And so we have Greek logic, Greek psychology, Greek cognitional theory, and Greek moral theory. Over a period of centuries, there occurred a process from what the French call the *vécu* to the *thématique*; from what the Scholastics call the *exercite* to the *signate*; from what the Germans call the *existentiell* to the *existential*; from what we would call experience and consciousness to knowledge in the fully objective sense of the word.

2 The Christian Apprehension of Christ

Now what occurred with regard to man in the development of Greek thought occurred in a similar way with regard to Christ in the history of the Christian apprehension of Christ. You will know from the older type of catechism or from the decrees of the Council of Chalcedon and the Third Council of Constantinople that in Christ Jesus there is one divine person and two natures: a human nature and a divine nature; and consequently, two different sets of properties: divine properties and human properties; two operations: divine operation and human operation; and two wills: a divine will and a human will. Those conclusions were arrived at roughly in the course of seven centuries. The Greek development was over a considerably longer period – it depends on where you place Homer. But that period of time was required for the Christians to come to think of Christ in that fashion. Because that development occurred through the decrees of ecumenical councils, we know that it is a development of dogma. But if it had not occurred through councils, if it had been simply the work of theologians, it would have been a development of doctrine without being a development of dogma. The development part is the essence of theology, and I propose to attempt to communicate to you some notion of what theology is and does, by considering principally the development of Christology in Christian thought.

2.1 *In the New Testament*

In the New Testament none of the expressions used to describe Christ in the later councils are to be found. The word 'person,' in the later technical sense, does not occur; there is the word *prosôpon* but it is not used in that later technical sense. The word 'nature' occasionally occurs, but not in any great technical sense; and certainly there is no mention of two natures in Christ, of a divine nature in Christ and a human nature in Christ. There is no talk about properties or operations in any technical sense, very little about wills, and nothing about two wills. What is the New Testament apprehension of Christ from which the development begins?

One may say schematically that there are four main apprehensions of Jesus of Nazareth in the New Testament. They tend to overlap, one to complement the other, but the four are fundamentally distinct. There is the conception of Christ as anticipated, as the Messiah, as Christ; he is the one expected by and promised to the people of Israel, the one who was to come. In this scheme, this first mode of apprehension, Christ is conceived and apprehended through the memories and expectations of the Chosen People, through their literature, and through their living faith and hope. In the tenth chapter of St John, the Jews are depicted as asking our Lord, 'Tell us, once and for all, whether or not you really are the Christ' (10.24).[4] Their question is about the Christ. Of course, the answer given there is not in terms of Christ; in 10.30 our Lord says, 'The Father and I are one.' The answer is in an entirely different scheme from the scheme of the question; the question deals with an apprehension of Christ through prophecy and promise.

There is a second mode of apprehending Jesus in the New Testament, and there the name is the Son of Man. The Son of Man is not someone who is expected, who is to come; he is not the memory of someone who has come and died and gone away again. The Son of Man, except for a single passage in the seventh chapter of Acts (7.56), is named only in the Gospels, and statements about the Son of Man are of three main types. There is the Son of Man as present before the eyes of the apostles, the disciples, the crowds, and the enemies of Jesus: 'Foxes have holes and birds have nests, but the Son of Man has not whereon to lay his head';[5] 'John the Baptist came, neither eating nor drinking, and you said he had a devil; the Son of Man has come, both eating and drinking, and you say, "Behold, a glutton and a wine drinker, a friend of publicans and sinners."'[6] There is

4 NRSV: 'How long will you keep us in suspense? If you are the Messiah, tell us plainly.'

5 NRSV: 'Foxes have holes, and birds of the air have nests; but the Son of Man has nowhere to lay his head' (Matthew 8:20).

6 NRSV: 'For John came neither eating nor drinking, and they say, "He has a demon"; the Son of Man came eating and drinking, and they say, "Look, a glutton and a drunkard, a friend of tax collectors and sinners!"' (Matthew 11.18–19)

the Son of Man who has power to forgive sins and proves it by telling the sick to rise, take up their beds, and walk. The same Son of Man is also the subject of prophecy; he will be betrayed, condemned, scourged, crucified; he will die and rise again; and he will come again upon the clouds of heaven in power and majesty. Hence a second mode of apprehending and presenting Jesus is in terms of the Son of Man, and that is the apprehension of him during his mortal life.

Thirdly, there is the Lord, the *Kyrios*, the risen Christ, who sits at the right hand of the Father, who intercedes for us as eternal priest, who sends his Spirit into our hearts. This third apprehension pertains to the Christian community, to the period after the resurrection.

So there is the apprehension of the Jewish community expecting our Lord, of the contemporaries of our Lord, who apprehend him as the Son of Man, and of the Christian community after the resurrection, who adore the risen Lord sitting at the right hand of the Father.

Finally, there is the Son sent by the Father, as mentioned in Romans 1.3, Galatians 4.4–6, Philippians 2.6–11, and the first chapter of Hebrews.

Those four apprehensions – the eternal apprehension, if I may use the word, of Christ who is sent by the Father, and the three temporal apprehensions – provide a fundamental scheme. The New Testament account of Jesus primarily regards his functions as Savior, Redeemer, Priest and Victim, Lord and Master and Teacher. But Christians could not eliminate the question, Just who is Christ? The history of Christian doctrine is a long series of decisions of the Christian community acting through its bishops and excluding what were considered erroneous opinions on Christ: erroneous, because not compatible with the word of God taught from the beginning and handed down in the apostolic churches. The word of God is on the level of statement.[7] Other statements may be in accord with it or

7 This is a true part of a doctrine the whole truth of which is more complex. A somewhat fuller account is given in this same chapter (p. 267), where Lonergan speaks of 'the multiple purposes' of the New Testament: devotion, preaching, meditation, and so on. But he had given a much more systematic listing of the uses of scripture two years earlier in the lecture 'De argumento theologico ex sacra scriptura' (Faculty Seminar, Gregorian University and Biblical Institute, Spring 1962); scripture may be taken as: 'usus linguae, unde studia philologica ... expressio, Ausdruck, unde hermeneutica romantica ... occursus, unde exsistentialis mutatio legentis, conversio ... fons multiplicis occursus, traditionis, doctrinae, systematis ... eventus, ut de eventibus, unde historia bibliae et biblica ... obscurae, male intellectae, unde labor exegeticus ... verbum Dei, cui contradicere est nefas, unde dogmata' (p. 3 of Lonergan's notes distributed at the seminar). Here, the word of God as statement is only one of seven ways of taking scripture.

opposed to it. The word as spoken has an implication and an implicit claim to truth, and it is that claim to truth implicit in the spoken word, in the word that is preached, that has the ontological (so to speak) implications of the Christian message.

2.2 *Christological Errors*

Now first of all, by way of an outline I shall list the principal Christological errors, as they are called. I mention these heresies, not because they are the main points of interest – for what positively was thought about Christ is the main point – but because they provide convenient landmarks.[8]

The difference between the Ebionites and the Adoptionists, roughly, is that the Ebionites were Jewish, the Adoptionists were Christian; the doctrine in both cases was the same, namely, Who was Jesus? – he was a man. He was inhabited by God, inhabited by the Holy Spirit, gifted with divine power, intimately related with God, but, all in all, he was just a man. That is the first point.

A second view rejected in the development of Christian doctrine was that of the Sabellians and Patripassianists who denied any distinction between the Father and the Son. Who was Jesus? He is just the same as God the Father; he not only is God, but is the same as God the Father.

A third view is that of the Arians, who acknowledged that the Logos is superior to all other creatures, yet held that he was a creature. The Word is not without any origin, any dependence on anyone else; he is Son, he depends upon the Father, and therefore he must be something made, a creature, although higher than any other angel or any other man or any other creature that can be imagined.

The Apollinarists present a converse to the position of the Adoptionists.

8 This short paragraph is greatly reduced from the recording, which is hard to follow at this point. Lonergan was listing on the blackboard the various errors in question – all of them familiar to him from the textbooks he had written for his Gregorian University courses *De Verbo incarnato* and *De Deo trino*. At the end of the list, he apparently went backwards to provide some information on councils and orthodox writings that dealt with the errors: the Council of Chalcedon in 451 on the Monophysites; the Council of Ephesus in 431 on Nestorius; a work of Athanasius, *Tomus ad Antiochenos*, against Apollinaris at a council in Alexandria in 362; the Council of Nicea against the Arians in 325. He concluded with the Ebionites and Adoptionists who belong to the first two centuries. Then he resumed his more regular lecturing style, taking up these errors in proper chronological order.

If you threw out the view that Jesus was just a man, in whom dwelt in a peculiar way the Holy Spirit, that he was a temple of God in some peculiar way, the simplest way of conceiving this would be to forget about the human soul. Or to put the matter differently, we may distinguish two Greek concepts of the soul, the Platonist and the Aristotelian. According to the Platonist doctrine, the soul is in the body the way a sailor is in the ship. According to Aristotle, the soul is a metaphysical coprinciple; it is the form of the body. To understand the Aristotelian opinion, one has to do what is called metaphysics. A soul is not a thing but a component in a thing; a human soul has peculiar properties, but still that is what it is. It is only by way of metaphysical thought that one can arrive at the Aristotelian notion of the soul.

That notion of the soul in general was unknown to the Fathers – 'in general' I say, at least up to this period of the fourth century. Athanasius explicitly acknowledges against the Apollinarists the existence of a human soul in Christ, but all his thinking about Christ prescinds entirely from any internal human process in Christ. He speaks about his body, his flesh – the Word was made flesh – and he insists the Word did not come into a man, because that would be adoptionism. The Word came into the flesh more or less as a Platonist soul, and the Platonist soul is not soul in the Aristotelian sense; it is a subject, it is the inner man, the one who is conscious, the one who experiences, the one who feels, the one who understands, the one who judges, the one who decides, the one who acts, the someone inside that vanishes when we are asleep and comes back again – the same one – when we awake. In Christ, there is the subject; there are not two subjects, a human person and a divine person. You cannot have two subjects in Christ; you would be positing two persons, you would have the Adoptionist doctrine of a man to whom the Word came. So you eliminate the human subject, and the tendency was, with the elimination of a human subject, to eliminate also a human soul. That is the error of Apollinaris, who taught that in Christ there is one person, one nature, one operation, one property, and one will. Apollinaris already had a stand on all the issues that were disputed for the following centuries.

Apollinaris, then, thought other than Athanasius. When the question is put explicitly, Did Christ have a human soul? Athanasius says that he had, and Apollinaris says he did not. In Athanasius, however, positive thinking about Christ's soul is lacking. The same is true in Cyril of Alexandria in the next century. In his earlier works, Cyril has practically nothing to say about Christ's human soul. He speaks of the Word and of the flesh: the Word was made flesh; but he does not speak explicitly of a human soul.

You see how that question, Did Christ have a human soul? ties in with the question of there being a human person there as well as a human soul. The question of anthropology becomes involved, with regard to Christ, right in the fourth century. Against the Arians, it was denied that the Word, the Son, was a creature; when that is denied, when a divine person is acknowledged in Christ, there arise questions about the humanity, and those questions are important. It makes a great difference whether or not Christ had a human soul, and whether there was a human subject there as well as a divine subject.

Those who wrote against the Apollinarists were found mainly in Asia Minor – Diodorus of Tarsus and Theodorus of Mopsuestia are significant examples. Their whole insistence was upon acknowledging two natures in Christ. They affirmed most stoutly the existence of the two natures: it is not the same that is eternal and is temporal; it is not the same that is immortal as God and is mortal as man; it is not the same who is eternally in heaven and who is incarnate temporally on earth; it is not the same who is omniscient as God and of whom St Mark says in 13.32 that of that day and hour no man knows, nor any angel, nor even the Son, but only the Father. They appeal to everything in the Gospels to refute the Apollinarist view that in Christ there was one nature. According to Apollinaris, the Word had the place of a human soul in the man Christ; and just as in us soul and body make one nature, so in Christ the Word and the flesh make one nature.

Those who wrote against Apollinaris had as one of their disciples Nestorius, who said, 'Well, if you have a nature, you have a person.' They did not think of a nature in some abstract fashion; nature meant this concrete reality. And this concrete reality, if intelligent, is a person. Consequently, if you have a nature, you also have a person; and the Nestorian insistence upon two natures resulted in an implication of two persons. There is no satisfactory way, except in terms of names or honor or adoration or some other fashion, in which they could say that there was just one person. And against the opposite view, the Monophysites and the Nestorians both refused any distinction between person and nature. Consequently, the Monophysites, to save the one person, insisted on a single nature in Christ.

So much, roughly, for our sketch. For Ebionites and Adoptionists, Jesus is just a man. For Sabellians and Patripassianists, there is no difference between God the Father and God the Son; God the Father was crucified – 'Patripassionists' literally means that the Father suffered on the Cross. The Arians denied the divinity of the Son; they admitted that the Son, the Logos, was above all creatures, but still he was not uncreated, he was generated. The Apollinarists, in order to deny the Adoptionist position which held a human subject in Christ, and consequently a human person in Christ to whom the Word came – just as the Holy Spirit came to the prophets, so the Holy Spirit came to the Son – eliminated the human subject and denied a human soul. So the Apollinarist doctrine is that there is no human soul in Christ; instead of a man we have someone who, in the words of St Paul, is according to the likeness of a man; Christ is made up of two principles, as we are; but we are made up of soul and body, Christ is made up of Word and flesh, and there is just one nature. Against the position of Apollinaris, the Nestorians affirmed two natures, but then were not able to save any unity. Finally the Monophysites, to save the one person, denied two natures; the sense in which they denied two natures is very complex.[9]

2.3 *The Development of Christological Dogma*

That sketch provides just landmarks on the process. The preaching of the apostles was to Jews and Gentiles. When anyone preaches he does not com-

9 Lonergan intended to break the lecture at this point, but first of all repeated his sketch as follows, indicating that the definition of issues is important for the next part of the lecture.

'Adoptionists, Ebionites: The question is, Just who is Christ? In the New Testament, we have the one anticipated by the Jews, the Son of Man who lived amongst us, the risen Lord who is *made* Lord, according to Acts 2.34. What is stated in the New Testament about the risen Lord suggests a deified man, someone who is made God after the resurrection; and counterbalancing that, we have the Son who was sent, the eternal Son. Those four presentations are not logically interrelated, do not provide a basis for systematic deduction (the New Testament is not a treatise; it is literature, literature written from different points of view).

'From that source, Christians asked, Just who is Christ? One answer: he's just a man. A second answer: he's the same as the Father, no difference between them; it was God the Father that became man. The Arians: he isn't God. The Apollinarists: he is God, God the Son, distinct from the Father; but he isn't a man as we are men: we are body and soul, he is Word and flesh. The Nestorians: on the contrary, he is not one nature such as human nature is one compound nature; he has two natures, he has all the properties of God, he is just as much God as God the Father, and he's just as much man as we are men; he has all the human properties, a human nature, all of the divine [properties], not some mixture of the two. But when the Nestorians [distinguished] two natures very clearly, they had no way of having just one person. And to get one person, the Monophysites swing back to some position, different from that of the Apollinarists, in which they affirm one nature; and the expression "one nature" is the one erroneous element in the Monophysite position. In their whole conception of Christ they hold exactly the same as the Council of Chalcedon, except they will not admit the expression "two natures."'

municate purely and simply everything he has in his mind. What he communicates, what he can communicate, depends about ninety-eight percent on what his listeners already know. The process of learning something, particularly learning something completely new – and Christian doctrine, the apostolic preaching, was something completely new – occurs when people apprehend in virtue of their already acquired habits of imagination and feeling and understanding and thought and conception. They have to put whatever they are told into their own mode of apprehension or they do not apprehend at all. They can make slight adaptations to what they already know, but they cannot make a total transformation of their own minds.

2.3.1 Jewish Christianity

An illustration of this was the way in which the Jewish Christians of the first centuries apprehended the Son and the Holy Spirit. They had several apprehensions but this one is illustrative. They knew the Old Testament, and they had to conceive the New in the light of the Old. To conceive the Son and the Holy Spirit, so frequently mentioned in the New Testament and distinguished there from one another and from God the Father, they went back to the vision of Isaiah in chapter 6, where the two seraphim stand before the Lord and cry unceasingly, 'Holy, Holy, Holy'; one of the seraphim is God the Son, and the other is the Holy Spirit. By this they did not mean that the Son and Holy Spirit were creatures; they meant that they were persons, that they were distinct from one another, that they were distinct from God the Father, that they were dependent on God the Father; but they were not thinking Greek thoughts in terms of creator and creature. In thinking of them as angels, they were using the resources of their own development to apprehend something new.

Still, in a sense this was not doing justice to the New Testament. Martin Werner wrote a work about 1940 on the beginnings of Christian doctrine,[10] in which he held that the early Christians conceived the Son and the Holy Spirit as creatures, merely as angels; but the experts – Catholic, Protestant, and non-Christian – more or less uniformly disagreed with his findings because he was imposing Greek categories upon Hebraic thought. What the early Christians meant when thinking of the Son and Holy Spirit as two seraphim was not thinking of them as creatures; they conceived them

10 Martin Werner, *Die Entstehung des christlichen Dogmas* (see above, chapter 4, note 13).

above all the other angels; but they were using a familiar Hebrew form of thought that they knew of from Isaiah, which enabled them to assimilate the new doctrine of the New Testament.

2.3.2 Gnosticism

The gospel was preached to the Gentiles, and this will give us a second variation. In the Gentile reception of the gospel, there were all the vagaries of what is known as Gnosticism. It was really a fantastic mode of thought, and it is not easily described, but it was totally undisciplined; it had no logical control, no scientific control of any sort; it was free speculation about God and the eons in God, and so on. The Gnostics thought they could fit Christianity into their preconceptions, but their views in general involved a total distortion of the Christian message. They were using as their tool for assimilating the gospel something that was radically alien to the gospel.

2.3.3 Tertullian

Apart from the excessive influence of the subject's prior knowledge upon what he is taught, illustrated by the Jewish Christians on the one hand and the Gnostics on the other, there were the inherent difficulties in conceiving what was meant by the Christian message.

Tertullian represents not only the opinion of a man whose doctrine later seemed heretical but also a mode of apprehension of the divinity of the Son that was largely current in the Western church during the second and third centuries and even into the fourth. The Son is God; Tertullian had no doubt about that. The Son is not the Father. Tertullian wrote a celebrated work, *Adversus Praxean*; nothing is known about this Praxeas except he is the man against whom Tertullian wrote. Praxeas held that God the Son and God the Father are one and the same, that there is no distinction between them; and that is a Sabellian or Patripassianist doctrine. Tertullian had to give some sort of explanation of how the Son could be God and yet not the Father, and to be able to give that explanation he had to have some criterion for saying that someone is divine. His criterion was very obvious. Why is the Son God? because he is made of the right stuff, he is made of the divine stuff.

This was a mode of thought quite congenial to the Stoic way of philosophic thinking current at the time; and it was the way in which Tertullian quite sincerely conceived the divinity of the Son. It was not a way that anyone found fault with among his contemporaries; they all thought more or less the same way. It was a naive-realist apprehension of God. Tertullian held that the Father is eternal and that the Son was emitted from the Father when the Father proposed to create; the Father is eternal, and the Son is not eternal. We would conclude from that that the Son was not God. Tertullian held that the Father is the whole and the Son is a part, that the Father is supreme and the Son is subordinate. From that we would conclude that the Son is not God, but that is because we have a different conception of God from Tertullian. Because Tertullian placed divinity in being made of, consisting of, divine stuff, the Son could consist of divine stuff, even though he were temporal and subordinate and partial. And if he consisted of divine stuff, then he really and truly was God. But because he was temporal while the Father was eternal, he was distinct from the Father.

This was Tertullian's way of meeting the difficulties, on the one hand of the Adoptionists, who held that the Son was not God, and on the other hand of the Sabellians, who held that the Son is exactly the same as the Father, that the Father as coming on earth is said to be sent as Son, but as existing in heaven is the one who sends.

It is in such a doctrine as Tertullian's that one sees the problems had by the Christians of the first centuries in answering the question, Just who is Christ? They could repeat wholeheartedly everything in the New Testament: all about the Christ that was anticipated, all about the Son of Man that was present corporeally before the eyes of the disciples, all about the risen Lord, all about the eternal Son. But that was not answering the questions that arose later. No matter how much you learn about anything, all you learn simply provides a basis for further questions. And when you answer those questions, those answers provide a basis for yet further questions. You can try to avoid the questions, dodge them, repeat what has been always said, but you leave people dissatisfied. And the theological effort arises insofar as a continuous effort is made to answer questions. Tertullian made an effort to answer questions, but he was not right. Further answers that were not right led to difficulties that will occupy the next period.[11]

11 A break occurs at this point in the lecture, following which Lonergan takes up the 'difficulties ... [of] the next period' of doctrinal development.

2.3.4 Origen

We spoke about Tertullian and his concept of God. Origen died in Alexandria about 250, so he was probably younger than Tertullian, who perhaps died about 220 or 230. He treated the same problem that Tertullian dealt with, but in a quite different manner. For Tertullian, what was real was a body, and consequently God was a body – not the kind of a body that we have, but at least he was real. Tertullian had a thoroughly coherent system, up to a point, with regard to spiritual matter and divine matter. The Son, being of divine matter, would be really divine. (I am simplifying Tertullian's manner of statement.)

Origen attacked the same problem, not from a Stoic type of background but from the background of Middle Platonism, which was a type of realism – a realism of the Ideas. In his commentary on St John, he goes into the question of the Son in considerable detail. It is there that one finds the clearest statements of Origen's thought. Of course, many of his works have been lost; and some exist only in Latin translations, and it is suspected that these translations are more orthodox than the original Greek. He was a man of incredible erudition; he edited what is known as the *Hexapla*: six versions of the Old Testament, one in Hebrew and five in Greek.[12] He wrote commentaries on practically everything. He wrote a work *De principiis* and endless homilies. He is perhaps the one who started the homily, and his homilies were thoroughly in the Hellenistic tradition. Origen was supposed to have been about the age of sixty before he gave a homily extempore; they were all highly ornate affairs.[13]

Origen, then, thought of God the Father and God the Son. He wanted them both to be supreme beings. One of his key texts was from St John, 'The Father is greater than I' (14.28). He held that the Son is truth, truth itself; the Son is wisdom itself. And the meaning of this 'itself' is the perfect exemplar, the Platonic Idea, the ultimate reality of what wisdom is, the ultimate primary reality of what truth is. Reality is the reality

12 'HEXAPLA ... The elaborate edition of the OT produced by Origen, in which the Hebrew text, the Hebrew text transliterated into Greek characters, and the four Greek versions of Aquila, Symmachus, the Septuagint (in a revised text with critical signs) and Theodotion were arranged in parallel columns.' *The Oxford Dictionary of the Christian Church*, 2nd ed., ed. F.L. Cross and E.A. Livingstone (London: Oxford University Press, 1974) 645.

13 Lonergan added a comment about 'the balanced periods that you get in the old third lessons of the breviary,' referring to the version of the Divine Office employed in the pre-Vatican II era.

of the Idea. And so on for a number of other things that are stated about the Son in the Gospels and Epistles, and particularly in St John. The Son was the Logos, the one embodiment of a series of eternal ideas, chief among them being truth and wisdom. But God the Father was beyond truth; truth involves some correspondence, some multiplicity between the knower and the known, some relationship. Similarly, the Father is beyond wisdom. The Father is divinity itself, goodness itself; and the Son is a participation of divinity, a participation of goodness itself. 'The Father is greater than I.'

In Origen, then, one has a subordinationism, as it is called, that is much stricter than in Tertullian. In Tertullian, while subordination of the Son is acknowledged, while the Father is eternal and the Son is temporal, still that subordination can be said to be accidental; it did not regard divinity, which was a matter of being of the right stuff. But in Origen, the Son participates divinity, the Son is the first to participate the divinity that is participated by all the saints, by all Christians.

Thus in Origen one has the use of a Platonist type of philosophy to put together the elements of a Christology. Just who is Christ? The Adoptionists said he is a man; the Sabellians said he is the same as the Father. Origen and Tertullian tried to find a way between these positions. I am not saying that Tertullian really knew Stoic philosophy, but he was thinking in the way in which the Stoics thought; he uses Stoic terms, but he does not use them in a fully technical sense. His mode of thought was that naive realism which is a more systematic thing in the Stoics. Origen drew upon the Middle Platonists and worked out another erroneous theory about the Son. But neither Tertullian nor Origen was thought to be a heretic because of his Christology; for while we would find fault with them in the light of later conciliar decisions, there was no one at that time who knew the later conciliar decisions and was able to say, 'They are heretics.' In other words, one must not judge earlier writings by later standards; one must not judge undeveloped thought by later developed thought; one has to see the whole, to understand the process of development, and it was to illustrate such a process that I spoke on the Greek discovery of mind. Things that seem obvious to us – that we are made of body and soul, that we have minds and wills, that we make decisions and we have free will – while they were experienced by the Greeks, were not objectified by all the Greeks but only through a slow process of development.

2.3.5 Nicea and Athanasius

A third person whom we may now consider is Athanasius. We have spoken of Athanasius in terms of the soul of Christ, but his fundamental contribution to Christology was on another score. The Council of Nicea had condemned the Arians in 325. The Eastern church was in turmoil until about the year 362. The ecclesiastical politics, the interference of the emperors in church affairs, the fact that Nicea was the first ecumenical council, and the difficulty of the question all complicated matters. But the difficulty of the question is the point we have to attend to. One is inclined to disagree with Tertullian: one must not have a materialist conception of God. One is inclined to disagree with Origen: the Platonist Ideas are not a satisfactory philosophy, and the Son is, according to us, truly God; he is not just a participation of God, as Origen conceived him. What is the right conception? The answer was worked out in connection with Nicea, in connection with a Greek term, *homoousios. Homoousios* is derived from *homos* (which is connected with *hama,* meaning 'at the same time,' 'together with') and *ousia,* which really means the being of a thing. The concrete being of a thing is normally translated by essence, but essence not in the later essentialist meaning of the word, but rather as connected with the Latin *esse, essentia.*[14]

What was meant by the word *homoousios?* According to G.L. Prestige, who has written a very useful work on God in patristic thought,[15] until the Council of Nicea, in non-Christian usage, in Gnostic usage, and in Christian usage *homoousios* had about the same meaning as Tertullian's idea of the divinity of the Son. Things are *homoousia* if they are made of the same stuff. For that reason, five of the bishops at the Council of Nicea refused to accept the decree, and were sent into exile by the emperor Constantine. They did not want to admit that God was material, that he was divisible, that a part of him could be named the Son and another part the Father; that did not make sense to them. And of course the advantage of Origen and his Platonism over Tertullian is that in Origen God – Father and Son – is conceived in a purely spiritual, immaterial fashion. That is the strength of Origen and of the Alexandrian school; they got completely beyond the naive realism and the materialism that are more or less a heritage of

14 On Lonergan's negation of essentialism, see editorial note *f* to Lecture 1 in *Understanding and Being* (see above, chapter 2, note 13).

15 George L. Prestige, *God in Patristic Thought* (London: W. Heinemann, 1936; 2nd ed., London: Society for Promoting Christian Knowledge, 1952).

human nature, of fallen human nature, with its *vulnus*, its wound, of ignorance.

What, then, was the meaning of *homoousios*, if those five bishops who rejected the decree of Nicea were mistaken? The simplest expression of the meaning of *homoousios* is familiar to all of you who read or recite the Preface of the Mass of the Trinity. You may recall hearing sung in church, or reading in your missals, the words 'Quod enim de tua gloria revelante te credimus, hoc de Filio tuo, hoc de Spiritu Sancto sine differentia discretionis sentimus.' What we believe because of your revelation (and God the Father is addressed) *de tua gloria*, about your glory, about the *kabôd* Yahweh, about that image of luminosity that was the Jewish apprehension of God, of divinity – what we believe on account of revelation about the glory of God the Father, *hoc de Filio tuo*, the same we accept of the Son, *hoc de Spiritu Sancto*, the same we accept of the Holy Spirit, without any discrimination, any difference.

In other words, the Son and the Holy Spirit are God, not because they are made of the same matter or stuff as the Father, not because of participation in some Platonic Idea of Godhead which would make them subordinate and not properly God according to the Platonist conceptions of Origen, but because the object of our faith is such that we make the same predications about Father, Son, and Holy Spirit. If the Father is eternal, the Son is eternal and the Holy Spirit is eternal; if the Father is omnipotent, the Son is omnipotent and the Holy Spirit is omnipotent; if the Father creates, the Son creates and the Holy Spirit creates; and so on: for everything we state about God the Father, the same is to be said of the Son and the Holy Spirit. *Homoousios*, consubstantial, means that the same predicates, the same predications, the same attributions are to be made about Father, Son, and Spirit.

You note that Monday night I distinguished three components in human knowing: experiencing, understanding, and judging.[16] As you compare Tertullian, Origen, and Athanasius or the Council of Nicea, you find (1) that Tertullian's thought is on the level of experience: the material is what we experience, what we put our hands on, what bears our weight – the sure and firm-set earth on which I tread, as Macbeth remarked, quaking with his fears; (2) on the second level there is understanding, and to

16 Lonergan here refers to his lecture, 'Philosophical Positions with Regard to Knowing,' given at the Thomas More Institute the previous Monday (above, chapter 10).

understanding correspond the Ideas – the Platonist-idealist type of thinking, and so Origen's position; and (3) there is the level of statement: making the same statements about Father, Son, and Spirit, saying that Father, Son, and Spirit are God in the same sense – and they are in the same sense because the same things are true about all three – is thinking of God on the level of judgment, of affirmation. It is the justification of the position of Nicea that the revelation given us through Jesus Christ is a revelation given us through statements – through the statements of our Lord, through the statements of the apostolic preaching, through the statements of the New Testament, through the statements of the teaching church. As long as one is stating, as long as the Christian message is a matter of statement, one can accept those statements only if one is thinking, not on the level of experience or on the level of understanding, but on the level of judgment. And that is the way in which God was conceived, the way in which the Blessed Trinity was conceived, at the Council of Nicea.

This was the fundamental step in the development of Christology. There is but one God. When you say the Son is God, what do you mean? Is it the one God, God the Father, that became man and lived among us? How can you conceive another who is God, and not the Father? What can you possibly mean by it? In time the notion that is most clearly expressed by Tertullian but that is to be found also in Hippolytus and in Dionysius of Rome and that seems to have been accepted pretty generally in the West – Hilary had a great time explaining the Council of Nicea to the Western bishops – gradually was eliminated. The conceptions of Origen were, after Nicea, dispensed by the semi-Arians under the leadership of Eusebius of Caesarea, and later, when Eusebius died, by Acacius, who succeeded him to the see of Caesarea. But conceiving of God on the level of affirmation – something distinct from an apprehension resting on experience or on understanding, something different from Tertullian and from Origen – was arrived at in Nicea and was propounded by Athanasius arguing against all the world in the years that followed Nicea.

Note that 'quod de tua gloria, hoc de Filio tuo' does not determine anything about God, Father or Son; it says that whatever is true of one is true of the other; it is a 'blank check' conception of God the Father and of the Son. Whatever has been revealed about the *kabôd* Yahweh, the glory of God, that is true of the Son as it is true of the Father, and it is true of the Holy Spirit as of Father and Son; but just what it is is another matter, which the Council of Nicea and Athanasius do not attempt to answer. That conception of Christ as God, that possibility of apprehending Christ as God in some precise fashion, in a manner that will make possible answers to questions, in a manner that would enable people to give some answer to the charge, 'You Christians are merely repeating a new myth, something that excites your imaginations and moves your emotions, but something that cannot bear scrutiny, something about which you are not able to answer the most elementary questions' – that answer was arrived at in the fourth century through the Arian controversy.

The logic of the necessity of our position has been illustrated in more recent years in a study of Anglican thought between the years about 1886, when *Lux Mundi* was published, and 1914, when another collective work, *Foundations*, was published.[17] The development of materialism, of positivism, and particularly of German and Kantian idealism brought new types of philosophy that seemed to do away entirely with the whole set of categories developed by Christian thought. The statement that Christ is God, that Jesus of Nazareth is God, created Christian philosophy; working from its presuppositions, you are forced to some sort of ontology. At Nicea, there was not an adequate basis provided by any Greek philosophy. The current philosophies of the time were Stoicism and Platonism and Epicureanism, and none of them would bear the type of thinking represented by the *homoousion*, the *consubstantiale*, of Nicea. A new type of philosophy would have to be developed to enshrine, to be able to include, that notion, a philosophy in terms of existence in the medieval sense. It was not something ready-made that the Fathers borrowed from the Greeks; there was no Greek philosophy they could borrow to express what they concluded from revelation. Aristotle never was much esteemed by the Greek Fathers; he was looked upon, at that time, as simply an empiricist – a judgment that has not a little foundation in the Aristotelian writings.

2.3.6 Further Questions

Answering the question that was raised at Nicea was not answering the whole question about Christ. It saved or established one fundamental point that had been developed about the year 200 in answer to the heresies of the Gnostics and particularly of Marcion: what we know as the Apostles'

17 *Lux Mundi: A Series of Studies in the Religion of the Incarnation*, ed. Charles Gore (New York: United States Book Company, 10th ed., n.d.; first published 1889); *Foundations: A Statement of Christian Belief in Terms of Modern Thought*, by Seven Oxford Men, B.H. Streeter, R. Brook, W.H. Moberly, R.G. Parsons, A.E.J. Rawlinson, N.S. Talbot, W. Temple (London: MacMillan, 1912).

Creed. At the Council of Florence in the fifteenth century, the Latins proposed to include the Apostles' Creed in the statement of faith, but the Greeks had never heard of any Apostles' Creed. From that time, the question of the precise dating of the Creed has been investigated at great length, but the common opinion at the present time seems to place it about the year 200. In the decree of Nicea, there were inserted the statements that one has in the Creed recited in the Mass, statements that regard the Son as God out of God, light out of light, true God out of true God, consubstantial with the Father, the one through whom all things were made; and then the Creed continues: conceived of the Virgin Mary, suffered under Pontius Pilate, died, and was buried. But the full affirmation of the divinity of the Son was added to the Creed at Nicea. The Apostles' Creed says, 'I believe in God the Father almighty, creator of heaven and earth, and in Jesus Christ, his only Son, our Lord.' It repeats what is said in the New Testament, where 'his only Son,' 'our Lord,' and 'Christ' are three principal titles of Jesus. The Apostles' Creed goes on immediately to his conception and suffering and death. At Nicea a further step is taken: into the Creed that about the year 200 affirmed against Gnostics and against the Marcionites (who separated the Old and New Testaments) that God is Creator of heaven and Creator of earth, there is inserted a fully explicit affirmation of the divinity of Christ.

Still, that did not answer all questions. Just who is Christ? He is God, but he is not just God, he is something else too, he is man; and what do you mean by that? Well, we have seen that the Greeks took a long time to figure out what is meant by a man, and they came up with a Platonist view of the soul as subject and an Aristotelian view of the soul as a metaphysical coprinciple of a single entity, a single being, named man. The Fathers did not know Aristotle or metaphysics. From St John's 'the Word was made flesh' (1.14)[18] and from expressions in St Paul such as 1 Corinthians 15.49 – 'As you have carried the image of the terrestrial man, of the old Adam, so now carry the image of the heavenly man'[19] – and from a number of other expressions, the Apollinarists argued that there is no human soul in Christ. There is the flesh, and there is the divine Word; there may be a vegetative soul and an animal soul, but there is no intellective soul in Christ. And a similar mode of speech can be found in Athanasius and in the earlier writ-

18 NRSV: 'The word became flesh.'

19 NRSV: 'Just as we have borne the image of the man of dust, we will also bear the image of the man of heaven.'

ings of Cyril of Alexandria because they wished to avoid Adoptionism, and were thinking of soul as subject.

That Apollinarist error led to a great development on the part of men whose memory later was obscured. Diodorus of Tarsus, in his lifetime, was a pillar of the church. I think there were over sixty works attributed to his name. He was a bishop of Tarsus, and he spent his life combatting Apollinarist doctrine in Asia Minor. But he was condemned later on because he was found to be Nestorian; he was considered, in the light of later developments, to have anticipated Nestorius's doctrine. But what he was doing was insisting on the true humanity of Christ against the Apollinarists, who denied in Christ a true humanity by denying him the human soul.

Similarly, Theodorus of Mopsuestia insisted on the two natures: Christ not only is God, he also really and truly is a man. He insisted upon the humanity of Christ. In Theodorus, and later in Theodoret of Cyr in Mesopotamia, there is a great insistence upon the humanity of Christ, and almost on the psychology of Christ. Theodorus has perhaps an exaggerated insistence upon the humanity of Christ, conceiving him as having moral conversion – not only moral evolution, but moral conversion.

Following upon the definition of Nicea and the error of the Apollinarists that simplified the question of who Christ is – Is he God? Yes. Is he man? Well, he is like a man, he is made of the Word and flesh; we are made of soul and body – there is a group in Asia Minor that insisted on the humanity of Christ. They insisted on it to the extent that they had no way of getting something that was one – one Jesus of Nazareth, one person, one reality – out of the two natures. The classic expression to their views was given by Nestorius.

The next main step after Nicea – I've been giving an outline of the development – was the Council of Ephesus. In the principal session of the Council of Ephesus, there was no argument from scripture. The action consisted mainly of five steps.[20] The decree of Nicea was read: 'I believe in God the

20 Lonergan's *De Verbo incarnato* (Rome: Gregorian University Press, 1964) 121–22 lists in great detail the steps taken at Ephesus, under the heading 'Gesta a concilio Ephesi ...' But they reduce to five main ones, as is clear from his 1972 lecture 'The Origins of Christian Realism'; these are (1) the reading of the Nicene Creed; (2) the reading of Cyril's second letter to Nestorius; (3) the verdict of the Council Fathers that Cyril's letter was in conformity with Nicea; (4) the reading of the second letter of Nestorius to Cyril; and (5) the verdict of the Council Fathers against Nestorius (see *A Second Collection* [see above, chapter 1, note 26] 255).

Father, creator of heaven and earth,' and so on; and then the predicates about the Son as God and the predicates about him as man. Cyril of Alexandria asked whether a letter of his to Nestorius was in accord with the Council of Nicea; and he was sure of his case. In the Council of Nicea, those who affirmed that the Son was really and truly God did not mean that someone was God called the Son, and someone else was conceived of the Virgin Mary, died, and was buried. There is just one and the same who is God and is conceived of the Virgin Mary, suffered, died, and was buried. And that was just the point that Nestorius attempted to evade. To insist on the two natures, he appealed to contradictory attributes: the eternal is not noneternal, it is not temporal; one and the same is not both temporal and eternal; one and the same is not both omnipotent and limited, and so on. Nestorius insisted upon contradictory attributes, and concluded to a negation that there was one and the same.

Cyril put his whole case on the fact that in Nicea there is no distinction between two – one who is God and another who is man; it is one and the same, and that insistence on one and the same is all that is ever meant by saying that Christ is one person. 'Person' is a technical term that makes the language simpler; but what is meant by a person is that radical 'one and the same' that is Jesus of Nazareth, that is the Savior, that is the Christ and the Son and the risen Lord. Obviously in the New Testament, it is one and the same that is the expected Christ, the present Son of Man, the risen Lord, and the Son who is sent. You do not get those all combining in different combinations if different individuals are meant, if one is not the other. But Cyril does not argue by going over the whole New Testament; he appeals to Nicea where there is no question of two. And on that ground, there was the decree of Ephesus which did not publish any symbol of faith, any creed, but simply stuck by the decree of Nicea and said that the doctrine of Nestorius was not compatible with the doctrine of Nicea.

There was considerable rivalry between Alexandria, where Cyril was patriarch, and Constantinople, where Nestorius was patriarch. And while the Council of Ephesus did justice to the fundamental truth contained in the Council of Nicea, still it left in abeyance what the bishops of Asia Minor had been struggling for against the Apollinarists during seventy years. To assert 'one and the same' is not to answer the question, 'What else was the Son besides being God?' Granted Nicea, one question is over and done with: he really and truly is God. Still, he lived amongst us, he taught us; what else was there besides God? The Apollinarist answer was not satisfactory. There still remained the question, What about the humanity? The predecessors of Nestorius had acknowledged the humanity of Christ to the full. Ephesus does not tell us much about it; it does not meet the point. So Ephesus in 431 was followed by Chalcedon in 451, in which finally was formulated the doctrine that in Christ there is one person and two natures. This doctrine easily is thought to be unhelpful, not useful for teaching, meaningless to the people. But if one conceives it as the outcome of an evolution that had been going forward for four centuries, as the evolution of a formula or expression that finally put an order in the answers to be given to fundamental questions about Christ, one is in a position, I think, to understand its significance and its value.

First of all, it is a means, a catch, a basket, so to speak, in which one combines the true humanity of Christ (he really and truly is man) and the true divinity of Christ (he really and truly is God). He is man as we are men; he is God as God the Father is God. He is not two persons; it is not someone who is God and someone else who is man; it is one and the same. Those are very elementary statements about Christ. They arise as a result of the fact that the word of God is statement, that preaching is statement, that we believe what is stated.

To go back to something that I started to say and that slipped my mind, I wanted to mention a work by J.S. Lawton entitled *Conflict in Christology*. The date is about 1947.[21] The contents have to do with the gradual disappearance from the Anglican Church of belief in the divinity of Christ because the influence of modern philosophy led to an elimination of any possible metaphysics, any possible meaning to the word 'is' apart from a useful copula for joining other words together, and consequently any possible meaning to the statement 'Jesus of Nazareth is God.'

As believers, we accept statements; and we accept statements not as acceptable modes of speech or obligatory modes of speech but as having a meaning. When a philosophy eliminates the possible meaning of fundamental elements in our statements, it can eliminate fundamental elements from our faith. And the elimination of, or the objection against, objective thinking, against metaphysical thinking, if taken seriously, eliminates dogma, eliminates Christian doctrine, for the simple reason that Christian

21 John S. Lawton, *Conflict in Christology: A Study of British and American Christology from 1889 to 1914* (London: Society for Promoting Christian Knowledge, 1947); Lonergan's initial reference, incomplete because of distraction, is on p. 262, and he resumes the reference later in answer to the first question (p. 269).

doctrine is doctrine; it is a message. The way that happened is depicted by Lawton in his book *Conflict in Christology.*

Let us make the point in a slightly different way. It is objected against theology and dogma that they are hopeless, that they are so obscure, so unhelpful. It is said that they do not help one to pray, they do not help one to lead a good life, and so on. It is said, too, that on the other hand the gospels are magnificently clear, they move our affections, they inflame us and open our eyes, they touch our hearts, and all the rest. That objection contains a number of elements that are completely true. It remains, however, that man is a rational being. If you tell him that his belief is just so much myth, that there is no essential difference between his sincere Christian belief and the beliefs of Hindus, of Confucians, of our primitive tribes, which are also sincere, his faith is completely devaluated. The New Testament speaks to us in vivid terms that move us in many ways, but the exact meaning of the New Testament is something on which exegetes and commentators have worked for nearly twenty centuries, and there is no proximate end in sight to their labors. The reason for that difficulty of interpretation lies precisely in the multiple purposes[22] – devotional purposes, purposes of preaching, purposes of meditation, affective, imaginative, volitional, cognitional and intellectual purposes – for which the New Testament may be used. Because it fulfils many ends at once, it does not contain the clarity and the precision that are necessary to eliminate the endless work of interpretation, exegesis, explanation, clarification that is renewed in every age of the church, and particularly in our own.

On the other hand, the doctrines of the church, while they have no meaning for people who are completely uneducated, still have a meaning that can be learned by a person of at least secondary education, with a little effort, in a fairly short time. And once they are learned, there is never any difficulty about understanding exactly what they mean. Historical work is done on the councils, and just what was meant, and so on; but there does not exist any series of commentators, each one disagreeing with his predecessors, on the meaning of the councils. It is the same with the meaning of Euclid's *Elements.* You have to study to know what Euclid meant, but once you know, there is no possible dispute about the meaning, because an effort is made in such a work at clarity and precision of meaning. It is not serving many purposes at once, it is serving just a single purpose. Similarly in the councils, there is that effort at clarity, and there is also the appearance of sterility. But there is

22 See above, note 7.

never any question of choosing between the dogmas and the scriptures, of choosing between theology and faith; one can have some of both, or all of faith and as much of theology as one cares for.

I have been attempting to communicate to you this evening a notion of theology. I have used the instance of the development of Christology, of the Christian apprehension of Christ; this is obviously a central question in Christianity. Development in the apprehension of ourselves is something that is going on, that occurs historically over a series of centuries; I illustrated it by the Greek discovery of mind as described by Bruno Snell. There occurs a similar development in the apprehension of Christ: before he came, he was apprehended as the Messiah; when he came, he was still apprehended as the Messiah but also as the present Son of Man; after his death, he was apprehended as the risen Lord, almost as a deified man, and remembered as the Son of Man in the Gospel narratives, and remembered as the Messiah announced in the Old Testament; and finally, by way of uniting all three, he is the Son sent by the Father, the Son through whom all things were made. The mere fact that this apprehension of the Son that is scattered throughout the books of the New Testament had to be assimilated by Jews and Gentiles made it insufficient just to repeat what was in the New Testament; one had to think it in one's own mode of thinking, and one gets the different thinking of the Jews and the Jewish Christians, and of the Gnostics among the Gentiles.

But apart from these merely subjective or preliminary difficulties, there were difficulties in putting together in a simple, coherent fashion just what the New Testament had to say about Christ. I illustrated that, first of all, by the series of errors: Adoptionists, Sabellians, Arians, Apollinarists, Nestorians, Monophysites;[23] and secondly, more positively, by trying to indicate the type of difficulty that made the process so interminably long and the disputes apparently so difficult: the difficulty from philosophy – a Stoic philosophy in Tertullian, a Platonist philosophy in Origen – and the subtlety, so to speak, of the solution arrived at at Nicea and presented by Athanasius with regard to the divinity of Christ. Then there were the questions that arose about his humanity: did he have a human soul, was he really and truly a man, and if he was really and truly a man, how could he also be God? And the answer to 'How could he...?' is not, 'We don't understand

23 The Monophysites were only mentioned in the summary we have retained in the text; but they are given more attention in the summary that we have moved to note 9 above.

mysteries.' At least we have to say precisely what it is that *is* the mystery. Is it someone else that is man and someone else that is God? If so, there is no mystery; if it is one and the same, are you not eliminating the two natures? Those are the questions that arose fundamentally in the Greek conciliar Christology, and perhaps they provide some illustration of a certain aspect of traditional theology.

If there are any questions that anyone may care to raise, I'll answer them now.

Question: You started to mention the development within Anglican theology, and you mentioned the reference to the development of German idealism as coming into England. Now I don't know whether you clearly finished this ...

Response: I started it and got distracted, and attempted to go back to it later. I started on it, probably in connection with the definition of Chalcedon. The definition reached in the middle of the fifth century at Chalcedon was accepted by all Christians practically up to the nineteenth century. Difficulties arose among Christians primarily from the liberal school, but especially in Germany and under the influence of the various German philosophies – the nineteenth-century development of philosophy. The issue penetrated into England toward the end of the century. Lawton recounts the gradual weakening or breaking down of clear affirmations of the divinity of Christ in the Anglican Church, the impossibility of giving any meaning to this formula of Chalcedon. That was the fundamental difficulty: what do you mean? You will find somewhat unfavorable allusions to it even in very conservative scriptural Anglicans or English non-Catholic exegetes, who say Christ is *indivise* and *immutabiliter* one; and there are two other adverbs that just slip my mind at the moment.[24] But what does it mean? You cannot give a meaning to it if objective thinking is a mistake. You cannot give a meaning to it if there is no possibility of metaphysics. Lawton just shows how the thing gradually broke down; the divinity of Christ disappears. You can say God was in Christ, reconciling the world to himself, as St Paul did in 2 Corinthians 5.19; and what do you mean by 'in'? – well, don't ask me hard questions! But if you say 'is,' for example, 'Jesus of Nazareth *is*

24 *DS* 302: 'Unum eundemque Christum Filium Dominum unigenitum, in duabus naturis inconfuse, immutabiliter, indivise, inseparabiliter agnoscendum ...'

God,' you're saying more than can be believed, and not merely more than can be believed but more than can have a meaning.

Those philosophic difficulties, which are difficulties of philosophic development in each individual but also difficulties on the level of philosophy itself, can eliminate meaning from any Christian doctrine. It is fundamentally on that point that theology has to work. You can say, 'Let's not bother about such abstruse points; what difference does it make?' Well, it doesn't make much difference to people who aren't concerned with meaning; but if you tell them that their faith – all they are believing – is a myth, they will be no end upset. And if you want to say, 'What do you mean if you don't mean a myth?' you'll have to get into this type of question to give an answer; or else, tell them, 'Well, just have simple faith.'

Question: When they said that the Father and the Son had the same nature, they said they had the same attributes to be predicated of the Son as of the Father; and it is said that our Lord is one person with two natures. Do they explain what that means? I mean, can you predicate the same operations, the same attributes?
Response: You predicate all the divine operations and human operations of the same person because there are two natures.
Question (continued): I didn't get that last part.
Response: Of the Son you predicate everything that can be predicated of every man because he is a man; but not of the Father: the Father is not a man; and not of the Holy Spirit: the Holy Spirit is not a man. The Son is consubstantial with us according to his humanity; he's consubstantial with the Father according to divinity; and it is one and the same that is divine and human.
Question (continued): So his divinity, can you predicate it?
Response: His divinity cannot be predicated of his humanity; they are both predicated of the one person. But the rules of predication there can be complex.

Question: It seems that the needs for doctrinal development were pushing the development of an anthropology. Today, in contemporary theologizing, isn't it happening the other way around: that what we are learning about human beings from social studies and from psychology is helping to push doctrinal development?
Response: Yes, pushing the anthropological side. In the last twenty-five

years, there has been in process a very fundamental development in Christology, namely, the transposition from one person with two natures, which has been interpreted mainly in a metaphysical fashion, to one subject of a divine consciousness and a human consciousness. The same thing is stated, but in psychological terms. And out of the psychological statement, you can have all the conclusions you have from the other, and a good deal more besides. Let us draw a four-termed analogy here in terms of nature: if I was not only myself but also a dog, I'd be one person with two natures; and if I were both myself and a dog, I'd have my own experiences and the experiences of the life of a dog – I'd lead a dog's life too. Subjectively, as the two natures are quite distinct, the two consciousnesses are quite distinct. In the incarnation, the Son emptied himself out, not in the sense that he dropped his divinity but that he lived a merely human life – which is more of a descent for him than it would be for us to lead the life of a dog; and leading the life, that is, from the internal viewpoint of being a subject.

Now the questions that are put about Christ today are psychological questions, they are historical questions: How did he think? What did he know as a boy? What did he know as a boy of twelve? What were the questions he was asking about? Was he learning something? When he asks Mary, 'Where was Lazarus lying? Where is the tomb?'[25] (see John 11.34) was he learning something, or was his question insincere? And so on. All those psychological questions come up, and insofar as anthropology develops, it becomes possible to give consideration even to those questions, because theoretical development makes the apprehension of the data possible. Without the theoretical development, you haven't got the questions to ask about the text – does it mean this or that? – because you have no 'this' or 'that' to put in your questions.

Question: Is there a development also from Christ to man, from knowledge that we have of the mystery of Christ to insights into the mystery that is man?

Response: Yes. That's another question, is it not? Christ in man, the anthropological front, the individual, the group, the destiny of man: all those are contemporary questions that are knocking at the theological doors.

25 NRSV: 'He said, "Where have you laid him?"' (John 11.34)

Question: From the standpoint of faith, how might it be more comfortable to think of Christ in the Eucharist?

Response: To think can mean to imagine, to conceive, to affirm. The fundamental way, the way that one can think the thing through and be coherent, is to put oneself on the level of Nicea: the true statement. Not the level of experience, not the level of understanding, but the level of true statement accepted in faith. And just as for the question about the divinity of Christ an answer of some sort is found, not on the level of experiencing matter, or understanding ideas, but making the same statements about Father, Son, and Holy Spirit, so the doctrine of transsubstantiation gives you the fundamental statements about the Eucharist on which everything else depends, and they are accepted on faith. This is my body, my body is not bread, this is no longer bread; 'this,' that which is designated by a demonstrative, and 'is my body': the transsubstantation of the substance of the bread into the body of Christ; and similarly with regard to the wine. That's the fundamental step, and it's on that level of statement. That provides an ultimate basis; you can ask further questions, and answer them on that level, and you're doing theology of a very strict type. It provides a framework within which your religious living can develop, a framework within which you can interpret your religious experience, and so on. But those answers may be schematic gestures without much meaning.

Lexicon of Latin and Greek Words and Phrases

Latin Words and Phrases

emanatio intelligibilis: intelligible emanation
ens: being
ens [est id] cui suo modo competit esse: being [is that] which has its own proper act of existence
id quod est: that which is
id quod non est: that which is not
in genere intelligibilium ... ut potentia tantum, ... ut actus: in the genus of intelligibles ... as potency only, ... as act
in his quae sunt sine materia idem est intelligens et intellectum: in the immaterial order, understanding and what is understood are identical
indivise, immutabiliter: indivisibly, unchangeably
intelligibile in actu est intellectus in actu: the intelligible in act is the intellect in act
libertas errandi: freedom for error
mobile: what can be moved
motivum: what can move – transitive
motum: what is moved
movens: what is moving – transitive
non creatus, non factus, sed genitus: not created, not made, but begotten
non creatus, non factus, non genitus, sed procedens: not created, not made, not begotten, but proceeding
omnia simpliciter: simply everything
sensus fidelium: common perception of the faithful
species intelligibilis: intelligible form

subsistens distinctum in natura intellectuali: a distinct subsistent in an intellectual nature
terminus ad extra: external term
una substantia: one substance

Greek Words and Phrases

ananké: fate
homoousios: consubstantial
mia ousia: one substance

Works of Lonergan Referred to in Footnotes

We list here only those works of Lonergan that are referred to in our footnotes. Some of the works are published, some are in the semipublished state of notes issued for students, some are not published in any sense, but all are available in the Library and/or Archives of the Lonergan Research Institute, Toronto. Where it is pertinent, we have indicated the number (anticipated or actual) for volumes appearing in the Collected Works (CWL).

The Analogy of Meaning. Lecture given at the Thomas More Institute, Montreal, 25 September 1963 (CWL 6).

'Analytic Concept of History.' *Method: Journal of Lonergan Studies* 11:1 (1993) 5–35 (CWL 17).

'Aquinas Today: Tradition and Innovation.' *A Third Collection* (*q.v.*) 35–54.

'Bernard Lonergan Responds.' *Foundations of Theology: Papers from the International Lonergan Congress 1970*, ed. Philip McShane. Dublin: Gill and Macmillan, 1971; Notre Dame: University of Notre Dame Press, 1972, 223–34 (CWL 17).

Bernard Lonergan: 3 Lectures. Ed. and with introduction by R. Eric O'Connor. Montreal: Thomas More Institute, 1975.

Caring about Meaning: Patterns in the Life of Bernard Lonergan. Ed. Pierrot Lambert, Charlotte Tansey, Cathleen Going. Montreal: Thomas More Institute Papers/82, 1982.

'Christology Today: Methodological Reflections.' *A Third Collection* (*q.v.*) 74–99.

Collection. 2nd ed., ed. Frederick E. Crowe and Robert M. Doran. Toronto: University of Toronto Press, 1988 (CWL 4).

'Cognitional Structure.' *Collection* (*q.v.*) 205–21.

'The Concept of *Verbum* in the Writings of St. Thomas Aquinas.' *Theological Studies* 7 (1946) 349–92; 8 (1947) 35–79, 404–44; 10 (1949) 3–40, 359–93 (CWL 2).

'Consciousness and the Trinity.' *Philosophy & Theology* 7:1 (1992) 3–22 (CWL 6).

De argumento theologico ex sacra scriptura. Notes for lecture at faculty seminar, Gregorian University and Biblical Institute, Rome, Spring 1962 (CWL 17).

De Deo trino: Pars analytica. Rome: Gregorian University Press, 1961.

De Deo trino. Vol. 1: *Pars dogmatica* (2nd ed.); vol. 2: *Pars systematica* (3rd ed.). Rome: Gregorian University Press, 1964 (CWL 9).

'The Dehellenization of Dogma.' *A Second Collection* (*q.v.*) 11–32.

De intellectu et methodo. Notes by students of theology course, Gregorian University, 1959 (CWL 19).

De methodo theologiae. Notes by students of theology course, Gregorian University, 1962 (CWL 19).

De Verbo incarnato. Rome: Gregorian University Press, 1960; 2nd ed., 1961; 3rd ed., 1964 (CWL 8).

'Dimensions of Meaning.' *Collection* (*q.v.*) 232–45.

Divinarum personarum conceptionem analogicam evolvit Bernardus Lonergan, S.I. Rome: Gregorian University Press, 1957; 2nd ed., 1959; (3rd ed. = *De Deo trino*, vol. 2).

Doctrinal Pluralism. Milwaukee: Marquette University Press, 1971 (CWL 14).

Exegesis and Dogma. Lecture given at Regis College, Willowdale, Ontario, 3 September 1963 (CWL 6).

Existentialism. Notes for lectures, Boston College, 1957 (CWL 18).

'*Existenz* and *Aggiornamento*.' *Collection* (*q.v.*) 222–31.

'Finality, Love, Marriage.' *Collection* (*q.v.*) 17–52.

'The Future of Thomism.' *A Second Collection* (*q.v.*) 43–53.

Georgetown University Lectures on The Method of Theology. Notes for a series of ten lectures, July 13–17, 1964 (CWL 19).

Grace and Freedom: Operative Grace in the Thought of St. Thomas Aquinas. Ed. J. Patout Burns. London: Darton, Longman & Todd, and New York: Herder and Herder, 1971 (CWL 1).

Hermeneutics. Lecture in the institute 'The Method of Theology' (*q.v.*).

'The Human Good.' *Humanitas: Journal of the Institute of Man* 15 (1979) 113–26 (CWL 14).

Insight: A Study of Human Understanding. 5th ed., ed. Frederick E. Crowe and Robert M. Doran. Toronto: University of Toronto Press, 1992. 1st ed., London: Longmans, Green and Co., 1957 (CWL 3).

'*Insight* Revisited.' *A Second Collection* (*q.v.*) 263–78.

Intelligence and Reality. Notes for lectures at the Thomas More Institute, Montreal, March–May, 1951 (CWL 21).

Interview of 30 March 1971. *Curiosity at the Center of One's Life: Statements and Questions of R. Eric O'Connor*, ed. J. Martin O'Hara. Montreal: Thomas More Institute Papers/84 (1984) 385–401.

Knowledge and Learning. Notes for lectures in an institute in the Graduate School of Gonzaga University, Spokane, Washington, 15–16 July 1963.

Lectures on *Insight*. Delivered at Loyola University, Los Angeles, 21–23 September 1964.

Lectures on *Method in Theology*. Delivered in the institute 'Transcendental Philosophy and the Study of Religion,' Boston College, 3–12 July 1968 (CWL 20).

Letter (22 January 1935) to Henry Keane (CWL 21).

Mathematical Logic. Notes for lectures, Boston College, 1957 (CWL 18).

'The Mediation of Christ in Prayer.' *Method: Journal of Lonergan Studies* 2:1 (1984) 1–20 (CWL 6).

'Metaphysics as Horizon.' *Collection* (*q.v.*) 188–204.

'Method in Catholic Theology.' *Method: Journal of Lonergan Studies* 10:1 (1992) 3–26 (CWL 6).

Method in Theology. London: Darton, Longman & Todd, and New York: Herder and Herder, 1972; 2nd ed., same publishers, 1973; latest reprint, Toronto: University of Toronto Press, 1994 (CWL 12).

The Method of Theology. Institute given at Regis College, Willowdale, Ontario, 9–20 July 1962 (CWL 19).

'Natural Right and Historical Mindedness.' *A Third Collection* (*q.v.*) 169–83.

'The Ongoing Genesis of Methods.' *A Third Collection* (*q.v.*) 146–65 (CWL 13).

'Openness and Religious Experience.' *Collection* (*q.v.*) 185–86 (CWL 4).

'The Origins of Christian Realism.' Seventeenth Annual Robert Cardinal Bellarmine Lecture, Saint Louis University School of Divinity (1972). *A Second Collection* (*q.v.*) 239–61.

'The Origins of Christian Realism.' Lecture given at Regis College, Toronto (1961). *Method: Journal of Lonergan Studies* 5:1 (1987) 1–12 (CWL 6).

Philosophical Positions with Regard to Knowing. Lecture at the Thomas More Institute, Montreal, 29 September 1964 (CWL 6).

'Philosophy and the Religious Phenomenon.' *Method: Journal of Lonergan Studies* 12:2 (1994) 125–46 (CWL 14).

'Philosophy and Theology.' *A Second Collection* (*q.v.*) 193–208.

Philosophy of God, and Theology: The Relationship between Philosophy of God and the Functional Specialty, Systematics. London: Darton, Longman & Todd, and Philadelphia: Westminster, 1973 (CWL 14).

The Philosophy of History. Lecture at Thomas More Institute, Montreal, 23 September 1960 (CWL 6).

'Questionnaire on Philosophy.' *Method: Journal of Lonergan Studies* 2:2 (1984) 1–35 (CWL 14).

'Questions with Regard to Method: History and Economics.' Interview in *Dialogues in Celebration*, ed. Cathleen M. Going (Montreal: Thomas More Institute, 1980) 286–314.

'The Redemption.' *Bernard Lonergan: 3 Lectures* (*q.v.*) 1–28 (CWL 6).

'The Role of a Catholic University in the Modern World.' *Collection* (*q.v.*) 108–13.

'St. Thomas' Thought on *Gratia Operans*.' *Theological Studies* 2 (1941) 289–324; 3 (1942) 69–88, 375–402, 533–78 (CWL 1).

A Second Collection: Papers by Bernard J.F. Lonergan, S.J. Ed. William F.J. Ryan and Bernard J. Tyrrell. London: Darton, Longman & Todd, and Philadelphia: Westminster, 1974 (CWL 11).

'Subject and Soul.' *Philippine Studies* 13 (1965) 576–85. Written without this title as introduction for the English and French editions in book form of the *verbum* articles (CWL 2).

'Theology and Praxis.' *A Third Collection* (*q.v.*) 184–201.

Theology as Christian Phenomenon. Lecture given at the Thomas More Institute, Montreal, 1 October 1964 (CWL 6).

'Theology in Its New Context.' *A Second Collection* (*q.v.*) 55–67.

A Third Collection: Papers by Bernard Lonergan, S.J. Ed. Frederick E. Crowe. New York: Paulist Press, 1985 (CWL 13).

Thought and Reality. Lectures at the Thomas More Institute, Montreal, 1945–46 (CWL 21).

'Time and Meaning.' *Bernard Lonergan: 3 Lectures* (*q.v.*) 29–54.

Topics in Education: The Cincinnati Lectures of 1959 on the Philosophy of Education. Ed. Robert M. Doran and Frederick E. Crowe, revising and augmenting the unpublished text prepared by James Quinn and John Quinn. Toronto: University of Toronto Press, 1993 (CWL 10).

Towards a Definition of Education. Lecture at Regis College (then Christ the King Seminary) 1949 (CWL 21).

Understanding and Being: The Halifax Lectures on INSIGHT. 2nd ed., ed. Elizabeth A. Morelli and Mark D. Morelli. Revised and augmented by Frederick E. Crowe with the collaboration of Elizabeth A. Morelli, Mark D. Morelli, Robert M. Doran, and Thomas V. Daly. Toronto: University of Toronto Press, 1990 (CWL 5).

'Unity and Plurality: The Coherence of Christian Truth.' *A Third Collection* (*q.v.*) 239–50.

Verbum: Word and Idea in Aquinas. Ed. David B. Burrell. Notre Dame: University of Notre Dame Press, 1967 (CWL 2).

The Way to Nicea: The Dialectical Development of Trinitarian Theology. Trans. Conn O'Donovan. London: Darton, Longman & Todd, and Philadelphia: Westminster, 1976 (CWL 9).

Index